Leaders'
Guide
Youth

Alpha

ACKNOWLEDGEMENTS

The *Youth Alpha Leaders' Guide* is a truly global project. Alpha International would like to thank the many people from the international Youth Alpha team who have been involved in the creation and development of this resource, including:

Andy Watkins (Australia)
Beth Fellinger (Canada)
Chia Wen Chien (Singapore)
Dominik Sandles (Germany)
Francis Dodd (Ghana)
Jonathan Westerkamp (Netherlands)
Gisele Zurcher (Switzerland)
Helen Lawson (Scotland)
Ian Clarkson (England)
Jamie Haith (England)
Louisa Jacob (England)
Nicola Marshall (England)
Phil Knox (England)
Rachael Heffer (England)
Rebecca Long (USA)
Richard Dawson (England)
Richard Drake (New Zealand)
Sandra Blair (Scotland)
Scarlett Sharp (England)
Shane Linford (England)

This Youth Alpha material is based on *Alpha – Questions of Life* by Nicky Gumbel and has been compiled by Matt Costley. It is an updated and modified version of the 2003 edition, which was written by Jonathan Brant.

Special thanks to the following contributing authors: Mike Pilavachi, Mark Oestreicher, Pete Greig, Gavin Calver, Al Gordon, Pete Wynter, Brad Hawkes, and Simeon Whiting and also to Sophie Godfree, Philomena Lufkin and Julia Evans for all of their hard work on this project.

The Youth Alpha team would also like to thank the Alpha Publications team, including: Katie Markham, Kate Crossland-Page, Jo Soda, Will Ahern, Jon Shippen, Phil Williams, Becky Cotter, Lauren Whig, Mary Melo and Joe Laycock.

youthalpha LEADERS' GUIDE

CONTENTS

INTRODUCTION

SECTION 1 – THE YOUTH ALPHA COURSE SESSIONS

SECTION 2 – HOW TO RUN A GREAT YOUTH ALPHA COURSE

SECTION 3 – EXPERT ADVICE ON RUNNING YOUTH ALPHA

COURSE ESSENTIALS

BEHIND THE SCENES

FOR YOUNG LEADERS

FOR YOUTH PASTORS

SECTION 4 – YOUTH ALPHA TEAM TRAINING

APPENDICES

INTRODUCTION

WELCOME

'Don't let anyone look down on you because you are young, but set an example for the believers in speech, in life, in love, in faith and in purity' (1 Timothy 4:12).

Hi! We're thrilled that you've got a copy of this *Leaders' Guide* and that you are interested in running a Youth Alpha course.

This resource is designed to help you run a Youth Alpha course which, in turn, will help you to share your faith with your friends. We hope and pray that it enables you to do just that.

Youth Alpha is designed to be flexible because every group is different. Our hope is that this guide will help you to tailor a unique course perfectly suited to your group.

In every session, you will notice that each teaching point has several illustration options. Hopefully it will be clear to you which of these is best for your group. Please remember, however, that this resource is just a guide – feel free to add bits of your own story as you go and/or include your own ideas for illustrating the points.

We would also encourage you to access the Youth Alpha TalkBuilder online at youthalpha.org

TalkBuilder is an exciting new tool that will allow you to:

- build and personalise your Youth Alpha talks online

- find more illustration options

- upload any illustrations that you have used to share with others

Before you get into the main part of the resource, we want to give you a few practical tips that will help you to run a successful Youth Alpha course:

1 **Run the whole course – don't cut sessions out**
Our experience is that this is the best way to run Youth Alpha – if it wasn't, we wouldn't have put all the sessions in! You will notice that there are two 'combined' talks, in which the topics of four sessions have been squeezed into two. This merging will allow you to cover all the course material over eight weeks, rather than ten, if you need to.

2 **Do the Youth Alpha Weekend or Day**
We know that the course Weekend or Day can be difficult to organise; it does require a lot of effort, but it is one of the most important parts of the course.

3 **Register your course online**
Go to youthalpha.org and sign up. This will mean potential guests wanting to do a course in your area can find you.

4 Get in touch with your local Youth Alpha Adviser
Youth Alpha Advisers are amazing people with a wealth of experience in running Youth Alpha. If you have any questions, or if you need a bit of help, contacting your local Youth Alpha Adviser is a great place to start. Go to youthalpha.org to find out who your local Adviser is.

5 Come to a Youth Alpha Conference or training day
This guide includes everything you need to know to run a great course, but it's even better if you can come and get some training: check out youthalpha.org for more information. We hope to see you at a training event soon!

The last thing we want to say is: please get in touch – we would love to hear from you! We especially enjoy hearing stories of lives being changed through Youth Alpha, so whatever it is, drop us a line at youth@alpha.org anytime.

We are praying for you, and we hope you have a fantastic time running Youth Alpha.

The Youth Alpha team

WHAT IS YOUTH ALPHA?

Youth Alpha is an adaptation of the Alpha Course. The Alpha Course gives people an opportunity to explore the meaning of life and the Christian faith.

A BRIEF HISTORY

The Alpha Course has been running at HTB (a church in central London) since the late 1970s, when it was started as a course for new believers. In the early 1990s, a clergyman called Nicky Gumbel (now vicar of HTB) took over the leadership of Alpha and soon noticed the potential to use it as an evangelistic tool.

After seeing so many people come to faith on the course at HTB, other churches in London also began running Alpha. It soon started to spread throughout the UK, and then all around the world. It is now running in over 160 countries, and it is estimated that over 18 million people have attended an Alpha Course.

A typical Alpha session starts with some food, which is followed by a 'talk' explaining a particular aspect of the Christian faith. This is followed by a discussion in small groups. Generally, the small group time is considered the most important part of the course, as it is a chance for guests to say whatever they like; they are encouraged to discuss the talk honestly.

YOUTH ALPHA

Youth Alpha is very similar to the Alpha Course in terms of teaching content, but it is presented in a way that is more appealing to young people.

Youth Alpha was started in 1996 as a response to the demand from churches for a youth version of the Alpha Course. It was redeveloped in 2002, and this version was launched in 2010.

Youth Alpha is now running all across the globe, from Uganda to the United Kingdom, from Singapore to Spain, and from Argentina to Australia.

The course is being used in all major denominations and in many different contexts: in schools, confirmation classes, young offenders institutions, youth groups, youth clubs, sports clubs, and cafés. Time and again we have been excited to see the number of young people starting to run the course in order to share their faith with their friends.

The first Youth Alpha Conference was held in 2004. Since then, many more have been held worldwide, and many thousands of delegates have attended these events.

The Youth Alpha course covers the following topics:

Introductory session – Christianity: Boring, Untrue, Irrelevant?
Session 1 – Who Is Jesus?
Session 2 – Why Did Jesus Die?
Session 3 – How Can We Have Faith?
Session 4 – Why and How Do I Pray?
Session 5 – Why and How Should I Read the Bible?
Session 6 – How Does God Guide us?

Youth Alpha Weekend/Day

Weekend Session 1 – What about the Holy Spirit?
Weekend Session 2 – How Can I Be Filled with the Holy Spirit?
Weekend Session 3 – How Can I Make the Most of the Rest of My Life?

Session 7 – How Can I Resist Evil?
Session 8 – Why and How Should I Tell Others?
Session 9 – Does God Heal Today?
Session 10 – What about the Church?

So, by running Youth Alpha, you are joining many others across the globe in using this tool to help share the good news of Jesus Christ. It's great to have you on board.

A TYPICAL YOUTH ALPHA SESSION

In one sense, there's no such a thing as a 'typical' Youth Alpha session, since every course will be different, but there are four key elements that should form the basis of every course, regardless of style and context: food, fun, the talk, and small groups.

FOOD

One of the reasons that the Alpha Course has worked so well is that at every session the guests eat together. We think there's something quite spiritual about people eating together. It is a way of helping people to feel comfortable and at ease, and it forms community. Eating together was definitely of high value for Jesus too – just look at the Gospels to see how much of Jesus' ministry was based around shared meals.

So we want to encourage you to fit the principle of eating together into the context of your Youth Alpha course. No doubt this will be very different from course to course. Think about what sort of food your friends are into, and where teenagers in your area eat together. Probably only you will know what is best.

It might be that you get takeaway pizzas, or recruit some parents to cook a great meal. Other courses have gone for the café feel with muffins and pastries, while some have bought fish and chips for everyone. In a school lunchtime, food is harder to do, so perhaps you might offer cookies to go with everyone's packed lunch. Our recommendation is that you make food a key part of the course, but how you do that is up to you.

NB: it's worth remembering that guests on the course aren't usually Christians and we need to make them feel as comfortable as possible. Therefore, we never pray before eating on Youth Alpha. This prevents people from feeling uncomfortable. There will be opportunities to pray later on the in course.

FUN

We believe that it is possible to learn about Jesus and have fun doing it (radical, aren't we?), so we would encourage you to make your course as fun as possible.

When you're inviting people to Youth Alpha, don't ask them to sign up for the whole course, just ask them to come to the first week. If they like it, they will come back. We have found this works best for two reasons: first, the idea of joining an eight- (nine- or ten-) week course can seem pretty intense; secondly, if we know that people will only come back next time if this session is fantastic, we will put more effort into making the first week fun. We recommend spending an extra twenty minutes or so making the venue look good, as this can really add to the fun feel of the course.

In this guide, each Youth Alpha session starts with a choice of ice breaker games. These are silly games, designed to get everyone involved and having fun. If you don't like them or don't feel they will suit your group, then don't use them – use your own ideas instead (don't forget to share these with us online at youthalpha.org!).

TALK/PRESENTATION

Obviously, what we're doing on Youth Alpha is a factual exercise: we are passing on knowledge – biblical truth – and encouraging people to explore this and think it through for themselves.

Over ten weeks (or eight or nine, depending on your course), everyone who does Youth Alpha is given a crash course in Christianity along with the basic building blocks of faith. We're passing on factual knowledge, but we do it in a more creative way than just talking at our guests.

There is no DVD for Youth Alpha. Unlike most regular Alpha sessions, which use DVDs of Nicky Gumbel, the Youth Alpha talks are always given live. This may be a scary thought for some of you (enough to make you think twice about running a course!) but it is definitely the best way. And you can do it!

The good news is that each of the talks is clearly laid out for you in this guide, as well as on TalkBuilder. There are lots of different options to choose from (movie clips, internet video clips, stories, games and activities) to help illustrate what you are saying. A Youth Alpha talk should be between ten and twenty minutes in length.

For further information on how to give a great Youth Alpha talk, please see page 341.

SMALL GROUPS

Following the talk (or as part of it) we always have small groups.

A typical small group consists of between six and eight guests, one or two leaders who facilitate the discussion, and one or two 'helpers' who are there to host and welcome people.

Small groups are arguably the most important part of the Youth Alpha course. The reasons are twofold:

1 Small groups can be the part of the course that really engages people; it is where the relational side of the course kicks in and where friendships develop. We all know how important it is to feel like we're part of a group

2 It is where we give space for the group to say what they really feel. We genuinely value the opinion of everyone on the course, regardless of how 'wacky' that may be. There's no better way to encourage learning and discovery than through discussion

There is an article in Section 3 of this guide called 'How to lead a Youth Alpha small group' (see page 338) which is absolutely essential reading for anyone running Youth Alpha. There is also a 'team training' talk outline called 'How to lead small groups on Youth Alpha' in Section 4 of this guide (see page 372).

IS YOUTH ALPHA FOR YOU?

This may not be the first question you'd expect to be asked at the start of this resource, but it could be one of the most important ones.

We want to begin by saying that Youth Alpha may not be the best course for you. If you want to run a course for a group of teenagers who have had no contact with you or with church before, or if you are just looking for a curriculum to occupy your youth group with, then this may not be the best starting point.

But if you want to share your faith with a group of people with whom you are already on a journey, then Youth Alpha might be a great thing to do together.

Some questions to ask yourself before you commit:

• Why do I/we want to run a Youth Alpha course?	GOOD IDEA ☐	GOD IDEA ☐
• Is this about converting people, or sharing my faith out of love?	CONVERTING ☐	SHARING ☐
• Do I/we have the time and resources to be able to do this?	NO ☐	YES ☐
• What next? What if all of my group become Christians? What about those who enjoy the course but don't become Christians?	NO IDEA ☐	GOT A PLAN ☐
• Do I/we have the support of my church, parents, friends, etc?	NO ☐	YES ☐
• Are there some people praying for me/us?	NO ☐	YES ☐
• Is my church willing to welcome any of our group who may want to join?	NO ☐	YES ☐

If you ticked any of the first column, then it might be worth giving a bit more thought to whether the timing is right for you to run a course. If you ticked all of the right-hand column, then you're ready to start planning your Youth Alpha course!

HOW TO USE THIS LEADERS' GUIDE

Whether you are fifteen or fifty-one (actually, especially if you are fifteen!), this resource has been written for you. One of the exciting things that God seems to have been doing with Youth Alpha over the last few years is inspiring teenagers to run the course for their friends.

We really want to encourage that, so if you are a teenager, know that we believe in you and want to support you. If you are a bit older, then we want to support you too – but why not involve some of your youth group in the planning and leadership of the course? Our experience shows us that this is the best way.

This *Youth Alpha Leaders' Guide* is full of helpful information and has been designed to give someone with no experience in leading this kind of course enough confidence to give it a go. On the other hand, you may well be a youth ministry veteran and a lot of this may seem very basic. We would encourage you to flick through all of the material and take in whatever is relevant to you.

The *Leaders' Guide* contains four main sections along with appendices:

SECTION 1 – THE YOUTH ALPHA COURSE SESSIONS

This contains all fourteen talks from the Youth Alpha course, written in a way that will allow you to easily give the talks yourself, direct from this resource. It includes hundreds of options to help you personalise your talks. Text that appears in an italicised font indicates instructions for leaders. Text that is not italicised indicates points that should be said by leaders as part of their talk.

SECTION 2 – HOW TO RUN A GREAT YOUTH ALPHA COURSE

This section tells you everything you need to know in order to run a great course. It includes helpful checklists to make sure all the details of your course are accounted for.

SECTION 3 – EXPERT ADVICE ON RUNNING YOUTH ALPHA

This section contains articles on the many different aspects of running a Youth Alpha course, all of which are written by youth ministry professionals.

SECTION 4 – TEAM TRAINING

This section contains full talk outlines for the two team training sessions. This will help you to equip your team to run the course successfully.

APPENDICES

This section contains all the appendices that are referred to throughout this *Leaders' Guide*. Each appendix contains additional information that will help you to run your course.

We hope that you will find this *Leaders' Guide* helpful. Enjoy!

SECTION 1

THE YOUTH ALPHA COURSE SESSIONS

INTRODUCTION TO SESSIONS

This section includes all of the Youth Alpha talk outlines.

The talks are written so that you can give them exactly as they are; all you have to do is choose which illustration you prefer for each teaching point. More recent illustrations are also available on TalkBuilder. Anything that is listed in *italics* is for leaders' reference only – italics represent instructions, and they are not part of the talk. Points that should be made in the talk are emphasised by appearing in regular type, usually with bullet points preceding them.

Feel free to expand any point, use more than one illustration, or add personal stories wherever you like. The aim of this guide is to be flexible!

ILLUSTRATION OPTIONS

Each option is represented by a different icon so you can immediately tell what there is to choose from. The icons are as follows:

 MEDIA – movie clip, internet video clip, picture, song or other type of media

 PRACTICAL – activity or demonstration

 GAME – a game (surprisingly!)

 STORY – either true or fictional

 ANALOGY – helps explain a teaching point

 TESTIMONY – a chance to add your own story to make it personal

 PRAYER – a chance for prayer

 REFLECTION – time for the group to reflect on what they've learnt

Most options are broken down into four elements to help you choose which to use:

Quick summary
An overview of the illustration

Equipment / resources needed
What you need

How it works
An explanation of what to do

How to link to talk
How to make the illustration do its job for you!

See how long each option takes to prepare by referring to this symbol:

PREPARATION TIME **0**
minutes

In addition to the illustration options, most sessions also contain two other optional aids which may help you further explain your teaching points. Please remember that these are in no way compulsory, and depending on your group you may choose to use them always, use them once in a while or never use them at all:

OPTIONAL EXTRA – GOING DEEPER

Helps you delve deeper into a particular point

OPTIONAL JOKES/QUOTES

Quotes from well-known people/jokes to help further illustrate a point

LIST OF SESSIONS

This is a complete outline of the entire Youth Alpha course, including the positioning of the Weekend/Day and its talks. You should give the talks in the order listed. If you want to run your course in eight weeks, rather than the standard ten, you should use the two combined talks 'How Can I Live Free?' (Session 7a) and 'What about the Church and Telling Others?' (Session 8a), omitting sessions 7, 8, 9 and 10. If you want to run your course in nine weeks, use 'How Can I Live Free?' (Session 7a) and omit sessions 7 and 9. For sample timings for your Youth Alpha course, please see Appendix 1 on page 400, or online at youthalpha.org/lgmedia

Introductory session	Christianity: Boring, Untrue, Irrelevant?
Session 1	Who Is Jesus?
Session 2	Why Did Jesus Die?
Session 3	How Can We Have Faith?
Session 4	Why and How Do I Pray?
Session 5	Why and How Should I Read the Bible?
Session 6	How Does God Guide us?

Youth Alpha Weekend/Day

Weekend Session 1	What about the Holy Spirit?
Weekend Session 2	How Can I Be Filled with the Holy Spirit?
Weekend Session 3	How Can I Make the Most of the Rest of My Life?

Session 7	How Can I Resist Evil?
Session 7a	How Can I Live Free? *[Sessions 7 and 9 combined – for use in 8/9 week courses]*
Session 8	Why and How Should I Tell Others?
Session 8a	What about the Church and Telling Others? *[Sessions 8 and 10 combined – for use in 8 week courses]*
Session 9	Does God Heal Today?
Session 10	What about the Church?

INTRODUCTORY SESSION

CHRISTIANITY: BORING, UNTRUE, IRRELEVANT?

INTRODUCTORY SESSION
CHRISTIANITY: BORING, UNTRUE, IRRELEVANT?

SUMMARY

AIMS OF THIS SESSION

- To encourage people to think about the bigger questions of life

- To explain that Christianity is not boring, untrue or irrelevant

- To explore the idea of doing a Youth Alpha course

NOTES

- It is really important that the talk is brief and to the point – any hint of it being long and boring and people won't want to join the course

- Get your team to hand out invitations after the talk and ask them to encourage/invite people to come on the course

SESSION OVERVIEW

- Launch event activity (eg, band or similar)
- Talk
    - Introduction
    - Point 1 – Boring?
    - Point 2 – Untrue?
    - Point 3 – Irrelevant?
    - Conclusion and invitation to join the next Youth Alpha course
- End of launch event

WELCOME

- Welcome to the Youth Alpha launch party!

- It's great to have you here with us

- Over the next few minutes, I'm going to look at a couple of questions that will encourage you to think about some important issues

Choose one of the following 3 options:

OPTION 1

VOX POPS: 'WHAT DO YOU THINK ABOUT CHRISTIANITY?'

PREPARATION TIME 5 minutes

Quick summary
Show the group a video in which members of the public share their views on Christianity – some of these views are controversial. The purpose of this is to give the group an idea of what other people think about Christianity.

Equipment / resources needed
The vox pops video can be found online at youthalpha.org/lgmedia
You may want to use a projector and a screen in order to show the film to the whole group.

> Suggested tip
> *If you have time, you could even make your own video showing the public's views on this topic. To create a low-tech version, you could take photos of people and put them on a wall with their thoughts written below.*

How to link to talk
- What do you think about Christianity? Why do people feel so strongly about religion?

OPTION 2

SURVEY

PREPARATION TIME 5 minutes

Quick summary
By asking people to answer several simple questions by a show of hands, you can demonstrate to the group that many people believe that Christianity is boring, untrue and irrelevant.

Equipment / resources needed
None.

How it works

I am going to ask you to answer three questions related to your feelings about Christianity.

One: put your hand in the air if you think Christianity is boring

Two: put your hand up if you think the claims of Christianity are untrue

Three: put your hand up if you think that Christianity is irrelevant to the life of a teenager in today's world

How to link to talk

- Some people feel that Christianity is no longer relevant to us today. What do you think about Christianity?

'BORING, UNTRUE, IRRELEVANT?' TESTIMONY

You might like to share a bit of your own story, especially if you can identify with anyone who considers Christianity to be boring, untrue or irrelevant. Encourage the group by explaining how your opinion changed over time. Tell them how you feel about Christianity now.

You may choose to use one or more of these quotes/jokes to help illustrate your point:

OPTIONAL QUOTES/JOKES

Abraham Lincoln (former president of the USA)

'If all the people who fell asleep in church on Sunday morning were laid out end to end … they would be a great deal more comfortable.'

(Abraham Lincoln, president of the USA 1861–1865.)

Robert Louis Stevenson (Scottish author and poet)

[To be stated with surprise:] 'I have been to church today, and am *not* depressed.'

(Robert Louis Stevenson, 1850–1894.)

Joke 1

A vicar was taking a small boy around his church, showing him the memorials of those who died in the World Wars. 'These are the names of all those people who died in the services,' said the vicar. 'Did they die at the morning or the evening service?' asked the boy.

- You may well be wondering why you're here, and that's okay …

- You may be thinking, 'This is the 21st century. What on earth does Christianity have to offer me?'

- Perhaps you're thinking that Christianity is simply boring, untrue and that it has nothing to do with us in our lives today – maybe you think it is irrelevant

- If you're thinking any (or all) of those things, then you are in the right place!

- I want to quickly address each of these objections to Christianity – the objections that suggest it is boring, untrue, and irrelevant

- Jesus Christ said: 'I am the way, the truth and the life' (John 14:6)

- I want to look at each of Jesus' claims but in reverse order, so: life, truth, and way

POINT 1 – BORING?

- Is Christianity boring?

Choose one of the following 2 options:

OPTION 1

THE SIMPSONS MOVIE

PREPARATION TIME **5** minutes

Quick summary

In this clip, we hear Homer loudly announce that he doesn't want to go to church, just as the family are on their way in to a service. This clip perpetuates common misconceptions about the church being boring.

Equipment / resources needed

A copy of the film The Simpsons Movie, *Twentieth Century Fox Film Corporation, 2007. Certificate PG.*

▷ *Chapter 3: 0:03:57*   ☐ *Chapter 3: 0:04:45*

Projector and screen (or a TV), and a DVD player.

How to link to talk

- I think many people feel this way about church – they think of it as boring

OPTION 2

STUDENT IN CHURCH

PREPARATION TIME **0** minutes

Quick summary
This joke demonstrates how some people feel about preachers in church, and how they feel about church in general – they assume it is always dull and boring.

Equipment / resources needed
None.

How it works
A student went to her college chapel, and after looking at the order of service, groaned aloud. The middle-aged lady next to her turned and asked what the matter was. The student replied, 'It's the man who's preaching today. He's one of my teachers. I have to go to his classes and he's the dullest man alive. Everything he says is utterly boring.'
'Oh,' said the older woman, 'Do you know who I am?'
The student looked at her and said she didn't.
'Well,' said the woman, 'I'm that preacher's wife!'
The student swallowed hard and said faintly, 'Well, do you know who I am?'
'No,' said the professor's wife.
'Well that's fortunate,' said the student as she got up and ran away!

How to link to talk

- That's the impression a lot of people have about church – that preachers are boring and church is dull

- Jesus said, 'I am the life' (John 14:6)

- Many people think that Christianity is about having no life. People believe that Christianity, and church in particular, is utterly boring

- But the reality is that Jesus says he came to give us life, and life to the full (John 10:10)

- Following Jesus is not only the most exciting way to live life to the fullest, but it is the reason you were created – it is why you are here. It's not meant to be boring!

POINT 2 – UNTRUE?

- Is Christianity untrue?

Choose one of the following 4 options:

OPTION 1

THE LION, THE WITCH AND THE WARDROBE

PREPARATION TIME 5 minutes

Quick summary
In this scene, we see the children enter the wardrobe and stumble into the winter of Narnia. When Lucy first tells her siblings what she has seen, they don't believe her, despite the fact she is telling the truth. Although at first it seems that Narnia is imaginary, it is actually real, and the others are challenged in their disbelief.

Equipment / resources needed
A copy of the film The Chronicles of Narnia: The Lion, the Witch and the Wardrobe, *Disney Enterprises, Inc. and Walden Media, LLC, 2005. Certificate PG.*

▶ *Chapter 7: 0:33:33*   ☐ *Chapter 8: 0:39:00*

Projector and screen (or a TV), and a DVD player.

How to link to talk
- There are millions of people (like Lucy) who think that Christianity is the real deal. Youth Alpha is about encouraging people to step into the wardrobe to see whether there is anything real there; it is about encouraging people to make up their own minds

OPTION 2

PEPE RODRIGUES

PREPARATION TIME 0 minutes

Quick summary
This story shows how easy it is for things to get lost in translation. Rather than relying solely on second hand messages, it is better to see things for yourself.

Equipment / resources needed
None.

How it works
Pepe Rodrigues, one of the most notorious bank robbers in the early settling of western America, lived in Mexico – just across the border from Texas. He regularly crept into Texan towns to rob banks, always returning to Mexico before the Texas Rangers could catch him. The frustrated lawmen were so embarrassed by this that one day they illegally crossed the border into Mexico. Eventually, they cornered Pepe in a bar that he frequented.

Unfortunately, Pepe couldn't speak any English, so the lawmen asked the bartender to translate for them.

The bartender explained to Pepe who these men were, and Pepe began to shake with fear. The Texas Rangers, with their guns drawn, told the bartender to ask Pepe where he had hidden all the money he had stolen from the Texas banks. 'Tell him that if he doesn't tell us where the money is right now, we're going to shoot him dead on the spot!' The bartender translated all this for Pepe.

Immediately, Pepe explained to the bartender in Spanish that the money was hidden in the town well. If they counted down seventeen stones from the handle, they'd find the loot hidden behind the seventeenth stone.

The bartender turned to the Texas Rangers and said in English, 'Pepe is a very brave man. He says that you are a bunch of stinking pigs, and he is not afraid to die!'

[Adapted from Wayne Rice, Hot Illustrations *(Youth Specialties, 1994).]*

How to link to talk

- Sometimes, things get lost in translation (in this example, deliberately!). If most of what you know about Christianity is just stuff you've heard from other people, then you should really check it out properly for yourself

OPTICAL ILLUSIONS

PREPARATION TIME **5** minutes

Quick summary
Show the group some optical illusions, and ask them questions related to what they see (or what they think they see).

Equipment / resources needed
You can find 'Optical illusions' on Sheet 1 at the end of this session, or online at youthalpha.org/lgmedia
You may want to use a projector and a screen in order to show the illusions to the whole group.

How to link to talk

- Things are not always as they first appear. The truth is sometimes hidden

EVERYTHING IS SPIRITUAL

PREPARATION TIME **5** minutes

Quick summary
In this clip, Rob Bell talks about the concept of a two-dimensional world called 'Flatland'. This shows how we can often come to the wrong conclusion over such big questions.

Equipment / resources needed
A copy of the film Everything is Spiritual, *Flannel, 2007.*

▷ Chapter 4: 0:35:30   ☐ Chapter 4: 0:39:28

Projector and screen (or a TV), and a DVD player.

How to link to talk

- Like Rob describes in that clip, we can often draw the wrong conclusions to the big questions because they are such difficult concepts to grasp. It is hard to imagine a God who is bigger than our dimensions and our thinking, but that doesn't mean it isn't true – so it is worth investigating

- Jesus said, 'I am the truth'

- Truth isn't such a popular concept in our culture today. We speak of things being true 'for me' – and we are happy with the idea that one person's truth is another person's untruth

- But Christianity doesn't work that way. Its claims are so big that it must either be true for everyone, or true for no one. What it cannot be is true for some and not others. It's either true, or it's not. Jesus said that he *is* truth – not *a* truth, but *the* truth

- I believe that Jesus helps us make sense of the world around us

- If you are up for joining us on Youth Alpha, part of what we'll be doing is looking into some of the claims Jesus made and seeing whether they are true or not. It's worth finding out

POINT 3 – IRRELEVANT?

- Is Christianity just plain irrelevant?

Choose one of the following 3 options:

OPTION 1

THE OFFICE

PREPARATION TIME **5** minutes

Quick summary
In this clip, David Brent does an impromptu dance and manages to embarrass both himself and his staff. His dance is completely irrelevant to anything else that is going on in this clip – it literally comes out of nowhere.

Equipment / resources needed
A copy of The Office Series 2, *episode 5, BBC Worldwide, 2003. Certificate 15.*

▷ Chapter 2: 0:09:52   ☐ Chapter 3: 0:11:56

Projector and screen (or a TV), and a DVD player.

How to link to talk

- David Brent thinks he is a cool manager and a good dancer! In reality, he is out of touch with his staff and his dance is irrelevant to popular culture

- Many people see the church in a similar light – they think that it is trying hard to be relevant, but really it is just out of touch with our culture

OPTION 2

'WC' LETTER

PREPARATION TIME **0** minutes

Quick summary
This story shows how it is possible to come to the wrong conclusion if you don't have enough information. If you only hear snippets of random information regarding Christianity, it is easy to conclude that it is irrelevant.

Equipment / resources needed
None.

How it works
An English lady wanted to buy a house in Switzerland. Following a viewing of the perfect property, she realised that she hadn't seen a toilet there. She wrote to the Swiss estate agent, and enquired about the location of the 'WC' [an old English abbreviation for 'water closet' – a polite way of saying toilet!].

The estate agent's knowledge of English was limited, so he asked the parish priest to translate the letter for him. The only meaning for the abbreviation 'WC' that the priest could think of was either Wayside Chapel or Wesleyan Chapel. As a result, the reply sent from the estate agent read:

'My Dear Madam,

I take great pleasure in informing you that the WC is situated nine miles from the house in a beautiful grove of pine trees surrounded by lovely grounds. It is capable of holding 229 people and it is open on Sundays and Thursdays only. As there are a great number of people expected during the summer months, it is an unfortunate situation, especially if you are in the habit of going regularly. It may interest you to know that my daughter was married in the WC and it was there that she met her husband. I can remember the rush there was for seats. There were ten people to every seat usually occupied by one.

You will be glad to hear that a good number of people bring their lunch and make a day of it, while those who can afford to go by car arrive just in time. I would especially recommend your ladyship to go on Thursdays when there is an organ accompaniment. The acoustics are excellent, even the most delicate sounds can be heard everywhere.

The newest addition is a bell donated by a wealthy resident of the district. It rings every time a person enters. A bazaar is to be held to provide plush seats for all, since the people feel it is long needed. My wife is rather delicate and she cannot attend regularly. It is almost a year since she went last, and naturally it pains her very much not to be able to go more often. I shall be delighted to reserve the best seat for you, where you shall be seen by all. For the children, there is a special day and time so that they do not disturb the elders. Hoping to be of some service to you. Yours faithfully, etc ...'

How to link to talk

- That story illustrates how easy it is to get the wrong idea from limited information. It is possible to jump to the wrong conclusion with quite spectacular results

- Many people have come to the conclusion that church and Christianity is irrelevant to their lives, but what if they have jumped to the wrong conclusion?

OPTION 3

'CHARLIE BIT ME'

PREPARATION TIME **5** minutes

Quick summary
This clip is called, 'Charlie bit me' and it is one of the most viewed videos ever in the history of the internet! It is very funny, but is totally irrelevant to today's topic.

Equipment / resources needed
To find the link for this clip, please visit youthalpha.org/lgmedia
You may want to use a projector and screen in order to show the clip to the whole group.

How to link to talk

- You might ask what relevance that clip has to our talk today. Well, it has no relevance at all! It's just funny

- The reason I showed it is because it is totally irrelevant to this subject. That is what many people say about Christianity: it is totally irrelevant to their life

- Jesus said, 'I am the way' (John 14:6)

- Jesus provides direction in our lives. Far from being irrelevant, he is totally relevant to all of us

- With Jesus to show us the way, we can have a life full of purpose and meaning – and fun!

- Living as a Christian is definitely not the easiest way of life, but it is the most fulfilling, because with Jesus in our lives we become more like the people that God created us to be

CONCLUSION

- Christianity is not boring – it is about living life to the full

- Christianity is not untrue – it is the truth

- Christianity is not irrelevant – it transforms the whole of our lives

- Let me ask you a final question: are you absolutely certain that your views on Christianity are based on solid, trustworthy information? Is there even a chance that you are jumping to conclusions based on limited information?

- I want to encourage you to check this out for yourself, so come and join us on our next Youth Alpha course. It starts *[insert date]*. We'll have some food, a short presentation, and then a chance to chat in small groups. It's a great way to begin to figure out some answers to this stuff. I hope you'll come!

- Thanks for listening

SHEET 1
OPTICAL ILLUSIONS

What do you see – two faces or a vase?

Which sphere is bigger?

Answer: They are the same size

SHEET 1 (continued)

Are these squares the same size or different?

Answer: They are the same

Are these lines parallel or crooked?

Answer: Straight

Which line is longer?

Answer: They are the same size

SESSION 1

WHO IS JESUS?

SESSION 1
WHO IS JESUS?

SUMMARY

AIMS OF THIS SESSION

- To encourage the group to think about who Jesus is (and in some cases, to correct false views)

- To explain that there is evidence for his life, death and resurrection

- To explore these questions together for the first time, have fun, and for small groups to get to know each other and begin discussion

NOTES

- Encourage small groups to start by getting to know each other. Some ideas are suggested in the session notes

- Remind leaders that if they ask each person in the group why they have come along to Youth Alpha, it is a good idea to start with the most negative person – this will make everyone else feel like they can be totally honest

- Stress that it is really important that leaders finish on time or even a bit early, especially as it is the first session

- Make sure you finish your prayer time and team meeting at least thirty minutes before the advertised start time, so that you are ready to welcome people as they arrive

SESSION OVERVIEW

- Food
- Welcome
- Ice breaker game
- Worship *(if applicable)*
- Talk
  - Introduction
  - Point 1 – Did Jesus actually exist?
  - Point 2 – Was Jesus more than just a 'good man'?
  - Point 3 – Is there any evidence to support Jesus' claims?
  - Point 4 – Is there any evidence for Jesus' resurrection?
  - Conclusion
- Small groups

WELCOME

- Welcome to Youth Alpha!

- It's great to have you here with us

- Before we get going, let's start with an ice breaker game

ICE BREAKER GAME

Choose one of the following 3 options:

NAME GAME

PREPARATION TIME **0** minutes

Quick summary
A very simple game which can be played to help the group quickly learn each other's names.

Equipment / resources needed
None.

How it works
Get into the small groups you will have discussion with later. Starting with the group leader, each person must say their first name, preceded by a word that starts with the same letter. The word must describe their personality, for example: Macho Matt, Super Sarah, Phunny Phil, etc. The next person must start by saying the name(s) and word(s) of those before them, and then say their own, so that the last person has lots to remember!

> ### Suggested tip
> *Vary this game by playing it in a random order. Throw a soft ball at people as a prompt.*
>
> *Alternatively, instead of allowing members of the group only one word to describe themselves, give them three words each (starting with any letter) – a real test of memory!*

FAMOUS NAME GAME

PREPARATION TIME **30** minutes

Quick summary
A game that encourages people to mingle through asking each other questions to help them guess the famous name. This will help group members to learn each other's names and to start to feel comfortable around one another.

Equipment / resources needed

Sticky labels with names of famous people written on them (eg: Kanye West, Mickey Mouse, Scarlett Johansson, etc).

How it works

Stick a label with a famous name on it onto each person's forehead. Then everybody should mingle, introducing themselves to each other before asking a question in order to try to figure out who's name is on their forehead. Each member of the group can ask only one question of each person, and it has to be a question with a 'yes' or 'no' answer (eg, 'Am I male?', 'Am I dead?', 'Am I a singer?' etc).
The first person to guess their name wins, but you should keep going until everyone has figured out their name.

WATER BALLOON GAME

PREPARATION TIME **15** minutes

Quick summary

Teams of people pass a water balloon up and down a line as fast as possible. This should help the groups to relax and begin to feel comfortable around one another.

Look out: teams may get wet!

Equipment / resources needed

A minimum of four water balloons.

How it works

Get everyone into two teams and line the members up one behind the other. Hand a water balloon to the first person in each line. The balloons must be passed backwards as fast as possible, over the head of the first person, then between the legs of the second, over the head of the third, and so on in an over, under, over pattern until the balloon reaches the back of the line. When it reaches the last person, he or she must run to the front of the line and restart the process.
The relay is finished when the original head of the line returns to the front. Feed spare water balloons into the lines whenever they burst.

> Suggested tip
> *Fill plenty of balloons with plenty of water.*
> *Remember: more balloons per line + more water per balloon = more wetness and more fun!*

INTRODUCTION

- Hopefully that game has helped you to get to know each other

- My name is *[insert name]*, and I will be giving the talk today

- *You may like to introduce yourself to the group [share a bit of your story]*

- Now let's talk about the reason we're all here today! Over the next few weeks we're going to be looking at some of the big questions of faith and life. There will be some short talks given from the front, and there will be loads of time for you to chat together and discuss what you really think about what we've said

- I'd encourage you to be open and honest with each other – that's the way to get the most out of Youth Alpha

- So, to kick off the course, we're going to look at the question, 'Who is Jesus?'

Choose one of the following 5 options:

OPTION 1

VOX POPS: 'WHAT DO YOU THINK ABOUT JESUS?'

PREPARATION TIME **5** minutes

Quick summary
Show the group a video in which members of the public share their views on who Jesus is – some views are controversial.
The purpose of this is to show the many different opinions that people have on Jesus.

> Suggested tip
> *If you have time, you could even make your own video showing the public's views on this topic.*

Equipment / resources needed
The vox pops video can be found online at youthalpha.org/lgmedia
You may want to use a projector and a screen in order to show the film to the whole group.

How to link to talk
- What is it about Jesus that leads people to continue talking about him over 2,000 years after he lived?

PICTURES OF JESUS

OPTION 2

PREPARATION TIME **5** minutes

Quick summary
Show the group pictures of Jesus as drawn by people from different cultures. This demonstrates the differing opinions worldwide.

Equipment / resources needed
The pictures you should show can be found online at youthalpha.org/lgmedia
You may want to use a projector and a screen in order to show the pictures to the whole group.

How to link to talk
- It's interesting, isn't it, how people view Jesus based on the ideas of their own culture?

WHAT DID JESUS LOOK LIKE?

OPTION 3

PREPARATION TIME **5** minutes

Quick summary
Give the group the chance to make their own picture of Jesus. This demonstrates how our own culture affects our ideas about what he looked like.

Equipment / resources needed
Magazines and newspapers.
Paper.
Scissors and glue.

How it works
Give the group a range of magazines and newspapers and allow them five minutes to cut, paste and create their own picture of what they think Jesus looked like.

How to link to talk
- It's interesting, isn't it, how our view of Jesus is based on our own culture's ideas?

JESUS AS A SWEAR WORD

OPTION 4

PREPARATION TIME **0** minutes

Quick summary
Give the example of using 'Jesus' as a swear word to demonstrate the widespread acknowledgement of Jesus as a pivotal figure in history.

Equipment / resources needed
None.

How it works

- Many of you will have heard the word 'Jesus' spoken as an expression of frustration or annoyance

- Have you ever wondered why this is? How often have you heard someone stub their toe and say, 'Buddha!' or, 'Mohammed!'?

How to link to talk

- What is it about Jesus that leads to his name being used so much more than any other name?

COIN ILLUSTRATION

PREPARATION TIME **0** minutes

Quick summary

Show the groups a coin and explain that the date on it has been measured from Jesus' birth. This demonstrates the impact that his birth has had on society.

Equipment / resources needed

A coin that has the year printed on it. If it doesn't have the year, the illustration will not work.

How it works

Ask if someone has a coin that you can borrow (have one ready in case they don't). Read out the year the coin was made. If, for example, the date reads 1996, ask:

- It's one thousand nine hundred and ninety-six years since what?

The answer is, '1996 years since the birth of Jesus Christ.' Once the illustration is over, give the coin back ... or don't!

How to link to talk

- Isn't it amazing that one man has changed the course of life so much, we even number our years after his birth?

- Christians follow Christ – hence the word 'Christian' – CHRIST-ian (obviously). It's about having faith in this man Jesus – but not blind faith, faith based on evidence

- Can we prove it beyond any shadow of a doubt? No. But the evidence is good

- Wait a minute – is there any point in looking at Jesus, as we are now, if we don't believe in God? Many believe that. But I would argue that without looking at who Jesus is, we can't find out who God is, or if there even is a God

POINT 1 – DID JESUS ACTUALLY EXIST?

- Yes. Most scholars, Christians and non-Christians alike, agree that the following points are true about the life of Jesus Christ:

    - he was a Jewish man, born in Bethlehem in Judea around 4 BC

    - he was famous for being a great teacher and miracle worker

    - he was crucified by the Roman authorities

    - his followers believed he was the Son of God and that he rose from the dead; they spread the good news

- Yes. The Bible points to him

You may like to work through this optional extra with your group, but it is not essential:

OPTIONAL EXTRA – GOING DEEPER
PREPARATION TIME (5) minutes

TEXTUAL CRITICISM

Quick summary
Through the science of textual criticism, we know that versions of the Bible through the ages have remained true to the original copy – they are more accurate than the copies of other well-respected historical works.

Equipment / resources needed
Leaders can find an additional copy of this table online at youthalpha.org/lgmedia You may want to use a projector and screen in order to show the table to the whole group.

WORK	WHEN WRITTEN	EARLIEST COPY	TIME LAPSE	COPIES
Herodotus	488–428 BC	AD 900	1,300 years	8
Thucydides	c.460–400 BC	AD 900	1,300 years	8
Tacitus	AD 100	AD 1,100	1,000 years	20
Caesar's Gallic War	58–50 BC	AD 900	950 years	9–10
Livy's Roman History	59 BC – AD 17	AD 900	900 years	20
New Testament	AD 40–100	AD 130 (full manuscripts AD 350)	30–310 years	5,000+ Greek 10,000 Latin 9,300 others

---

How it works

- Professor F. F. Bruce, from the University of Manchester in the UK, is an expert in the field of what's known as textual criticism – a science that can determine whether the copies of ancient texts we read now are the same as when they were written

- There are two main questions to ask in order to find out:

  1. How quickly after the original was written was the earliest copy made?
  2. How many copies are there?

How to link to talk

- So, Herodotus and Thucydides were both written in the 5th century BC. The earliest copies that we have are from around AD 900, so there's a 1,300 year gap. For each of these works we have only eight copies, and yet no classical scholar would doubt *their* authenticity

- Tacitus: 1,000 year gap between the original and the first copy – a total of twenty copies

- Caesar's Gallic War: 950 year gap between the original and the first copy – a total of nine or ten copies

- Livy's Roman History: 900 year gap between the original and the first copy – a total of twenty copies

- The New Testament: written between 40 and 100 AD. The earliest copy we have is AD 130, and we have full manuscripts at AD 350. So, at most, there's a 300 year gap. And we don't just have eight or even twenty manuscripts – we have: 5,309 Greek manuscripts, 10,000 Latin manuscripts and 9,300 others

- You can see that the New Testament stands absolutely and unapproachably alone amongst ancient writings – and no serious historian would disagree with that conclusion

POINT 2 – WAS JESUS MORE THAN JUST A 'GOOD MAN'?

- Two big questions to consider are: who did Jesus think he was? And, of course, was he right?

Choose one of the following 3 options:

CHANGELING

PREPARATION TIME **5** minutes

Quick summary
This clip shows how Christine is forced, by a manipulative policeman, to take home a boy who isn't her own son. This can be used as an example of a manipulative leader.

Equipment / resources needed
A copy of the film Changeling, 2008 Universal Studios. Certificate 15.

▷ *Chapter 4: 0:20:00*   ☐ *Chapter 4: 0:24:15*

Projector and screen (or a TV), and a DVD player.

How to link to talk
- Some people believe that Jesus was like this – that he deliberately deceived people about who he was and simply told them what they wanted to hear

TRUTH OR LIES

PREPARATION TIME **0** minutes

Quick summary
This game tests how well people can lie about themselves. Use this to demonstrate how easy it is to do.

Equipment / resources needed
None.

How it works
In small groups, each person must say three things about themselves, two of which are true and one of which is totally made up. The others have to guess which of the facts is false. Try to make them as grand as possible – 'I like cornflakes' as your false fact doesn't quite work. So, if you've met Justin Timberlake or done a parachute jump, make those your true facts and think up an equally improbable one as your lie!

How to link to talk
- It is easy for us to deceive each other, isn't it? But was Jesus deceiving his followers? Many would say that some of his claims were so outrageous that he must have been playing games

TEACHER AT SCHOOL

PREPARATION TIME 0
minutes

Quick summary
Tell the following story to encourage people to think about how they might feel if they heard someone today making the claims that Jesus made.
This demonstrates why some people may have thought Jesus was crazy.

Equipment / resources needed
None.

How it works
'Imagine a new teacher arriving at a school. The school is failing – an educational disaster area. Unlike the rest of the zombies and wannabe-dictators the school employs, this new man is dynamic. He's interesting, he's brilliant and he cares about you, the students, not just about results, the girls fancy him and in time, the boys start talking and dressing like him. In short, he's the best thing that's happened to the school since they started serving chips in the cafeteria.

Then it happens. In the middle of Wednesday morning assembly he gets to his feet and announces: "I am the bread of life. Whoever comes to me will never go hungry." There's a stunned silence. Ms Frittle, the tone deaf music mistress who has a bit of a thing for the new teacher, is so shocked that her mouth drops open and her false teeth fall out.

The new teacher hasn't finished though. Turning to Form 10C, the biggest bunch of delinquents in the school, he declares: "I am the light of the world. Whoever follows me will never walk in darkness." The headmaster's notes drop to the floor with a crash and the first of many giggles ripple around the room.

Still the new teacher is not finished. "I am the resurrection and the life. He who believes in me will live even though he dies; and he who lives and believes in me will never die." By now the school secretary is on the phone to the nearest mental hospital and the head of Year 7 is quietly ushering the petrified 11 and 12 year-olds out of the fire exit. Unconcerned, the new teacher turns to where the PE teachers are seated. "Your sins are forgiven," he says.'

(*Jonathan Brant*, My Whole World Jumped, *pp.38–39, Alpha International 2002.*)

How to link to talk
- How would you feel if that happened to you? You'd think the guy was mad, wouldn't you? Well, some of the stuff that Jesus came out with must have sounded a lot like that 2,000 years ago

- So who did Jesus think he was?

- Let's look at what he said about himself. Jesus was humble, yet he said some outrageous stuff. He said:

  - 'I am the bread of life' (he can satisfy our spiritual hunger, John 6:35)

  - 'If the Son sets you free, you are free indeed' (John 8:36)

  - 'I am the light of the world' (John 8:12)

  - 'I am the resurrection and the life' (he will overcome death and give us eternal life, John 11:25)

  - 'I am the way, truth and the life' (we get to God through him, John 14:6)

  - 'If you have seen me, you have seen God' (John 14:9)

- He also made some pretty big claims that show he thought he was God:

  - he claimed that he could forgive sin – in Mark 2:5 he said to someone, 'Your sins are forgiven.' People knew that only God could forgive sin. It was this sort of comment that annoyed the religious types and led to Jesus being killed

  - he claimed to be the one who would judge the world (Matthew 25:31–32, 40, 45)

  - he claimed to be the Messiah (Mark 14:61–62)

  - he claimed to be Son of God (Mark 14:61)

  - there's the story of Jesus appearing to 'doubting Thomas' after his resurrection (John 20), and Thomas says, 'My Lord and my God', and Jesus basically says, 'Yeah, that's me'

- But of course it is possible that Jesus' claims were wrong

- There are three logical options:

  - Jesus wasn't God, and knew he wasn't, so he was lying: he was a fraudster, an evil, deceptive person **(BAD)**

  - Jesus wasn't God but thought he was: he was genuine, but deluded – insane **(MAD)**

  - Jesus was telling the truth: he is **GOD!**

  - what do you think? Was he bad, mad, or God?

You may choose to use one or both of these quotes to help illustrate your point:

OPTIONAL QUOTES

C. S. Lewis (author of the 'Narnia' books)

'A man who was merely a man and said the sort of things Jesus said wouldn't be a great moral teacher; he'd either be insane or else he'd be the devil of hell. You must make your choice. Either this man was and is the Son of God or else insane or something worse. But don't let us come up with any patronising nonsense about his being a great human teacher. He hasn't left that open to us. He didn't intend to.'

(C. S. Lewis, Mere Christianity, *Macmillan/Collier, 1952.)*

Bono (lead singer of Irish rock band U2)

An interviewer asked: 'Christ has his rank among the world's great thinkers. But Son of God, isn't that far fetched?'
Bono replied, 'No it's not far fetched to me. Look, the secular response to the Christian story always goes like this: he was a great prophet, obviously a very interesting guy … But actually Christ doesn't allow you that. He doesn't let you off that hook. Christ says "I am God incarnate" … So what you are left with is either Christ was who he said he was or a complete nutcase. I'm not joking here. The idea that the entire course of civilisation for over half the globe could have its fate changed and turned upside down by a nutcase, for me *that's* far fetched.'

(Michka Assayas, Bono on Bono – Conversations with Michka Assayas, *Riverhead, 2005.)*

POINT 3 – IS THERE ANY EVIDENCE TO SUPPORT JESUS' CLAIMS?

- Jesus' teaching supports his claims – 'Love thy neighbour', 'Love your enemies', etc, is generally accepted as the best teaching ever, and no one has ever spoken any wiser words since

- His life and works support his claims – people sometimes say Christianity is boring. Jesus was *never* boring! Imagine going with Jesus to a

    - party (he turns the tap water into wine!)

    - picnic (five loaves and two fish become a feast for thousands!)

    - hospital (the sick and lame get up and go home!)

    - funeral (the dead man gets out of his coffin and walks out!)

- His character supports his claims:

    - living for others, a selfless life

    - courageous – dying for others

    - so perfect, his enemies couldn't find anything to convict him of

- His fulfilment of prophecy supports his claims:

    - he fulfilled 300 Old Testament prophecies – 29 in a single day!

- could he have made some of these happen so it *looked* like he was the promised Messiah? Maybe – but only if he could have planned his birth, birthplace, mother, death and burial with perfect accuracy … no easy feat!

• His resurrection from the dead supports his claims:

- if true, it is proof he is God. The physical resurrection of Jesus is the cornerstone of Christianity

You may choose to use this quote to help illustrate your point:

OPTIONAL QUOTE

The writer and atheist, Richard Dawkins, was quoted by Matthew Parris as saying this: 'If the resurrection is not true, Christianity becomes null and void', and he's right! The resurrection is the foundation of Christianity.

(Matthew Parris, 'Another Voice', The Spectator, 22 April 2006.)

POINT 4 – IS THERE ANY EVIDENCE FOR JESUS' RESURRECTION?

Let me run through four quick bits of evidence before we finish:

• Jesus' body wasn't in the tomb

- did his followers take it? No, they all died for Jesus; would they have died for a lie?

- did the authorities take it? No, as they could have simply shown his body to stop rumours about Jesus rising again (think how quick the Iraqi authorities were to prove that they had executed Saddam Hussein by showing his body)

- did thieves steal it? No, because all that was left in the tomb were Jesus' grave clothes (the most valuable item, and the only thing graverobbers wanted in those times)

• Jesus' presence with the disciples

- in the Bible he appeared eleven times after his resurrection, once to over 500 people. It's hard for 500 people to have the same hallucination at the same time!

• The immediate impact afterwards

- when Jesus died, the disciples were scared and went into hiding. Their leader, who they thought was going to fight the Roman authorities on their behalf, had just died. Yet just days later, they were ready to change the world!

- Christian experience over last 2,000 years

    - millions, even billions, have followed Christ over the years and have experienced a relationship with him

CONCLUSION

- And that is my experience too …

 'RELATIONSHIP WITH JESUS' TESTIMONY

Speak personally about what having a relationship with Jesus means to you.

- So to sum up what I've talked about today:

- Jesus is real. He is a real figure in history, he existed

    - he claimed to be the Messiah – God's son

    - he died on the cross and rose again

    - trusting Jesus is a step of faith – but there is proof to help us make that step

You may choose to use one or more of these quotes to help illustrate your point:

OPTIONAL QUOTES

Sir Arthur Conan Doyle (author of the 'Sherlock Holmes' novels)

'When you have eliminated the impossible, whatever remains, however improbable, must be the truth.'

(Arthur Conan Doyle, 1859–1930.)

C. S. Lewis (author of 'Narnia' books)

'We are faced, then, with a frightening alternative. The man we are talking about was and is just what he said or else insane or something worse. Now, it seems to me obvious that he was neither insane nor a fiend; and consequently, however strange or terrifying or unlikely it may seem, I have to accept the view that he was and is God.'

(C. S. Lewis, Mere Christianity, *Macmillan/Collier, 1952.)*

Jade Goody (the late British celebrity, weeks before she died)

'I'm absolutely exhausted but I've got to keep going for my boys. I want them to believe in Jesus and God.'

(Ben Leach, 'Jade Goody vows to attend sons' christening', The Telegraph, 25 February 2009.)

QUICK PRAYER TO CLOSE

PREPARATION TIME **0** minutes

Quick summary
Pray to end your session.

Equipment / resources needed
None.

How it works

- I am just going to say a short prayer to close

- Lord, thank you for everyone who has come today. I pray that you would be with us over this course and that you would help each of us to be open to you and honest with each other. Please be with us all this week, in Jesus' name, Amen

How to link to talk

- Now we're going to have a quick break and then go into our small groups

- I want to encourage you to be really honest and say what you really think about what I've said. Have fun, and I'll see you next time

QUOTES ABOUT LIFE

PREPARATION TIME **0** minutes

Quick summary
Some poignant quotes about life.

Equipment / resources needed
The quotes can be found online at youthalpha.org/lgmedia
You may want to use a projector and a screen in order to show them to the whole group.

How to link to talk

- Now we're going to have a quick break and then go into our small groups

- I want to encourage you to be really honest and say what you really think about what I've said. Have fun, and I'll see you next time

---

Suggested tip
You could play the quotes to some music. Coldplay's 'Yellow' fits well.

SESSION 1
WHO IS JESUS?

SMALL GROUP DISCUSSION QUESTIONS

[These can be combined at the end of the talk or interspersed after each teaching point. You can find an additional copy of this sheet online at youthalpha.org/lgmedia]

We suggest you begin your small group discussion by getting to know each other a bit. Here are some ideas to help break the ice:

1. *Play the name game. As listed in the 'Ice breaker games' section at the start of the session, starting with the group leader, each person must say their first name preceded by a word that starts with the same letter. The word must describe their personality, for example: Macho Matt, Super Sarah, Phunny Phil, etc. The next person must start by saying the name(s) and word(s) of those before them, and then say their own, so that the last person has lots to remember!*

2. *Each person must say their name, and then tell the group what their favourite film/ book/TV programme/song is*

3. *Each person must say their name, followed by the name of the person they'd most like to be stuck in a lift with (this person could be famous, dead, alive … there are no restrictions)*

4. *Each person must say their name, and then tell the group what one luxury item they'd take with them if they were stranded on a desert island*

POINT 1 – DID JESUS ACTUALLY EXIST?

- If someone had asked you this morning 'who was Jesus?' what would you have said?
- If you had a chance to meet Jesus, what would you ask him?
- Why do you think the life of one man has had such an impact on the world, whether you believe he was God or not?
- What is the one big question you would like to have answered on this course?
  [It might be good to write these down for future group discussions]

POINT 2 – WAS JESUS MORE THAN JUST A 'GOOD MAN'?

- How do you feel about the idea that Jesus was either bad, mad, or God?
- Do you think he was evil and trying to mislead people?
- Do you think he was insane?
- Do you think that maybe he was who he said he was?
- What do you think about Jesus claiming things like, 'I am the way'?

POINTS 3 & 4 – IS THERE ANY EVIDENCE TO SUPPORT JESUS' CLAIMS / IS THERE ANY EVIDENCE FOR JESUS' RESURRECTION?

- What do you feel about each of the arguments given?

    - Jesus' teaching: never bettered since

    - his life: perfect, sinless

    - his miracles

    - his fulfilment of prophecies made years before he was born

    - his resurrection

    - the fact that the disciples went from scared to fearless

    - the fact that we are here today talking about this!

- Have a look at the 'Conspiracy theories' hand out *[see Sheet 2; or download from youthalpha.org/lgmedia]* and talk about the different suggestions and how likely/ unlikely they may be

SHEET 2
CONSPIRACY THEORIES
HAND OUT

These facts about Jesus are agreed by everybody, believer and skeptic alike.

Fact 1   The Romans crucified Jesus

Fact 2   Jesus' body was placed in a tomb that was closed with a large stone and guarded by soldiers

Fact 3   On the third day after Jesus' death, the tomb was found to be empty

Fact 4   The belief that Jesus had been raised from the dead spread through the known world

CONSPIRACY THEORY ONE – JESUS DIDN'T REALLY DIE

Some people have argued that Jesus didn't really die on the cross – he only passed out from the pain and exhaustion. They believe that when he was taken off the cross and laid down in a comfortable position in a cool tomb he simply recovered consciousness, got up and walked off into the sunset to live happily ever after.

CONSPIRACY THEORY TWO – THE DISCIPLES STOLE THE BODY

Some people believe that in the middle of the night the disciples crept up and overpowered the sleepy Roman guards. They then rolled the stone away from the entrance to the tomb, picked up Jesus' lifeless body and disappeared into the night. They started the rumours that Jesus had risen from the dead in order to make themselves seem more important. Throughout the rest of their lives they never let on to anyone what they had done.

CONSPIRACY THEORY THREE – THE AUTHORITIES SECRETLY REMOVED JESUS' BODY

Some people think that the Jewish and Roman authorities worked together to steal and get rid of Jesus' body; perhaps because they didn't want the tomb to become a religious shrine or holy place constantly crowded with Jesus' old followers. They simply took the body and buried it somewhere else, somewhere secret.

PROBLEMS WITH THESE CONSPIRACY THEORIES

CONSPIRACY THEORY ONE – JESUS DIDN'T REALLY DIE

Even before being hung on the cross Jesus was brutally beaten and tortured.
Roman soldiers, who knew when their victim was dead, carried out the crucifixion. Dead bodies in those days were wrapped like mummies in cloth and sticky spices. To escape the tomb Jesus would have had to get out of the grave clothes, roll away a heavy stone and fight the soldiers.

CONSPIRACY THEORY TWO – THE DISCIPLES STOLE THE BODY

The disciples were scared and confused; they weren't thinking of a daring rescue.
The disciples could not have overpowered the soldiers guarding the tomb. It is believed that all the disciples were eventually killed for their belief in Jesus' resurrection. Surely at least one of them would have confessed the truth to save his own skin?

CONSPIRACY THEORY THREE – THE AUTHORITIES SECRETLY REMOVED JESUS' BODY

The authorities hated the fast spreading belief that Jesus was alive and had risen from the dead. If they had had the body, or had known where it was, they would simply have produced it and thrown it down in a public place to prove to everyone that Jesus really was dead. They didn't do this, so we have to assume that they didn't have the body.

NOTE

None of these theories can account for the fact that over 500 people are reported to have seen Jesus alive in the weeks following his crucifixion.

SESSION 2

WHY DID JESUS DIE?

SESSION 2
WHY DID JESUS DIE?

SUMMARY

AIMS OF THIS SESSION

- To encourage the group to know that God loves us and wants to have a relationship with us

- To explain that we have all fallen short of God's standards, but Jesus, in dying for us, took our sins upon himself

- To explore how Jesus' death and resurrection give us eternal life

NOTES

- You may want to briefly mention the Youth Alpha Weekend/Day at the start of this session and give out information packs about this. If you think it is a bit early, then wait until next week

- Remind leaders that it is important that they finish on time

- Make sure you finish your prayer time and team meeting at least thirty minutes before the advertised start time, so that you are ready to welcome people as they arrive

SESSION OVERVIEW

- Food
- Welcome
- Ice breaker game
- Worship *(if applicable)*
- Talk
  - Introduction
  - Point 1 – What's the problem?
  - Point 2 – What's the solution?
  - Point 3 – What are the results?
  - Conclusion
- Small groups

WELCOME

- Welcome back to Youth Alpha!

- It's great to have you here with us again

- Before we get going, let's start with an ice breaker game

ICE BREAKER GAME

Choose one of the following 4 options:

TURN THE CARPET

PREPARATION TIME 0 minutes

Quick summary
Teams must try to maintain their balance while turning over the carpet they are standing on.

Equipment / resources needed
Between one and three (depending on the number of teams) rugs, carpets, tarpaulins or bed sheets (they must be big enough for eight people to stand on at a squeeze).

How it works
Divide everyone into groups of about eight people and give each group a rug (or equivalent). The group must try to turn over the rug, flipping it from top-side up to bottom-side up, without anyone stepping off it until it is perfectly turned over and flat again.
The game totally restarts if any group member touches the floor with any part of their body.
We suggest you spend no longer than ten minutes on this game.

FINGER COUNT

PREPARATION TIME 0 minutes

Quick summary
A simple elimination game with a bit of maths thrown in for good measure.

Equipment / resources needed
None.

How it works
Your groups should start by dividing into pairs. They should stand facing each other, with their hands behind their backs. On the count of three, each person should draw their hands out in front of them, showing the other person a combination of fingers. The winner is the first one to add up the total number of fingers on show on all four hands.
The winner stays standing, the loser sits down. The winners play each other, and the game should continue until you have one ultimate champion.

THE DOUGHNUT GAME

PREPARATION TIME 5 minutes

Quick summary
Volunteers try to eat hanging doughnuts without using their hands.

Equipment / resources needed
Between three and six ring doughnuts (or apples), depending on the number of players.
Between three and six long pieces of string from which to hang the doughnuts.

How it works
Attach a string to three (or more, if necessary) ring doughnuts (or to the stalks of three apples) and hang them from the ceiling (or you can have people stand on a chair and hold them). Ask for three volunteers who will try to eat the doughnuts/apples while keeping their hands behind their backs. Set a time limit for completion (we suggest spending no more than one minute on this game); at the end of this time, the person who has eaten the most of their doughnut/apple is the winner!

> ### Suggested tip
> *To make things even more difficult, you could blindfold the volunteers.*

SPEED MEETING!

PREPARATION TIME 5 minutes

Quick summary
Like speed dating, minus the dating.

Equipment / resources needed
A chair for each person in your group.

How it works
This should be done in your pre-arranged small groups.
Divide the chairs into equal groups and arrange each set in a circle – one inside the other, with the inner ring facing the outer ring (creating pairs). Ask people to take their seats, and read out the first question on the list below. Allow each member of every pair thirty seconds to answer the question.
When one minute is up, one of the rows should take a step to the right so they are facing someone different and new pairs are formed. Read the next question.
Continue to rotate every sixty seconds until all the questions have been answered.

Here are some examples of questions you could ask:

1. Where do you go to school, and what do you think of it?

2. What are your favourite TV programmes and why?

3. What has been the greatest moment of your life so far?

4. Who is the person you know best in this room and why?

5. What is your favourite animal and why?

6. How did you come to be here today?

INTRODUCTION

- Hopefully that game has helped you to get to know a few more people

- Welcome to week two of Youth Alpha – if this is your first week and you've just joined us, this is the perfect time to begin the course!

- My name is *[insert name]* and I will be giving the talk today

- *You may like to introduce yourself to the group [share a bit of your story]*

- Last week we asked, 'Who is Jesus?' We looked at some evidence which shows that Jesus did exist, and we also heard some of the stuff he said about himself

- This week we're looking at the central part of the Christian faith – Jesus' death on the cross. But why did Jesus die?

Choose one of the following 4 options:

OPTION 1

THE MIRACLE MAKER

PREPARATION TIME **5** minutes

Quick summary
This clip depicts Jesus' crucifixion, demonstrating his violent death.

Equipment / resources needed
A copy of the film The Miracle Maker, *SAF and Christmas Films, 2000. Certificate U.*

▷ *Chapter 17: 1:10:08* ☐ *Chapter 17: 1:13:27*

Projector and screen (or a TV) and a DVD player.

How to link to talk
- Do you ever find it strange that Christianity is based entirely around the brutal death of one person? Isn't that kind of weird? Why is Jesus' death so prominent for Christians?

FOUR WOMEN WITH JEWELLERY ON

PREPARATION TIME **5** minutes

Quick summary
Show a picture of four women with different types of jewellery on, in order to demonstrate that the cross, once a means of execution, has now become a fashion symbol.

Lady one – hang man's noose earrings
Lady two – pearl necklace
Lady three – electric chair earrings
Lady four – cross around neck

Equipment / resources needed
The pictures you should show can be found online at
youthalpha.org/lgmedia
You may want to use a projector and a screen in order to show the pictures to the whole group.

How to link to talk
- So looking at these ladies, which is the odd one out?

- The odd one out is the lady with the pearls, because she isn't wearing an instrument of death and torture as jewellery

- Why do so many people (including loads of celebrities) wear a tool of torture around their neck? Why is it that an instrument of execution is the most common and recognisable symbol of the Christian faith? Why is the cross at the heart of Christianity?

GALLOWS JEWELLERY

PREPARATION TIME **45** minutes

Quick summary
Wear a gallows around your neck to show that the cross, too, is like that – a symbol of death. This demonstrates that the cross, once a means of execution, has now become a fashion symbol.

Equipment / resources needed
Make yourself a mini gallows using wood or plasticine.

How it works
Place your homemade gallows around your neck as if it is fashionable to do so.

How to link to talk
- How would you all feel if I wore this to school every day? It would be odd, wouldn't it?

- But yet many people wear crosses as pretty jewellery, perhaps often without thinking about what a cross actually is – a means of execution! Is that strange?

- Why is an instrument of execution the symbol of the Christian faith?

IMAGES OF THE CROSS

PREPARATION TIME **5** minutes

Quick summary
Show several pictures of Jesus on the cross in order to demonstrate to the group a number of different representations. You could play some music while you look at the images.

Equipment / resources needed
The pictures you should show can be found online at youthalpha.org/lgmedia
You may want to use a projector and a screen in order to show the pictures to the whole group.

How to link to talk
- Death by crucifixion, on a cross, was probably the cruellest and most painful way to die

- So why do Christians base their faith on, and even wear a symbol of, the painful death of one man 2,000 years ago?

You may like to work through this optional extra with your group, but it is not essential:

OPTIONAL EXTRA – GOING DEEPER

PREPARATION TIME **0** minutes

CRUCIFIXION

Quick summary
Tell the group the true story of Jesus' crucifixion.

Equipment / resources needed
None.

How it works
Cicero described crucifixion as 'the most cruel and hideous of tortures.
Jesus was stripped and tied to a whipping-post, he was flogged with four or five strips of leather interwoven with sharp, jagged bone and lead'
Eusebius, the third-century historian, described Roman flogging in these terms:
'The sufferer's veins were laid bare, and the very muscles, sinews and bowels of the victim were opened to exposure. He was then taken to the Praetorium, where a crown of thorns was thrust on his head. He was forced to carry a heavy crossbar

on his bleeding shoulders until he collapsed

'When they reached the site of crucifixion he was again stripped naked. He was laid on the cross and six-inch nails were driven into his forearms just above the wrists. His knees were then twisted sideways so that the ankles could be nailed between the tibia and the Achilles tendon. He was lifted up on the cross, which was then dropped into a socket in the ground. There he was left to hang in intense heat and unbearable thirst, exposed to the ridicule of the crowd. He hung there, in unthinkable pain, for six hours while his life slowly drained away. It was the height of pain and depth of shame'

How to link to talk

- As you can see, death by crucifixion, on a cross, was probably the cruellest and most painful way to die

- So why do Christians base their faith on, and even wear a symbol of, the painful death of one man 2,000 years ago?

POINT 1 – WHAT'S THE PROBLEM?

- God made the world and designed us to be in relationship with him. What he really wants is to have a friendship, a relationship, with us

- But we can only be friends with God if we manage to live up to the standards he sets for us

- If you've read the newspapers at any point recently, you'll see it's pretty obvious that the world isn't perfect. There is plenty of bad stuff going on around us

- Humans have a problem – we have all done wrong. The Bible, and Christians who follow the Bible, call this sin (Romans 3:23)

- Sin is an old-fashioned and unpopular word, but it refers to all that we do wrong (Romans 3:23). Here's an example:

DISTORTION ILLUSTRATION

PREPARATION TIME **5** minutes

Quick summary

A visual example of how sin has distorted the world since its creation.

Equipment / resources needed

An image or a video to project on a screen – could be a picture or film of a person in your group.

A projector, or a TV and DVD player, depending on whether you want to show an image or a film.

How it works

Start off with a perfect image on the screen. Gradually tweak the focus controls (or in the case of a video, the tracking controls) so that the image becomes more and more distorted.

How to link to talk

- When God first made humans, he made them perfectly – in his image. As people disobey God and do wrong (sin) the image becomes more and more blurred (a bit like the picture on the screen). The world is broken, and this is not how God intended it to be

- When God made the world, he made it perfect. He gave humans the authority to take charge of it, but human sin has distorted the natural world. This sin puts a barrier between us and God (Mark 7:21–23)

T-SHIRT ILLUSTRATION (PART 1)

PREPARATION TIME **5** minutes

Quick summary

A t-shirt gets messed up, demonstrating how easily we become 'unclean' before God. (Later in this session it gets swapped for a clean one.)

Equipment / resources needed

Two white t-shirts.

Different spreads (jam, honey, peanut butter, etc).

Baby wipes for cleaning up with.

How it works

Wear one of the t-shirts over your clothes. Explain the following:

- God's plan for humankind is that we have a perfect relationship with him. God created us perfect, or clean, like this t-shirt. As long as we are clean, we can have a relationship with him. But the problem is that none of us, not one, is perfect – all of us have sinned (Romans 3:10). As we sin against God, or go against his plan for us, we become dirty and cut ourselves off from him (Mark 7:21–23)

As you explain that we have all sinned (you might ask people to shout out the bad stuff that happens in the world), use your hands and cover yourself in jam, marmite, peanut butter, and other messy spreads. Leave the t-shirt on until later in the talk.

How to link to talk

- When we are like this, with dirt all over us, we can't have a right relationship with God

> **Suggested tip**
> *As a variation, get each person to name a sin and then smear the spread on to the t-shirt themselves. Leave the t-shirt on until later in the talk.*

BANANA BLOW OUT

PREPARATION TIME **0** minutes

Quick summary
Volunteers must try to blow a banana through a pair of tights! This demonstrates the human need for Jesus in our bid to have a right relationship with God.

Equipment / resources needed
Two bananas.
Two pairs of (cheap) tights.
Baby wipes to clean up with.

How it works
Have a volunteer (or two), who doesn't mind getting messy, come to the front. Get them to shove as much of a (peeled!) banana as possible into their mouth and chew it up without swallowing it (and without being sick!). At this stage, they should be unable to speak.
Put a pair of tights over their head (while their mouth is still full of banana) and ask them to try to blow the banana out through the tights. They will be unable to do it. The banana will go all over their faces, and the rest of the group will see this through the tights.

Remove the tights and give them baby wipes to clean their faces with.

How to link to talk

- At the start of that game, our friend represented humanity as it originally was – without sin

- The banana represents sin, and, when we sin, we are unable to communicate with God

- Through our own efforts we are unable to get rid of sin – just as *[name of volunteer]* couldn't get rid of the banana when *[he/she]*

was in the tights! We need help

- With Jesus' help we are able to get rid of sin and live cleaner (less messy) lives

WALL OF FAME AND SHAME

Quick summary
How 'good' do you believe other people are? This game demonstrates how ALL human beings fall short of God's standards.

Equipment / resources needed
Name labels (or post-it notes) – with the names of people past and present written on them (see list that follows).

How it works
Have name labels made up in advance with names written on them (the names below are just suggestions):

- *Mother Teresa*
- *Barack Obama*
- *Bart Simpson*
- *Osama Bin Laden*
- *Ned Flanders*
- *Adolf Hitler*
- *Wayne Rooney*
- *[Your youth leader/teacher]*
- *Your mum*
- *Feel free to add other names*

Ask the group to tell you where to put each name on the 'wall of fame and shame' – the higher up the wall, the better that person's life is/has been; the lower down on the wall, the worse. Start with Mother Teresa. Put each person's name in the appropriate place (as decided by the group) until all are done.

How to link to talk
- It all depends on who we are comparing ourselves to, doesn't it? Some people may seem 'good' and others 'bad'

- But God's standard isn't the ceiling, it's the sky. Even the 'best' person (perhaps someone like Mother Teresa) is still a long way off from God's standards

- We might think we are better than a terrorist (or Bart Simpson!), but we are still imperfect (Mark 7:21–23). None of us are good enough to earn God's love, or to have a relationship with him, because we have all messed up

POINT 2 – WHAT'S THE SOLUTION?

Choose one of the following 6 options:

LORD OF THE RINGS

PREPARATION TIME **5** minutes

Quick summary
In this clip, Gandalf sacrifices himself to save the others. This shows someone dying to save people that they love.

Equipment / resources needed
A copy of the film Lord of the Rings: The Fellowship of the Ring, *New Line Productions, Inc., 2001. Certificate PG.*

▷ *Chapter 30: 1:59:18* ☐ *Chapter 30: 2:01:43*

Projector, screen (or a TV) and a DVD player.

How to link to talk
- Every once in a while someone is noble enough to die or suffer for somebody else. Usually it is for someone they love or someone they feel responsibility for (refer to the video clip you have just watched)

- God loved us SO much that he took our place, substituted himself for us, and suffered the results of our sin. Because Jesus lived a perfect life, he was able to die and take our sin upon himself

- Jesus did not die for just one or two people, but for all those who *have* ever lived and for all those who *will* ever live. Jesus' death on the cross took care of the results of sin once and for all (1 Peter 2:24)

T-SHIRT ILLUSTRATION (PART 2)

PREPARATION TIME **5** minutes

Quick summary
The messy t-shirt from earlier is replaced by a fresh white one, demonstrating that through Jesus' death, our sins are forgiven and God sees us as clean again.

Equipment / resources needed
One white t-shirt.

How it works
Ask a friend on the team to wear a perfectly white t-shirt over their clothes. Get them to come forward and then explain the following:

- God's son Jesus was the only human to ever live a perfect life. He was the only person who ever died without committing a single sin. When Jesus died on the cross, he took upon himself all the sins of the world (1 Peter 2:24)

At this point, both you and the other person should take off the t-shirts you are wearing.

- When Jesus died, he died the death that each of us deserved – the death that we would have had to die, because we have fallen short of God's standards. Jesus died in our place, and gave us his own sinlessness to live in

Give the dirty t-shirt you were wearing to your friend and get them to put it on; you put on their perfectly clean shirt. (Be careful not to get the clean one dirty or it will slightly spoil the point!)

How to link to talk

- Because Jesus took our sin upon himself, when God looks at us he sees us as clean and perfect. We can have a relationship with God through the sacrifice that Jesus made for us

'EVERYTHING' SKIT

PREPARATION TIME **5** minutes

Quick summary
A musical mime showing the battle between God and the devil, with the song 'Everything' by Lifehouse playing in the background. This demonstrates that though we may sin, through Jesus, we can still have a relationship with God.

Equipment / resources needed
To find the link for this clip, please visit youthalpha.org/lgmedia
You may want to use a projector and a screen in order to show the clip to the whole group.

How to link to talk

- As you saw in that clip, we (humankind) were separated from God. Jesus came to reunite us through his death – he took all of our sin upon himself and died in our place, so we may now know God

T-SHIRT ILLUSTRATION MIME

PREPARATION TIME **5** minutes

Quick summary
A mime of someone's dirty t-shirt, representing sin, being replaced with a clean t-shirt to show the difference that Jesus' death has made to us.

Equipment / resources needed
To find the link for this clip, please visit youthalpha.org/lgmedia
You may want to use a projector and a screen in order to show the clip to the whole group.

How to link to talk

- God's son Jesus was the only human to ever live a perfect life. He was the only person who ever died without committing a single sin. When Jesus died on the cross, he took upon himself all the sins of the world (1 Peter 2:24). In other words, he died wearing our dirty t-shirt

- When Jesus died, he died the death that each of us deserved – the death that we would have had to die, because we have fallen short of God's standards. Jesus died in our place, and gave us his own sinlessness to live in

- Because Jesus took our sin upon himself, when God looks at us he sees us as clean and perfect. We can have a relationship with God through the sacrifice that Jesus made for us

OPTION 5

FOOD COLOURING ILLUSTRATION

PREPARATION TIME 5 minutes

Quick summary

A jug of coloured water is made clear again, demonstrating how Jesus' death cleanses us so that we may have a right relationship with God.

Equipment / resources needed
One glass jug filled with water.
Food colouring.
One bottle of bleach (not lemon or colour-fast).

How it works
Take a clear jug of water.

- God created us to live with him, but we ruined his image when we messed up. It's a bit like polluting this water by doing this:

Add one or two drops of (preferably) red food colouring. You only need to add a small amount of colouring and the water should change quickly.

- Jesus died and took our sins – our dirtiness – upon himself. He paid the price for our sins (1 Peter 2:24)

Pour in the bleach and wait a bit – it takes about a minute or two to turn clear again.

How to link to talk

- Because Jesus died for our sins, we are able to be 'clean' again in God's eyes; we are free to have a perfect relationship with him

- Jesus died so that we might be clean in God's eyes

MAXIMILLIAN KOLBE

PREPARATION TIME **0** minutes

Quick summary
This is a true story about a man who gave his own life to save the life of another man. This demonstrates the significance of Jesus' sacrificial death on the cross.

Equipment / resources needed
None.

How it works
On 31 July 1941, a prisoner escaped from Auschwitz (the German concentration camp in World War Two). As a reprisal, the Gestapo arbitrarily selected ten men to die in a underground starvation bunker. One of the men who was selected was a man called Francis Gajowniczek. When Gajowniczek was selected, he cried out. He said, 'Ah, my poor wife and my children. They'll never see me again.' And at that moment, a Polish man – very unimpressive-looking in many ways, with round glasses in wire frames – stepped out, and he said, 'Look, I'm a Catholic priest. I don't have a wife and children.' He said, 'I want to die instead of that man.' And to everyone's amazement, his offer was accepted.

Maximilian Kolbe was the name of the Catholic priest. He was forty-seven years old at the time. And he went with the others to the starvation bunker.

He was a remarkable man – apparently, he got them all praying and singing hymns that transformed the atmosphere in that bunker. He was the last to die – he was given a lethal injection of carbolic acid on 14 August 1941.

Forty-one years later, on 10 October 1982, Maximilian Kolbe's death was put in its proper perspective. In St Peter's Square in Rome, present in a crowd of 150,000 people – including 26 cardinals, 300 bishops and archbishops – was that man, Francis Gajowniczek. The Pope described the death of Maximilian Kolbe in these terms. He said, 'It was a victory, *like* that won by our Lord, Jesus Christ.'

When Gajowniczek himself died in 1995, *The Independent* newspaper published his obituary – it said that he had spent the rest of his life going around telling people what Maximilian Kolbe had done for him, because he'd died in his place.

(*Felix Corley, 'Obituary: Francziszek Gajowniczek',* The Independent, *23 March 1995.*)

How to link to talk
- And in an even more amazing and wonderful way, Jesus offered to die instead of us, so that any who choose to follow him will never have to pay the price of sin themselves

POINT 3 – WHAT ARE THE RESULTS?

- It isn't just that Jesus died for us – plenty of people have given their lives for others

- Jesus came through death and was resurrected – he *conquered* death. This means that we don't need to fear death. Jesus' death and resurrection gives us eternal life

- Surely all of us prefer to follow a guide who has already been on the same path themselves. Jesus knows what he is doing

Choose one of the following 4 options:

OPTION 1

SHREK
PREPARATION TIME 5
minutes

Quick summary
In this clip, Shrek rescues the princess from the tower; he sets her free. This demonstrates the similar way in which Jesus has set us free from the captivity of sin.

Equipment / resources needed
A copy of the film Shrek, Dreamworks LLC, 2001. Certificate U.

▷ *Chapter 8: 0:35:00*   ☐ *Chapter 8: 0:39:52*

Projector and screen (or a TV) and a DVD player.

How to link to talk
- That, in a way, is a bit like what Jesus did for us. He has freed us from captivity, he has rescued us

OPTION 2

LIONEL RICHIE
PREPARATION TIME 0
minutes

Quick summary
This is a true story about Lionel Richie setting his father free from debt. This demonstrates how Jesus has 'paid the debts' of our sins through his death.

Equipment / resources needed
None.

How it works
The singer Lionel Richie (you probably know him better as the father of Nicole Richie from TV's *The Simple Life* with Paris Hilton) was interviewed on television by Jeremy Vine, the British TV presenter. He explained that he came from a very poor background but once he'd started to make money out of his singing, he gave his father this huge birthday present. His father was really excited about it, but as he took off the wrapping paper, he found there was more wrapping paper inside. When he took off another layer, there was more wrapping paper, and more wrapping

paper inside that. The present just got smaller and smaller and smaller, and Lionel could see his father's face falling.

Eventually he got to the heart of it, where he found a little tiny piece of paper. It just said this: 'All debts paid.' His father said, 'What, you've paid my credit card debt?' Lionel said, 'Yeah, I've paid off all your credit cards.' His father said, 'Well, what about the car?' Lionel said, 'Yeah, I've paid off the car.' His father said, 'Well, what about the mortgage?' Lionel said, 'Yeah, I've paid off your mortgage.'

('Jeremy Vine meets … Lionel Richie', BBC, 2004.)

How to link to talk
- All debts paid – that's what Jesus did for us on the cross: he paid all of our debts. Jesus said: 'If the Son sets you free, you will be free indeed' (John 8:36)

THE JUDGE AND THE CRIMINAL   PREPARATION TIME 0
minutes

Quick summary
This story, about a judge and his friend – a criminal – helps to show that although we must pay for our sin, God loves us enough that he gave his only son to cleanse us.

Equipment / resources needed
None.

How it works
There once were two little boys who were best friends. They played together, went to school together, they even went to university together. They were inseparable, until their careers took them in very different directions.

One became a lawyer, the other a criminal. While one eventually became a judge, the other disappeared deeper and deeper into a life of crime. Eventually the criminal was caught and sent to trial.

On the fateful day in the courtroom he came face to face with his old best friend, the judge.

So the judge had a dilemma. He loved his friend but he had to do justice. So the judge handed down the appropriate penalty for the offence – a huge fine. There was no way that his old friend could ever afford to pay what he owed.

But then the judge took off his robes, went down, stood with his friend, and wrote out a cheque covering the cost.

He paid the penalty himself.

How to link to talk
- That, in a way, is a bit like us and God. God loves us, but at the same time, there needed to be a price paid for our sin. God can't just say (just like that judge couldn't just say), 'It's okay, don't worry about it.' But he paid the penalty himself – through Jesus

OPTION 4

THE JUDGE AND THE CRIMINAL ANIMATION   PREPARATION TIME **5** minutes

Quick summary
A cartoon animation of the judge and the criminal story (above). This demonstrates that although we must pay for our sin, God loves us enough that he gave his only son to cleanse us.

Equipment / resources needed
To find the link for this animation please visit youthalpha.org/lgmedia
You may want to use a projector and a screen in order to show the animation to the whole group.

How to link to talk
- That, in a way, is a bit like us and God. God loves us, but at the same time, there needed to be a price paid for our sin. God can't just say (just like that judge couldn't just say), 'It's okay, don't worry about it.' But he paid the penalty himself – through Jesus

---

- Exactly how it works is a mystery, but the Bible teaches that the death of Jesus (who was sinless, who had never done wrong) makes a wonderful difference to us (Romans 3:21–26)

- Jesus' death on the cross took away our sin and made us clean again. We are unstained by all the things we have done wrong

- Jesus' death on the cross means that God is no longer separated from us, and we can begin a relationship with him (2 Corinthians 5:19). Jesus was the last sacrifice

CONCLUSION

- So, let's quickly summarise today's topic:
  - each of us was drowning in our own sin; we were dirty, being sucked under, about to die and become separated from the God who loves us, but in Jesus, God came to our rescue
  - God has made a way for the results of our sin to be dealt with so we can enter into a relationship with him. If we believe that Jesus suffered on the cross for us, and if we say sorry for the things that we have done wrong (our sins), we can begin to know God (Galatians 2:20)
  - if you had been the only person in the world, Jesus would have died for you

'FORGIVENESS' TESTIMONY

Finish by sharing some of your story (or perhaps the story of someone else who is also running the course). Focus on the difference it has made knowing that God has forgiven you for all your sins, and what having a relationship with God through Jesus means for your life.

Choose one of the following 4 options:

OPTION 1

QUICK PRAYER TO CLOSE

PREPARATION TIME **0** minutes

Quick summary
Pray to end your session.

Equipment / resources needed
None.

How it works
- I am just going to say a short prayer to close

- Lord, thank you for everyone who is here today. I thank you for what for what we've talked about in this session and I thank you that you died on a cross so that we could know you. I pray you would guide our discussion as we go into our groups. Amen

How to link to talk
- Now we're going to have a quick break and then go into our small groups

- See you next time!

OPTION 2

PRAYER OF COMMITMENT

PREPARATION TIME **0** minutes

Quick summary
A chance to give members of your group the opportunity to ask Jesus to come into their lives and forgive their sins by leading them in an appropriate prayer.

Equipment / resources needed
None.

How it works
If appropriate, you may wish to give your guests an opportunity to respond to this week's message by asking Jesus to forgive their sins and come into their lives. If you need a model for that prayer you could use this:

- If you feel that you would like to ask Jesus to come into your life and to forgive your sins, then just echo this short prayer in your heart

- Lord Jesus Christ, thank you for dying for me on the cross. I'm sorry for the things in my life that have been wrong. I now turn away from everything that I know is wrong and I now receive your gift of forgiveness. I put my trust in what you did on the cross for me. Please come and fill me with your Holy Spirit and give me the strength to lead the kind of life that deep down I'm longing to lead. Thank you, Lord Jesus. Amen

How to link to talk
- Now we're going to have a quick break and then go into our small groups

- See you next time!

OPTION 3

CROSS ILLUSTRATION

PREPARATION TIME **10**
minutes

Quick summary
Encourage the group to attach their sins to the cross and ask God for forgiveness.

Equipment / resources needed
One big wooden cross.
One small piece of paper per person.
One pen per person.

How it works
Give everyone some paper and a pen. Ask each person to write down one thing in their lives that they know has come between them and God. Get them to fold up their paper and pin it to the cross. This is a symbolic gesture in which we are asking Jesus to forgive us for our sin.

- We are going to have the chance to attach our sins to the cross. Write your sin on a piece of paper, fold it up, and pin it to the cross

How to link to talk
- Now we're going to have a quick break and then go into our small groups

- See you next time!

OPTION 4

LISTEN TO A SONG

PREPARATION TIME **5**
minutes

Quick summary
Ask the group to reflect on what has been talked about this session while listening to a song about the cross.

Equipment / resources needed
An appropriate song to play.
Possible suggestions include, although are not limited to, as you may well know a more fitting/more recent song to use:

- 'Happy day' – Tim Hughes (*from the album* Happy Day, *2009, Survivor Records*)

- 'When I survey' – Tim Hughes (*from the album* Happy Day, *2009, Survivor Records*)

- 'Nothing but the blood' – Matt Redman (*from the album* Facedown, *2004, Sparrow/Sixstep Records*)

A CD player/iPod with speakers.

How it works
- We are going to have some time to reflect upon what we've heard today, while listening to a relevant song

Encourage the group to close their eyes, listen to the words of the song, and/or to talk to God about their lives.

How to link to talk
- Now we're going to have a quick break and then go into our small groups

- See you next time!

SESSION 2
WHY DID JESUS DIE?
SMALL GROUP DISCUSSION QUESTIONS

[These can be combined at the end of the talk or interspersed after each teaching point. You can find an additional copy of this sheet online at youthalpha.org/lgmedia]

POINT 1 – WHAT'S THE PROBLEM?

- What do you think about the idea of wearing a cross now that you've heard what it represents? Is it weird?

- How do you feel about the idea that God wants to have a relationship with you?

- Would you agree that humanity has a problem?

- Do you think the word 'sin' is too old-fashioned? How would you explain the word 'sin' to a friend?

POINT 2 – WHAT'S THE SOLUTION?

- Can you see how the death of Jesus on the cross can solve the problem of sin?

- How do you feel about the idea that Jesus had to die a painful death on the cross in order for you and me to be forgiven of our sins?

POINT 3 – WHAT ARE THE RESULTS?

- What did you think of the example used to show the results of what Jesus did?

- Do you think that having a relationship with God is something positive?

- What did you think of *[speaker]*'s testimony? Did any of that make sense to you?

SESSION 3 –
HOW CAN WE
HAVE FAITH?

SESSION 3
HOW CAN WE HAVE FAITH?

SUMMARY

AIMS OF THIS SESSION

- To encourage the group to know that although following Jesus is a step of faith, it is not a blind step

- To explain what we can base our faith on, and give the group confidence to know that they can make that step

- To explore the idea of the Trinity

NOTES

- You will definitely want to start promoting the Youth Alpha Weekend/Day at the start of this session, and (if you haven't already) give out information packs about this

- Remind leaders that it is important that they finish on time

- Make sure you finish your prayer time and team meeting at least thirty minutes before the advertised start time, so that you are ready to welcome people as they arrive

SESSION OVERVIEW

- Food
- Welcome
- Ice breaker game
- Worship *(if applicable)*
- Talk
    - Introduction
    - Point 1 – What the Father promises
    - Point 2 – What Jesus did
    - Point 3 – What the Spirit does
    - Conclusion
- Small groups

WELCOME

- Welcome back to Youth Alpha!

- It's great to have you here with us again

- Before we get going, let's start with an ice breaker game

ICE BREAKER GAME

Choose one of the following 4 options:

TRIPOD BUILDING COMPETITION

PREPARATION TIME **0** minutes

Quick summary
Teams must try to build the highest tripod using only straws and sellotape.

Equipment / resources needed
Lots of drinking straws.
Sellotape – thirty centimetres per group.
One pair of scissors per group.

How it works
Give each small group lots of drinking straws, a thirty centimetre long piece of sticky tape and a pair of scissors. In the time you have set for them (we suggest spending no more than ten minutes on this game), each group must try to build the strongest tripod possible, using only the materials they have been given. When the time is up, test the tripods by placing books on top of them. The group with the strongest tripod wins.

> Suggested tip
> *To make the competition more challenging, give groups uncooked spaghetti noodles and marshmallows to build their tripods with, instead of straws and tape.*

HUMAN TRIPOD

PREPARATION TIME **0** minutes

Quick summary
Teams must try to build a 'human tripod' using three team members' legs.

Equipment / resources needed
Three trays.
Three plastic jugs of water.

How it works

Create two or three teams of three people. Get them (exclude those in skirts!) to lie on their backs, each with one leg in the air. They must balance a tray with a plastic jug of water on it as long as possible, using only their legs. The team that lasts the longest wins! We suggest you spend no longer than five minutes on this game.

Look out: teams may get wet!

NO CHAIRS TRICK

PREPARATION TIME **0** minutes

Quick summary
A funny game to play with four people.

Equipment / resources needed
Four chairs.

How it works
Set up four chairs in a square formation (the chair seats should face each other, with chair backs facing out, so that they can be easily removed). Ask four volunteers, all of whom should be roughly the same size, to sit on the chairs with their right arm facing the back of the chair. Each should lie back, so their head and the top of their back is resting on the knees of the person behind them. The chairs should be removed, and the strength of the formation is such that the four volunteers can hold their positions without the support of the chairs. (Please visit youthalpha.org/lgmedia to find a link for a clip that you can use for a guide.)

STAND UP, SIT DOWN

PREPARATION TIME **0** minutes

Quick summary
Pairs interlock arms, back to back, and attempt to sit down and stand up together.

Equipment / resources needed
None.

How it works
Start off with two volunteers standing back to back and ask them to lock their arms together. Get them to sit down and stand up without letting go of each other (this is a lot harder than it sounds!). When the original pair get back up to a standing position, add another pair to the game. Continue to add pairs at this 'return to standing' point throughout the game, until the whole group is involved. We suggest you spend no longer than five minutes on this game.

INTRODUCTION

- Hopefully that game has helped you get to know a few more people

- Welcome to week three of Youth Alpha – if this is your first week and you've just joined us, it's great to have you with us

- My name is *[insert name]*

- *You may like to introduce yourself to the group [share a bit of your story]*

- Last week we asked, 'Why did Jesus die?' and we looked at the cross and what Jesus' death means for us

- This week we're looking at the question, 'How can we have faith?' What can we base our faith upon?

Choose one of the following 4 options:

VOX POPS: 'WHAT IS FAITH?' PREPARATION TIME 5 minutes

Quick summary
Show the group a video in which members of the public share their views on faith. This will give the group an idea of what other people base their faith on.

> #### Suggested tip
> *If you have time, you could even make your own video showing the public's views on this topic.*

Equipment / resources needed
The vox pops video can be found online at youthalpha.org/lgmedia
You may want to use a projector and a screen in order to show the film to the whole group.

How to link to talk
- So what do we base our faith on?

COKE TASTE TEST PREPARATION TIME 5 minutes

Quick summary
A blind taste test – can your group spot the real thing? It is hard to know whether something is real if you haven't tried it first.

Equipment / resources needed
Three glasses.
Three types of soft drink – we suggest Coke, Diet Coke and Dr Pepper.

How it works
Lay out three glasses with different types of coke or cola in them – three drinks that look the same but taste different. Make sure no one sees which bottle you pour into which glass – we suggest you pour them before the session. Ask for a volunteer (should be someone who likes soft drinks). Without letting the volunteer touch or smell the drinks, ask which glass has the real coke in it. They should be unable to tell. Ask how they can find out which glass contains real coke. They should say, 'By tasting it.' Let them taste each drink, and hopefully they will be able to tell the difference! Give the volunteer a prize at the end.

> **Suggested tip**
> *As a variation, ask the whole group to come and walk past the glasses and then decide together, rather than just using one volunteer.*

How to link to talk

- It's easy to have an opinion on something without checking it out properly

- It's only when you taste something that you are able to tell the difference between the real thing and imitations

- I believe that it is the same with Christianity. On this course, you will have the chance to 'taste' Christianity, and see for yourself that Jesus is the way

- But how can we ever be sure of our faith?

OPTION 3

PEPSI ADVERT

PREPARATION TIME **5** minutes

Quick summary
A Pepsi advert in which a girl is insulted at being offered an 'imitation' drink. It is hard to know whether something is real if you haven't tried it first.

Equipment / resources needed
To find the link for this advert, please visit youthalpha.org/lgmedia
You may want to use a projector and a screen in order to show the advert to the whole group.

How to link to talk
- The girl in this clip was obviously was able to tell the real from the fake once she tasted her drink!

- It's only when you taste something that you are able to tell the difference between the real thing and imitations

- I believe that it is the same with Christianity. On this course, you will have the chance to 'taste' Christianity, and see for yourself that Jesus is the way

- But how can we ever be sure of our faith?

OPTION 4

URBAN MYTHS

PREPARATION TIME **0** minutes

Quick summary
Tell your group some urban myths to show that, sometimes, it can be tricky to tell the difference between truth and elaborate lies.

Equipment / resources needed
You can find some interesting urban myths to read aloud to your group on Sheet 3 at the end of this session, or online at youthalpha.org/lgmedia

How it works
- Let's take a look at some of these stories

Read the myths aloud to your group.

- Which of these myths do you think is most believable/least believable?

- Why?

- What criteria do you use to decide whether something is true or not? (For example, does the credibility of the witness, our view of the world and the way it works, inconsistency in the story, a better explanation, etc, make a difference to our overall judgment?)

How to link to talk
- In some ways, it is the same with faith. We need to decide if Christianity is the 'real thing' or just an elaborate hoax

- We all have different experiences, so can we ever be sure of our faith?

- Today's session is looking at how we can know that our faith is based on something more than just a fairytale

- So what does it mean to be a Christian? Is it about being a good person? Hopefully – but that's not enough on its own. There are plenty of nice atheists!

- Some people say, 'Well, my parents are Christians, so I guess I am too.' Others say, 'I believe in God – that's enough', but the Bible says, 'Even the demons believe [in God]' (James 2:19). That alone doesn't make you a Christian

- Actually, even going to church doesn't make you a Christian any more than going to McDonalds makes you a Big Mac!

- Being a Christian – a CHRIST-ian – means that you are a follower of Jesus Christ; it means that you have a relationship with God

- In 2 Corinthians 5:17, the Bible explains that those who become Christians become new people. They're not the same any more; the old life is gone and a new life has begun

- How this happens is different for each person. Some know the exact day they became a Christian, whereas some have always been Christians. For others, it is more of a process with no definite 'moment' of change

- Our confidence in our faith can be based upon three things, a bit like a tripod. They are the Father, the Son, and the Holy Spirit – this is called the 'Trinity'. *[If you have time, you may like to give an illustration of the Trinity to make it clearer]*

- The first thing we can base our faith on is the word of God – what the Father promises

POINT 1 – WHAT THE FATHER PROMISES

- I don't know about you, but my feelings go up and down depending on the day, the week and the mood I'm in. But we don't base our faith on how we are feeling day-by-day, although that is important. We can base our faith on what God promises us in the Bible

Choose one of the following 5 options:

OPTION 1

INDIANA JONES

PREPARATION TIME **5** minutes

Quick summary
Indiana Jones takes a step of faith using the instructions from his father's Grail diary. We see Indiana trusting in the map he has been given, stepping out into what seems like a dead end ... and finding that there is a path after all. This is an example of a leap of faith that is based on something, rather than nothing.

Equipment / resources needed
A copy of the film Indiana Jones and the Last Crusade, *Lucasfilm Ltd, 1989. Certificate PG.*

▷ *Chapter 33: 1:42:44* ☐ *Chapter 33: 1:44:32*

Projector and screen (or a TV), and a DVD player.

How to link to talk
- In this clip we see Indiana Jones trusting that the map is right and that there is a path, even though it looks like there isn't

- Faith is taking God's promises and daring to believe them

OPTION 2

TESTS OF FAITH

PREPARATION TIME **0** minutes

Quick summary
Give some practical illustrations of tests of faith. For example, sitting on a chair.

Equipment / resources needed
A chair, for the leader to sit on.

How it works
- You all came in here and sat down on a chair – did any of you ask for any proof that the chairs would work before you sat down? No, because we have such faith in these things to work, we don't even question them anymore

Demonstrate your own trust by sitting down on the chair you have ready.

How to link to talk
- Faith is taking God's promises and daring to believe them

OPTION 3

MARRIAGE ILLUSTRATION (PART 1)

PREPARATION TIME **0** minutes

Quick summary
Use the example of marriage to show how a hard copy record (in this case a marriage certificate) can remind you that you are married, and that your husband/wife loves you.

Equipment / resources needed
None.

How it works
- Marriage is meant to be considered as the ultimate form of relationship between two humans. In today's culture, though, I know that this may not be your experience. I want you, however, to think of a married couple you know. If you asked them how they could prove that they were married, they might say, 'Well, I have a marriage certificate – have a look.' Even if one of them was grumpy and wasn't talking to their husband/wife, they would still be married, and they'd have the marriage certificate to prove it. Hopefully they wouldn't ditch their marriage just because they had one bad day

How to link to talk
- In the same way, we have God's written word – the Bible. This is a written record of his love for and commitment to us. If, at any point, we aren't feeling loved, we can *know* that God loves us because he has written it down

JOHN PATTON

PREPARATION TIME **0** minutes

Quick summary
This is a story about a man who translated the Bible into a tribal language. This illustrates the fact that faith means we can 'lean our entire weight' on God.

Equipment / resources needed
None.

How it works
John Patton was a Scot who travelled all the way from Scotland to a group of islands in the South West Pacific in order to tell the tribal people about Jesus.

The islanders were cannibals and his life was in constant danger. When he tried to translate the Bible into their language he found there was no word for 'belief' or 'trust'. Nobody trusted anybody else.

Finally, when one of the tribal people came in to his study, he thought of a way to find the word he was looking for. Patton raised both his feet off of the ground, leant back in his chair and asked the man, 'What am I doing now?' The servant gave him a word, which means 'to lean your whole weight upon'. This was the word Patton used in his translation of the Bible.

How to link to talk
- That's what faith is – leaning our entire weight on God

TRIPOD ILLUSTRATION (PART 1)

PREPARATION TIME **5** minutes

Quick summary
The three legs of a tripod represent the three parts of the Trinity.

Equipment / resources needed
A tripod or three-legged stool with removable/resizable legs.
A glass of water.

How it works
Bring out a three-legged stool or a camera tripod with the legs removed/contracted. Explain that each leg of the tripod/stool represents each member of the Trinity. As you are speaking, screw one of the legs into the stool, or extend it out of the tripod. Ask for a volunteer to sit on the stool (without putting their feet down) or try to balance a glass of water on top of the tripod.

- *Ask your volunteer: are you sure you can do this? (They won't be)*

If you have a real daredevil who's determined to give it a try, make sure they don't hurt themselves!
You will repeat this for each of the three points in this session. By point

three, you will be able to balance the water on the tripod, and/or someone will be able to sit on the stool.

How to link to talk
- Faith is taking God's promises and daring to believe them. But one leg of the tripod/stool alone isn't enough to give us confidence, is it? In a minute, we'll look at the other two legs in more depth

- So what does God promise us in the Bible?

- God promises that he will come in to our lives if we ask him. 'I will come in' (Revelation 3:20). So if you have sincerely asked him to come in, you can be sure he has

You may like to work through this optional extra with your group, but it is not essential:

OPTIONAL EXTRA – GOING DEEPER   PREPARATION TIME 5
minutes

THE LIGHT OF THE WORLD

Quick summary
Show your group a copy of this famous painting that depicts Jesus standing at a door with no handle on the outside. Explain that this demonstrates that Jesus will never force his way in to someone's life. He will only enter if asked.

Equipment / resources needed
A copy of The Light of the World *can be found online at* youthalpha.org/lgmedia. *You may want to use a projector and screen in order to show the picture to the whole group.*

How it works
- Holman Hunt, a famous artist, painted a picture of this verse (Revelation 3:20) which he called *The Light of the World*. It is a very famous painting

- Jesus, the Light of the World, is standing at the door of someone's house. And the house represents your life, or my life

- The owner of this house has never opened their life to Christ; this is shown by the fact that the door is over-run with weeds and thorns that have grown up around it

- When Holman Hunt painted this picture, someone said to him, 'Hang on a second. You've made a mistake.' He replied, 'What's that?' The person said, 'Well, you've left off the handle. There's no handle on the door.' And Holman Hunt replied, 'That's not a mistake. There is a handle, but it is on the inside'

How to link to talk
- Jesus doesn't force anyone to let him in to their lives – the choice is ours

- God promises that he will be with us forever. 'I am always with you' (Matthew 28:20)

- God promises to give us eternal life with him in heaven. 'I give them eternal life' (John 10:28). Jesus has died for us and conquered death – who better to believe than someone who has already been given eternal life?

POINT 2 – WHAT JESUS DID

- As we discussed in the first and second sessions, Jesus was unique. He saved us when we couldn't save ourselves, he made a relationship with God possible for us

- We can never earn God's forgiveness, but Jesus died to destroy the barrier between us and God

- God loves us and Jesus died to prove it (John 3:16)

- He took our sins upon himself (Isaiah 53:6; 2 Corinthians 5:21)

Choose one of the following 5 options:

OPTION 1

X-MEN

PREPARATION TIME **5** minutes

Quick summary
In this clip we see Jean sacrifice herself to save others. This is an example of a person saving someone through a unique power.

Equipment / resources needed
A copy of the film X2: X-Men United, Twentieth Century Fox Film Corporation, 2006. Certificate 12.

▷ *Chapter 36: 1:49:11*　　☐ *Chapter 36: 1:53:34*

Projector and screen (or a TV), and a DVD player.

How to link to talk
- Jean sacrifices her life to save the lives of others

- Like we talked about last session, Jesus sacrificed himself on the cross so that we could have a relationship with God

OPTION 2

BLONDIN

PREPARATION TIME **0**
minutes

Quick summary
This true story about Blondin wheeling his mother across a tightrope over the Niagara Falls shows that she is the only person who is willing put her complete trust in him. Think how much safer it is for us to put our complete trust in the Lord.

Equipment / resources needed
None.

How it works
Blondin, whose real name was Jean-François Gravelet, was born in 1824. He was a tightrope walker, and his big party trick was to walk an 1,100 foot long tightrope, 160 feet above the Niagara Falls. Every time he walked across this rope he'd do something different.

One time he took a frying pan and some eggs and stopped in the middle of the Falls to cook an omelette!

One time, a royal party, including the Duke of Newcastle, came over from England to watch him perform this trick. On this occasion, having walked across and back once, Blondin took a wheelbarrow and wheeled it across and back. The huge crowd cheered. Blondin went up to the royal party, and he said, 'Do you believe that I could put somebody in the wheelbarrow and wheel *them* across?' They all said yes. Blondin turned to the Duke of Newcastle and said, 'Hop in!'

Of course, the Duke didn't want to get in. Blondin asked the crowd if anyone else wanted to – no one did. Except for one person – Blondin's mother! She was the only one willing to trust him.

How to link to talk
- It may not be that wise to put your faith in a tightrope walker, but putting your faith in Jesus is very wise, because he is completely and utterly trustworthy

OPTION 3

BLONDIN ANIMATION

PREPARATION TIME **5**
minutes

Quick summary
Cartoon animation of the story about Blondin (see previous option).

Equipment / resources needed
The animation can be found online at youthalpha.org/lgmedia
You may want to use a projector and a screen in order to show the clip to the whole group.

How to link to talk
- It may not be that wise to put your faith in a tightrope walker, but putting your faith in Jesus is very wise, because he is completely and utterly trustworthy

MARRIAGE ILLUSTRATION (PART 2)

PREPARATION TIME **0** minutes

Quick summary
The example of marriage shows that we can look to an event in history to know that something is true.

Equipment / resources needed
None.

How it works
Going back to the example of marriage: if you asked a married person how they know their marriage is real, they might refer you to their wedding day; an actual event that happened

Normally, a wedding day involves the couple's family and friends coming to see them commit their lives to each other. Often, they give each other a ring as a visible sign of what they did that day

How to link to talk
- In the same way, we can look back to a single day in history – the death of Jesus on the cross – as a day that changed everything. That's why, as we looked at last week, many Christians wear a symbol of the cross to remind them of what Jesus did on that day

TRIPOD ILLUSTRATION (PART 2)

PREPARATION TIME **0** minutes

Quick summary
The three legs of a tripod represent the three parts of the Trinity.

Equipment / resources needed
A tripod or three-legged stool with removable/resizable legs.
A glass of water.

How it works
Pick up the stool again and screw another leg in, or, if you're using a tripod, pull out a second leg.

Ask another volunteer to try sitting on the stool (without putting their feet down) or try balancing the glass of water on the tripod.

- *Ask your volunteer: are you sure you can do this? (They won't be)*

How to link to talk
- With only two legs we still can't have complete faith. Although we are much closer, we can't yet 'lean our whole weight upon' the tripod

POINT 3 – WHAT THE SPIRIT DOES

- Whenever someone becomes a Christian, God's Holy Spirit comes to live within them (Romans 8:9)

Choose one of the following 3 options:

TRUST FALLS

PREPARATION TIME 0 minutes

Quick summary
Do the people in your group trust each other enough to fall into each other's arms?

NB: be very careful when trying this illustration!

Equipment / resources needed
Table/chair to stand on.

How it works
You could do this in small groups, or with just one person at the front. Have a volunteer stand on a table/chair, and between six and eight (strong!) people ready to catch them. Three or four pairs of people facing each other with their arms interlocked, is the best way to catch the falling person. Have the person who is falling face away from the catchers (so they land on their back), put their arms across their chest, close their eyes, and fall!

NB: if you have a smaller group, you could do this in pairs on ground level.

How to link to talk
- When you experience being caught, you are more likely to build trust in these friends

- In the same way, as we experience God's Spirit living within us, we find it easier to trust God

MARRIAGE ILLUSTRATION (PART 3)

PREPARATION TIME 0 minutes

Quick summary
The example of marriage shows us is that in order to maintain a healthy relationship, we need to communicate and spend time together.

Equipment / resources needed
None.

How it works

- Back to the example of marriage: if you asked someone how they knew they were married, another answer you'd hope to hear is that they have a day-to-day relationship with their husband/wife in which they speak regularly, spend time together, and live together

How to link to talk

- In a similar way, Christians have the Holy Spirit living in them. We can know God and experience a relationship with him every day

- We can have faith because of his presence with us

TRIPOD ILLUSTRATION (PART 3) PREPARATION TIME 0

minutes

Quick summary
The three legs of a tripod represent the three parts of the Trinity.

Equipment / resources needed
None.

How it works
Put the final leg of the stool in place and again ask for a volunteer to sit on the stool (without putting their feet down). In answer to your asking, 'Are you sure you can do this?' they should answer with an emphatic 'yes!' Have them take a seat, or, if using the tripod, extend its final leg and balance the glass on it. Give your volunteer a prize for their help.

How to link to talk

- With three legs to stand on – the three parts of the Trinity – we can be sure about our faith

---

- When the Holy Spirit lives in us, we begin to live and act more like Jesus. This is described in the Bible as the 'fruit' of the Holy Spirit

- The fruit of the Spirit is love, joy, peace, patience, kindness, goodness, gentleness and self-control (Galatians 5:22)

- This doesn't happen overnight, but it will begin to happen in us if we wait

- The Bible also says that 'the Spirit himself testifies with our spirit that we are children of God' (Romans 8:16). Having God's spirit in us helps us to know for certain that he loves us

CONCLUSION

- Becoming a Christian does involve faith, but not blind faith

- Faith is taking the promises of God and choosing to believe them

- We can trust in the promises of God in the Bible, we can look to the cross and see his love for us, and we can know God through his Holy Spirit living inside us

Choose one of the following 3 options:

OPTION 1

QUICK PRAYER TO CLOSE

PREPARATION TIME **0** minutes

Quick summary
Pray to end your session.

Equipment / resources needed
None.

How it works
- I am just going to say a short prayer to close

- Lord, please help us to have faith in you. Thank you for your promises in the Bible, thank you for that day in history where you died for us, and thank you that your Holy Spirit is available to all who believe in you. Please be with us all this week, in Jesus' name, Amen

How to link to talk
- Now we're going to have a quick break and then go into our small groups

OPTION 2

PRAYER OF COMMITMENT

PREPARATION TIME **0** minutes

Quick summary
A chance to give members of your group the opportunity to ask Jesus to come into their lives and forgive their sins by leading them in an appropriate prayer.

Equipment / resources needed
None.

How it works
If appropriate, you may wish to give your guests an opportunity to respond to this week's message by asking Jesus to forgive their sins and come into their lives. If you need a model for that prayer you could use this:

- If you feel that you would like to ask Jesus to come into your life and to forgive your sins, then just echo this short prayer in your heart

- Lord Jesus Christ, thank you for dying for me on the cross. I'm sorry for the things in my life that have been wrong. I now turn away from everything that I know is wrong and I now receive your gift of forgiveness. I put my trust in what you did on the cross for me. Please come and fill me with your Holy Spirit and give me the strength to lead the kind of life that deep down I'm longing to lead. Thank you, Lord Jesus. Amen

How to link to talk
- Now we're going to have a quick break and then go into our small groups

TIME TO REFLECT

PREPARATION TIME **0** minutes

Quick summary
Give the group an opportunity to reflect on what they have heard in this session.

Equipment / resources needed
None.

How it works
Have a moment of quiet. Invite people to close their eyes and ask someone to read the following verses from the Bible. You may want to play some music in the background.

- We are just going to take a moment to reflect on what we have heard today. *[Insert name of reader]* is going to read some Bible verses aloud for us now

- 'Do you not know? Have you not heard? The Lord is the everlasting God, the Creator of the ends of the earth. He will not grow tired or weary, and his understanding no one can fathom' (Isaiah 40:28)

- 'For the Lord is good and his love endures forever' (Psalm 100:5)

- How priceless is your unfailing love! Both high and low find refuge in the shelter of your wings' (Psalm 36:7)

- 'Can a mother forget the baby at her breast and have no compassion on the child that she has borne? Though she may forget, I will not forget you!' (Isaiah 49:15)

- 'For God so loved the world that he gave his one and only Son, that whoever believes in him shall not perish but have eternal life' (John 3:16)

- 'But God demonstrates his own love for us in this: While we were still sinners Christ died for us' (Romans 5:8)

- 'Whoever does not love does not know God, because God is love. This is how God showed his love among us: He sent his one and only Son into the world that we might live through him' (1 John 4:8–9)

How to link to talk
- Now we're going to have a quick break and then go into our small groups

SESSION 3
HOW CAN WE HAVE FAITH?
SMALL GROUP DISCUSSION QUESTIONS

[These can be combined at the end of the talk or interspersed after each teaching point. You can find an additional copy of this sheet online at youthalpha.org/lgmedia]

GENERAL DISCUSSION POINT – YOUR RELATIONSHIP WITH GOD

Give the group a chance to think about where they are in their relationship with God at this point by using the swimming pool illustration. The picture you should show can be found on Sheet 4 at the end of this session, or online at youthalpha.org/lgmedia. Print a copy of the hand out for each small group.

- Where do you feel you are in your relationship with God?

- Does the swimming pool illustration relate to how you feel?

POINT 1 – WHAT THE FATHER PROMISES

- What would you put if you had to fill in a questionnaire that asked, 'What is your religion?'

- Who or what do you have faith in? How do you feel about faith?

- How important are feelings in our everyday lives?

- How do you feel about the promises God makes in the Bible?

    - that he will come into our lives if we ask him

    - that he will always be with us

    - that he will give us eternal life

- Do you trust what the Bible says?

POINT 2 – WHAT JESUS DID

- Do you agree that belief in God is 'a leap of faith'?

- Does the idea that Jesus died for you change how you feel about Christianity?

POINT 3 – WHAT THE SPIRIT DOES

- How do you feel about the idea that God's Spirit can live in you?

- The talk mentioned that being a Christian changes us – our personality and character. What sort of person would you really like to be?

- Would you say you have a relationship with God? If so, how strong does your relationship with God feel?

You may like to include this optional extra, but it is not essential:

OPTIONAL EXTRA – GOING DEEPER

SESSION 3 BIBLE STUDY

Quick summary
This is an advanced option for small groups who may be ready for Bible study.

Equipment / resources needed
A Bible.

How it works
Read: 1 Peter 1:3–8 – Praise to God for a living hope

Then, in your small group, discuss the following questions:

- What do you think Peter means when he talks about a 'new birth' (v.3)?

- What do Christians have to look forward to (vv.4–5)?

- Should this affect the way we deal with difficulties in our lives (vv.6–7)?

- What does verse 8 tell us about the kind of relationship we can have with Jesus?

SHEET 3
URBAN MYTHS

Here is a list of popular urban myths. Read these aloud to your group before asking them which they think are the most/least believable.

- Humans use less than ten per cent of their brain (false)
  http://en.wikipedia.org/wiki/10%25_of_brain_myth

- The Great Wall of China is the only man-made object viewable from space (false)
  http://geography.about.com/od/specificplacesofinterest/a/greatwall.htm

- The average person needs to drink between eight and ten glasses of water a day (false)
  http://www.snopes.com/medical/myths/8glasses.asp

- The modern image of Father Christmas was created by the Coca-Cola Company (false)
  http://www. snopes.com/holidays/christmas/santa/cocacola.asp

- A tooth left in a glass of Coca-Cola will dissolve overnight (false)
  http://www.snopes.com/cokelore/tooth.asp

- Coca-Cola was originally green (false)
  http://www.snopes.com/cokelore/green.asp

- Chewing gum takes seven years to pass through the digestive system (false)
  http://snopes.com/oldwives/chewgum.asp

- Multiplying your dog's age by seven will produce the equivalent number of human years (false)
  http://snopes.com/critters/wild/dogyears.asp

Which of these do you think are most believable/least believable? Why?

SHEET 4
SWIMMING POOL
ILLUSTRATION HAND OUT

WHERE DO YOU FEEL YOU ARE IN YOUR
RELATIONSHIP WITH GOD?

SESSION 4

WHY AND HOW DO I PRAY?

SESSION 4
WHY AND HOW DO I PRAY?

SUMMARY

AIMS OF THIS SESSION

- To encourage the group to realise that prayer is about communicating with God

- To explain the idea that God always has the best plan for us. This sometimes results in prayers not being answered as we hoped

- To explore how to pray, and possibly have a go in our small groups

NOTES

- Mention the Youth Alpha Weekend/Day from the front and ask leaders to talk about it in their small groups

- Remind people to bring in their permission forms

- The end of this session might be a good moment to try praying in small groups. It is worth leaders remembering the following tips:

    - tell the group that no one has to pray aloud, but they can if they like

    - it is suggested that leaders say the first prayer, keeping it simple to prevent group members from feeling that they can't compete. Pray something like, 'Thank you God for the weather. Amen'

    - then others will think, 'That was easy … I could do better than that!'

SESSION OVERVIEW

- Food
- Welcome
- Ice breaker game
- Worship *(if applicable)*
- Talk
    - Introduction
    - Point 1 – What is prayer?
    - Point 2 – Why pray?
    - Point 3 – Does God always answer my prayers?
    - Point 4 – How do we pray?
    - Conclusion
- Small groups

WELCOME

- Welcome back to Youth Alpha!

- It's great to have you here with us again

- Before we get going, let's start with an ice breaker game

ICE BREAKER GAME

Choose one of the following 3 options:

JELLY BEAN FLOUR CAKE

PREPARATION TIME **5** minutes

Quick summary
Ask your group to try and cut the 'flour cake' without disturbing the jelly bean!

Equipment / resources needed
One plate.
One bowl.
One large packet of flour.
Jelly beans.
One blunt knife.
One ground sheet (to catch mess).

How it works
Before your session starts, get a small bowl and pack it tightly full of flour. Put a plate on top of the bowl and, holding both together, turn the bowl upside down so that you end up with a solid flour 'cake' on the plate. Place a jelly bean on top of the flour.
Give a member of your group a blunt knife and ask them to make one cut through the flour cake without knocking the jelly bean off. Go around the group getting each person to do the same. The person who knocks the jelly bean off has to eat it … the catch is that they cannot use their hands (they will have to stick their face in the flour!).

TOILET ROLL RACE

PREPARATION TIME **0** minutes

Quick summary
Teams race each other to unroll toilet paper and then roll it back up again.

Equipment / resources needed
One toilet roll per team.

How it works
Split your group into two teams (or more). Line the members up, one

behind the other, and give each team a toilet roll. When you say 'go', the first person in line must hold on to the end of the toilet paper, and then pass the roll between their legs to the next person (so the roll starts to unravel). The next person must pass the roll over their head to the person behind them. This continues in an over, under, over pattern until the roll reaches the back of the line. It is then passed back down the line, and the paper must be re-rolled back onto the tube until it reaches the front again. If the toilet paper breaks at any point, the team must start again. The first team to get the roll to one end of the line and back again, re-rolled, are the winners!

OPTION 3

SMALL GROUPS

PREPARATION TIME **0** minutes

Quick summary
Spend some time in your small groups discussing recent good/bad news. We suggest you spend no longer than ten minutes in your small groups.

Equipment / resources needed
None.

How it works
In your small groups, ask each person to share one piece of recent good news and one piece of recent bad news. Let them know that if they do not feel comfortable sharing this information with everyone else, they do not have to do so.
Once they have all shared, ask them the following questions:

- How did you handle the bad news?

- Did you need to blame somebody? Who did you blame?

- How did you respond to the good news?

- Did you give credit to anyone for the good news?

INTRODUCTION

- Hopefully you enjoyed that game/small group time!

- Welcome to week four of Youth Alpha

- My name is *[insert name]*

- *You may like to introduce yourself to the group [share a bit of your story]*

- Last week we looked at what we could base our faith on, and we talked about how becoming a Christian isn't just a blind step of faith

- This week we're looking at the topic of prayer: what is prayer, and why and how do we pray?

O BROTHER, WHERE ART THOU? PREPARATION TIME ⑤

minutes

Quick summary
In this clip, we see Everett praying in desperation as some men are about to be hanged. This demonstrates how, in the face of disaster, people often turn to prayer.

Equipment / resources needed
A copy of the film O Brother, Where Art Thou?, Universal Studios, 2000. Certificate 12.

▶ *Chapter 17: 1:30:32* ☐ *Chapter 17: 1:34:02*

Projector and screen (or a TV), and a DVD player.

How to link to talk
- Often, when bad things happen, people turn to prayer

- But is there more to prayer than that?

- Why and how do Christians pray (Matthew 6:5–13)?

EXAM SCENARIO PREPARATION TIME ⓪

minutes

Quick summary
How would you react in a crisis?

Equipment / resources needed
One large sheet of paper or a whiteboard.
Marker pens.

How it works
Ask for five volunteers. Get them to leave the room and then call them back in, one at a time. When they return, explain to them that you are going to set the scene, give them a piece of information and they must tell you how they would react in this situation.

Suggested scenarios:

- You are in an exam. You've turned over your paper, you've read it all through and you've realised you don't know the answer to a single question

- Your car is about to crash

- You've just sent a text about a guy/girl you fancy to that person by mistake, and not to your best friend as you intended

- You've just been told that there is a meteor heading for earth

As each volunteer gives his or her answer, write it down on a big sheet of paper or on a whiteboard.

How to link to talk

Prayer may or may not be mentioned by your volunteers, but in either case make the following point:

- In such a horrible situation, many people would pray. In fact, surveys show that seventy-five per cent of the population admit to praying at least once a week. Many of those people wouldn't even consider themselves 'believers'

- So what is so special about prayer? Why and how do Christians pray?

PICTURES OF SUFFERING

PREPARATION TIME **5** minutes

Quick summary

Show some pictures that depict different kinds of suffering. Use these pictures to make the point that suffering is often a cause for prayer.

Equipment / resources needed

The pictures you should show can be found online at youthalpha.org/lgmedia
You may want to use a projector and screen in order to show the pictures to the whole group.

How to link to talk

- Seeing people suffer may make us want to pray. But does God always answer prayer?

POINT 1 – WHAT IS PRAYER?

Choose one of the following 3 options:

TALLADEGA NIGHTS

PREPARATION TIME **5** minutes

Quick summary

In this clip, we see a family sit down for dinner and say a very random grace. This is an example of an unsuccessful prayer.

Equipment / resources needed

A copy of the film Talladega Nights, *2006 Columbia Pictures Industries, Inc. Certificate 15.*

▷ *Chapter 4: 0:13:38*   ☐ *Chapter 4: 0:15:58*
Projector and screen (or a TV), and a DVD player.

How to link to talk

- Often, though our prayers are formal, they are insincere – but God wants us to be honest with him

VOX POPS: 'WHAT IS PRAYER?' PREPARATION TIME 5 minutes

Quick summary
Show the group a video in which members of the public share their views on prayer. This will give the group an idea of what other people think about prayer.

Equipment / resources needed
The vox pops video can be found online at youthalpha.org/lgmedia
You may want to use a projector and a screen in order to show the film to the whole group.

> **Suggested tip**
> *If you have time, you could even make your own video showing the public's views on this topic.*

How to link to talk
- Many people have a false impression of what prayer is. But what is it?

NON-VERBAL COMMUNICATION PREPARATION TIME 0 minutes

Quick summary
This exercise will help the group to explore non-verbal communication. Just as there are many ways to communicate with other humans, so there are many ways for God to communicate with us.

Equipment / resources needed
Paper and pens (optional).

How it works
For this exercise you will need to pick one simple sentence and then explore the different ways – of which speaking is only one – that it can be communicated:

- *Speaking it*
- *Writing it*
- *Drawing it with symbols*
- *Drawing a picture*
- *Actions*
- *Sign language*
- *Acting it out in a mime*
- *By touch*

Get the group to brainstorm different systems of communication (like the ones listed above). Then, see if anyone can use one of these systems to communicate a relational sentence to someone else.

Suggested sentences include:

- I love you
- I really need the toilet
- I'm cross with you
- You're funny
- I'm sorry, I just farted

How to link to talk
- When we think about relating to God in prayer, we must be aware that God can speak to us in many different ways. We don't have to wait for an audible voice

- Prayer is the most important activity of our lives

- It is like having a 'hot line' to God – you can speak to him at anytime and in any place

- We pray:

    - to the Father – God is our 'dad', but he is also holy and powerful (Matthew 6:6)

    - through the Son – Jesus is always our link to God the Father (Ephesians 2:18)

    - by the Holy Spirit – the Holy Spirit helps us to pray (Romans 8:26)

- You might ask, 'But can I really build a relationship with God through prayer? I won't hear a voice or experience God speaking to me that way, will I?'

POINT 2 – WHY PRAY?

Choose one of the following 3 options:

OPTION 1

VOICE RECOGNITION ILLUSTRATION

PREPARATION TIME **0** minutes

Quick summary
Can your group recognise their friends' voices? As we grow closer to Jesus, we will start to recognise his voice, too.

Equipment / resources needed
None.

How it works
Have a volunteer join you at the front. Ask them to stand with their back to the rest of the group. Explain that when you point at someone, they must call out, 'Hello!' and the volunteer should try to guess who spoke.

How to link to talk

- When a friend that we know well says something – even just one word – we can recognise their voice. As our relationship/friendship with Jesus grows, we can learn to recognise him speaking to us

HUMAN RELATIONSHIPS

OPTION 2

PREPARATION TIME **0** minutes

Quick summary

Discuss the importance of communicating regularly with people you are in a relationship with. This will show the group that it is necessary to communicate with God through prayer.

Equipment / resources needed

None.

How it works

- Think of your girlfriend or boyfriend (some of you might have to imagine!). How would they feel if you decided you weren't going to speak to them, text them, chat with them online or see them for a month? Do you think they would call that a 'relationship'? Perhaps not

How to link to talk

- Communication is the key to a healthy relationship, and a breakdown of communication is often the reason relationships fail

- If we don't communicate with God, our relationship with him will stagnate and eventually die

PRAYER WORKS!

OPTION 3

PREPARATION TIME **0** minutes

Quick summary

This true story about St Augustine demonstrates the power of prayer.

Equipment / resources needed

None.

How it works

A Christian named Monica was having real problems with her rebellious teenage son. He was lazy, bad-tempered, a cheat, a liar and a thief. Although he became a very respectable lawyer, his life was dominated by worldly ambition and a desire to make money. His morals were 'loose' (as they would say in old English). He lived with several different women and had a son by one of them. At one stage, he joined a weird religious cult and adopted all kinds of strange practices.

Throughout this time, his mother continued to pray for him. One day, the Lord gave her a vision. She wept as she prayed, because she saw the light of Christ shining on her son; his face was smiling at her with great joy. This encouraged her to keep on praying. It was nine years before her son finally gave his life to Christ, at the age of twenty-eight.

That man's name was Augustine, now known as Saint Augustine: converted in 386 AD, ordained in 391, bishop in 396: perhaps the greatest theologian of the church ever.

How to link to talk
- St Augustine always attributed his conversion to the prayers of his mother. Her prayers literally changed the course of history

- Prayer is a very powerful thing!

- So why should we pray?

  - because Jesus prayed – and he told us to do the same (Mark 1:35; Luke 6:12, 9:18, 28, 11:1)

  - because it is how we develop a relationship with God – friendship is about spending time together

  - because it brings us joy and peace – even in difficult times (John 16:24; Philippians 4:6–7)

  - because it changes situations – prayer works (Matthew 7:7–11)

POINT 3 – DOES GOD ALWAYS ANSWER MY PRAYERS?

- Yes, I believe he does – but not always in the way we ask him to

Choose one of the following 3 options:

OPTION 1

BRUCE ALMIGHTY

PREPARATION TIME **5** minutes

Quick summary
This film clip shows Bruce answering all prayers with an email saying 'YES', and tragedy ensues. It is impossible for God to answer 'yes' to all prayers.

Equipment / resources needed
A copy of the film Bruce Almighty, *Buena Vista Home Entertainment, Inc. Certificate 12.*

▷ *Chapter 15: 1:12:05* ☐ *Chapter 15: 1:15:29*
Projector and screen (or a TV), and a DVD player.

How to link to talk
- Sometimes God cannot answer all prayers with a 'yes', because it is impossible. In this example, everybody won the lottery but each person only won $17!

- Other times, God says 'no' or 'wait', because the prayers we pray are not good for us, and he knows better than we do (Matthew 7:11)

SPORTING PRAYERS

PREPARATION TIME **0** minutes

Quick summary
Ask people to pray for opposing teams to win a specific sports match. This will show that it is impossible for God to answer all prayers with a 'yes'.

Equipment / resources needed
The jerseys that represent the opposing teams you wish to pray for.

How it works
Have two of your team members wear different football/rugby/other sports jerseys. Get both to come up and pray simultaneously that their team would win the league/match, etc.

How to link to talk
- Sometimes God cannot answer all prayers 'yes' because it is impossible – like in this example: both teams cannot win the same match!

- Other times, God says 'no' or 'wait', because the prayers we pray are not good for us, and he knows better than we do (Matthew 7:11)

RUTH GRAHAM

PREPARATION TIME **0** minutes

Quick summary
This true story about Ruth Graham demonstrates that God only answers 'yes' to prayers that are good for us.

Equipment / resources needed
None.

How it works
- Billy Graham was a famous Christian preacher/evangelist in the 1970s and '80s. You probably haven't heard of him before, but trust me, he was a big deal! His wife, Ruth, to whom he has been happily married for over fifty years, once said: 'God has not always answered my prayers. If he had, I would have married the wrong man, several times!'

How to link to talk
- Sometimes God says 'no' because the things we pray for are not good for us. We may want to have a new car, or to marry a certain person, or get a particular job, but God always knows better than we do (Matthew 7:11)

- So God doesn't always answer our prayers the way we would like him to

- Sometimes he doesn't answer our prayers because we can let things create a barrier between ourselves and God:

    - if we are disobedient (1 John 3:21–22)

    - if we don't forgive (Matthew 6:14–15)

    - if we haven't said sorry to God for the things we have done wrong (Isaiah 59:2)

    - if our motives are wrong (James 4:2–3)

POINT 4 – HOW DO WE PRAY?

Choose one of the following 2 options:

OPTION 1

MEET THE PARENTS

PREPARATION TIME **5** minutes

Quick summary
What is prayer? This clip shows Greg saying grace before a family dinner. This is an example of an unsuccessful prayer.

Equipment / resources needed
A copy of the film Meet the Parents, *Universal Studios, 2000. Certificate 12.*

▷ *Chapter 5: 0:23:27*   ☐ *Chapter 5: 0:25:11*

Projector and screen (or a TV), and a DVD player.

How to link to talk
- One thing I do know about prayer is that we definitely *don't* have to try to sound religious or 'spiritual' and we don't have to use long words!

OPTION 2

TEXT SPEAK PRAYER

PREPARATION TIME **0** minutes

Quick summary
The Lord's prayer translated into 'text speak'.

Equipment / resources needed
You may want to type up the prayer and use a computer or a projector in order to show it to the whole group.

How it works
Hand out a copy of this text message prayer to the group, or display on screen:

'dad@hvn,urspshl.we want wot u want@urth 2b like hvn.giv us food&4giv r sins lyk we 4giv uvaz.don't test us!save us!bcos we kno ur boss, ur tuf&ur cool 4 eva!ok?'

Ask the group to read it and translate it. See if anybody recognises it.

How to link to talk

- This is the most famous prayer in the world: the Lord's Prayer that Jesus taught us to pray

- To help us to pray we can follow a pattern. The shorthand for the cooking term 'teaspoon' is TSP and it is helpful to remember this when we pray:

    - **T** – thank you: praise God for all he has given you

    - **S** – sorry: apologise to God for what you have done wrong

    - **P** – please: ask God for what you, and others, need

- You can pray at any time and in any place, while doing anything (1 Thessalonians 5:17)

- But, it is also good to have a regular time when you can pray alone and not be distracted (Matthew 6:6). It is also good to have times when you pray with other people (Matthew 18:19)

CONCLUSION

'PRAYER' TESTIMONY

Finish by sharing a story (your own, or perhaps the story of someone else who is also running the course) about how God has answered prayer.

- So prayer is how we communicate with God, and how we build our relationship with him

- God always answers prayer, but not always in the way we'd expect or like him to

- Prayer should include being thankful to God, saying sorry, and asking him for what we need

QUICK PRAYER TO CLOSE

PREPARATION TIME 0 minutes

Quick summary
Pray to end your session.

Equipment / resources needed
None.

How it works
- I am just going to say a short prayer to close

- Lord, please help us learn to speak to you. Thank you that we can talk to you in prayer at any time, anywhere. Please teach us how to pray. Please be with us all this week, in Jesus' name, Amen

How to link to talk
- Now we're going to have a quick break and then go into our small groups

- Thanks so much for coming to Youth Alpha today – see you next time!

TEXT PRAYER

PREPARATION TIME 0 minutes

Quick summary
Each member of your group should write a text message prayer.

Equipment / resources needed
None.

How it works
Allow every person in the group some time to compose a text message prayer on their mobile phone. (You may want to play worship music in the background while they do this.) They can either keep this private, or text the prayers to your phone so you can read them out (you may not have time to read them all). If you do decide to read them out, remember to include your own.

- Each of us is now going to write our own text message prayer to God. If you like, you can text your prayer to my phone *[give number]* and I will read some of them aloud. If you would prefer to keep it private, that's fine too. I will read my own out

How to link to talk
- Now we're going to have a quick break and then go into our small groups

- Thanks so much for coming to Youth Alpha today – see you next time!

PRAYERS AS INCENSE

PREPARATION TIME   **0**   minutes

Quick summary
Each member of the group writes a short prayer that will later be set alight.

Equipment / resources needed
One small piece of paper per person.
Enough pens to go round.

How it works
Give each person a pen and paper and invite them to write down an honest prayer to God. Place all the prayers in a metal bucket, take them outside, and set fire to them. Explain that burning them a) makes the prayers confidential, and b) is a sign of us sending them up to God. Obviously we know that prayers don't need to go 'up' to him, but it can be a helpful symbol.

- Each of us is now going to write a short prayer on a piece of paper. We are going to put all the prayers in a bucket, and then we are going to burn them. This will ensure that the prayers are totally confidential, and it will also symbolise our prayers 'going up' to God *[you may wish to explain that prayers needn't go up to God, it's just one of the ways of visualising God receiving them]*

How to link to talk
- Now we're going to have a quick break and then go into our small groups

- Thanks so much for coming to Youth Alpha today – see you next time!

BALLOON PRAYER

PREPARATION TIME   **0**   minutes

Quick summary
Each member of the group writes a short note that will be put in a balloon and prayed for by one of their friends.

Equipment / resources needed
One small piece of paper person.
Enough pens to go round.
One balloon per person

How it works
Give each person a pen, a small piece of paper, and a balloon. Ask them to write a short prayer point, or the name of a person to pray for, and fold their paper up. They should put this folded paper inside their balloon, blow it up and tie it. When everyone has done this, explain that when you say 'go', they are to throw their balloon up, grab another balloon, pop it, and pray for the prayer request inside it. Say a quick prayer yourself and off you go! It is noisy, messy and fun.

- Each of us is now going to write a short prayer point on a piece of paper. We are going to put our prayers in a balloon, throw our balloon up, grab someone else's balloon, pop it and pray for them according to what they have written on their paper

How to link to talk

- Now we're going to have a quick break and then go into our small groups

- Thanks so much for coming to Youth Alpha today – see you next time!

SESSION 4
WHY AND HOW DO I PRAY?
SMALL GROUP DISCUSSION QUESTIONS

[These can be combined at the end of the talk or interspersed after each teaching point. You can find an additional copy of this sheet online at youthalpha.org/lgmedia]

POINT 1 – WHAT IS PRAYER?

- Do you pray? Would you consider trying prayer?

- What do you find most attractive about the idea of prayer?

POINT 2 – WHY PRAY?

- Do you agree that we should pray because Jesus prayed and told us to do the same?

- How do you feel about the idea that prayer helps us develop a relationship with God?

- Do you believe that prayer works?

POINT 3 – DOES GOD ALWAYS ANSWER PRAYER?

- Do you find it hard to imagine God actually answering prayer?

- Have you ever seen answers to prayer, or coincidences that happened after you prayed?

POINT 4 – HOW DO WE PRAY?

- Shall we have a go at praying together?

You might want to go around the group and encourage each person to pray a short prayer out loud. Be aware that this can be really scary and some may not want to do this – respect that. We would suggest you pre-arrange for one of your team to say the first prayer and ask them to pray the simplest, shortest prayer they've ever prayed!

You may like to include this optional extra, but it is not essential:

OPTIONAL EXTRA – GOING DEEPER

SESSION 4 BIBLE STUDY

Quick summary
This is an advanced option for small groups who may be ready for Bible study.

Equipment / resources needed
A Bible.

How it works
Read: Matthew 6:5–13 – The Lord's Prayer *(you can use different translations)*

Then, in your small group, discuss the following questions:

- Why does Jesus think that private praying is often better than public praying (vv.5–6)?

- From looking at the prayer that Jesus taught us, what kind of things do you think it is right to ask God to give us (vv.9–13)? *[As the leader, take some time to talk about answers to prayer that you have seen in your life. Then encourage other members of the group to tell of any they have experienced]*

SESSION 5

WHY AND HOW SHOULD I READ THE BIBLE?

SESSION 5
WHY AND HOW SHOULD I READ THE BIBLE?

SUMMARY

AIMS OF THIS SESSION

- To encourage the group to understand that God speaks to us through the Bible

- To explain that the Bible is God's word

- To explore the idea that we can have a relationship with God through reading the Bible

NOTES

- Mention the Youth Alpha Weekend/Day from the front and ask leaders to talk about it in their small groups again

- Collect any permission forms that have already been brought in, and encourage everyone else to bring them next week

- Suggest that any small groups who haven't yet had a go at praying together might try at the end of this session

SESSION OVERVIEW

- Food
- Welcome
- Ice breaker game
- Worship *(if applicable)*
- Talk
    - Introduction
    - Point 1 – An instruction manual for life
    - Point 2 – A way to relationship
    - Point 3 – How do we hear God speak through the Bible?
    - Conclusion
- Small groups

WELCOME

- Welcome back to Youth Alpha!

- It's great to have you here with us

- Before we get going, let's start with an ice breaker game

ICE BREAKER GAME

Choose one of the following 4 options:

BOTTLE GAME

PREPARATION TIME **0** minutes

Quick summary
Teams must help a volunteer to spoon dried lentils into a bottle balancing on someone's head.

Equipment / resources needed
Two glass bottles (milk bottles work best as the opening isn't too small).
Two teaspoons.
A large bag of dried lentils, peas or similar.
Two blindfolds.
Two ground sheets for keeping the floor tidy.

How it works
Split the group into two teams. Each group should form a circle, and a volunteer from each team should sit in the middle. Give this volunteer a glass bottle, which they should hold on top of their head with both hands. A second volunteer from each team must then be blindfolded — they will try to spoon the lentils into the bottle using only one hand. The rest of the team should cheer them on and help tell them where to direct the spoon. The team with the most lentils in the bottle at the end wins. We suggest you spend no longer than five minutes on this game

> **Suggested tip**
> *It might be a good idea to have the volunteer with the bottle sitting on a sheet, as it will help with clearing up.*

'I'M ALL RIGHT, JACK!'

PREPARATION TIME **0** minutes

Quick summary
Card game with crazy actions.

Equipment / resources needed
One pack of playing cards.
One chair for each person, set in a circle.

How it works

This is a card game which involves action and is quite amusing to watch and play. Sit the players in a circle and give the dealer a pack of cards. The dealer simply slaps the cards down, face up, in the centre of the circle while the rest of the group watch intently.

When the dealer turns up a Jack, the group must shout, 'I'm all right, Jack!'

When the dealer turns up a Queen, the group must get to their feet and curtsey.

When the dealer turns up a King, the group must get to their feet and salute.

When the dealer turns up an Ace, the group must stand and move around to the next seat in the circle.

When the dealer turns up a seven, the group must do all of the above in the order listed.

We suggest that you spend no longer than five minutes on this game.

> ### Suggested tip
> *You could play this as an elimination game – the last person to react is out. If you want to, you can let people invent more rules for other cards as they go.*

OPTION 3

'IF I …'   PREPARATION TIME **0**
minutes

Quick summary
A fun game to help people get to know each other.

Equipment / resources needed
None.

How it works
Each member of the group has to complete these four sentences. They must complete three truthfully and one falsely.

- If I could marry any famous person, I would marry …

- If I had all the money in the world, I would drive …

- If I could live in any part of the world, I would live in …

- If I could have any job, I would be a …

Once the group have had a few minutes to work on their answers, get each person to complete their sentences out loud, while the rest of the group try to pick which statement is false.

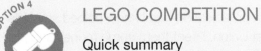

LEGO COMPETITION

PREPARATION TIME **5** minutes

Quick summary
Get groups to try to put a Lego set together without instructions.

Equipment / resources needed
One small Lego set per group.

How it works
Buy enough little Lego sets for each small group to have one. Hand them out. Explain that this is a competition, and that on the word 'go' each group must build whatever is in their box as fast as possible. (The trick is that you will have removed the instructions and the picture from all but one of the boxes.) See how the groups get on. The assumption is that the group who have the instructions will finish the task the quickest.

Say to your group:

- It is much easier to do when you have instructions, right?

INTRODUCTION

- Welcome to week five of Youth Alpha

- My name is *[insert name]*

- *You may like to introduce yourself to the group [share a bit of your story]*

- Last week we looked at why and how we pray

- This week we're looking at the question, 'Why and how should I read the Bible?'

Choose one of the following 3 options:

BIBLE SMUGGLING

PREPARATION TIME **0** minutes

Quick summary
A story about Nicky Gumbel, the man who started Alpha, smuggling Bibles into Russia.

Equipment / resources needed
None.

How it works
Nicky Gumbel, the man who started the Alpha Course, told this story:

'In 1976, after I had recently become a Christian, I went on a family trip with my parents to Russia. I had read that in the Soviet Union, as it was then, Christians were persecuted and it was very hard to get hold of Bibles.

Full of enthusiasm, I wrote to an organisation that I knew helped smuggle Bibles into places like the Soviet Union. I sent them some money and said that I wanted to take some Bibles with me when I went to Russia.

I got two replies. One was the *official* reply. The official reply was, "So sorry, we can't supply you with any Bibles — it's illegal to take them into Russia, and we suggest that you don't do so." The second was the *unofficial* reply: I saw on the doorstep an unmarked brown paper parcel containing Russian Bibles. So, feeling like James Bond, I packed these Bibles into my case. They were printed on very thin paper and contained both the Old and the New Testament.

When I got to Russia, we went into a church. In those days, the KGB (the Russian Secret Police) often infiltrated the churches. In the congregation, I tried to spot someone who looked like a genuine Christian. I saw a man, probably in his sixties, who looked as though he had the light of Christ shining in his face. I followed him out of the church and down the street where it was completely deserted.

There, I took out of my pocket a complete Russian Bible and handed it to him. In turn, he took out of his pocket what *he* had — a copy of the New Testament, probably a hundred years old, and almost totally worn out; the pages were threadbare. When he saw a whole Bible, he was elated! He was literally jumping and dancing for joy. He hugged me! I didn't speak a word of Russian and he didn't speak a word of English but we hugged each other and we ran up and down the streets, jumping for joy!'

How to link to talk

- Why was that man so excited to receive the Bible?

BEST SELLING BOOKS

PREPARATION TIME **0** minutes

Quick summary

Get the group to put the following list of books in order of number of copies sold.

Equipment / resources needed

None.

How it works

Get the group to put these books in order of copies sold, from most to least:

- *Lord of the Rings* – JRR Tolkien *(2nd: 150 million)*

- The Bible *(1st: between 2.5 billion–6 billion – unknown exactly)*

- *Charlie and the Chocolate Factory* – Roald Dahl *(5th: 13 million)*

- *Harry Potter and the Deathly Hallows* – JK Rowling *(4th: 44 million)*

- *The Da Vinci Code* – Dan Brown *(3rd: 57 million)*

- *The Cat in the Hat* – Dr Seuss *(6th: 10 million)*

(As listed on Wikipedia – http://en.wikipedia.org/wiki/List_of_best-selling_books)

How to link to talk
- You probably guessed right from the beginning that the Bible would turn out to be the biggest seller, but why?

IS IT IN THE BIBLE?

PREPARATION TIME **5** minutes

Quick summary
Is the phrase in the Bible or not? Get the group to indicate whether they think the following phrases are in the Bible or from other sources.

Equipment / resources needed
The slide with the phrases on can be found online at
youthalpha.org/lgmedia
You may want to use a projector and screen in order to show the slide to the whole group

How it works
Read out the following phrases and ask the group to decide which ones come from the Bible (IN), and which ones do not (OUT). You could get them to call out their answers, move to one side of the room (eg: left means IN, right means OUT) or you could provide signs for them to hold up.

- In the beginning God created the heavens and the earth – **IN** (*Genesis 1:1*)
- God helps those who help themselves – **OUT**
- Cleanliness is next to godliness – **OUT**
- You must not steal – **IN** (*Exodus 20:15*)
- There is a time for everything – **IN** (*Ecclesiastes 3:1*)
- Everyone is equal under the sun – **OUT**
- Father forgive them for they don't know what they are doing – **IN** (*Luke 23:34*)
- For what we are about to receive, may the Lord make us truly thankful – **OUT**
- Money is the root of all evil – **OUT** (*But 'the love of money' is described as 'a root of all kinds of evil', 1 Timothy 6:10*)
- Hell hath no fury like a woman scorned – **OUT** (*Shakespeare*)
- Don't judge other people or you will be judged – **IN** (*Matthew 7:1*)
- Turn or burn – **OUT**
- Do all you can to lead a peaceful life – **IN** (*1 Thessalonians 4:11*)
- He who would valiant be, 'gainst all disaster – **OUT** (*hymn by John Bunyan*)
- Do not be fooled: you can't cheat God – **IN** (*Galatians 6:7*)

How to link to talk

- Many of these phrases are pretty well known and are generally still considered good advice. In fact, the Bible is the best-selling book of all time!

- How can a book that was written around 2,000 years ago still have any relevance to our lives in the 21st century?

- Why do Christians put so much value and importance on the Bible?

- Why should we read the Bible?

POINT 1 – AN INSTRUCTION MANUAL FOR LIFE

- The Bible is, above all, a book full of stories. It is the story of God, his love for the world and the humans who live in it. It is full of stories about amazing people and events. All the elements that make soap operas and films so gripping also appear in the Bible. There is romance, war, revenge, love, sacrifice, murder and sex

- Key fact: this is no ordinary book. The Bible is uniquely God's book. The Bible is 'God-breathed' or 'God-inspired'. Even though humans wrote the words, it was God who inspired and guided them (2 Timothy 3:15–17)

- The Bible is an essential method of communication between ourselves and God

Choose one of the following 5 options:

OPTION 1

ROBOTS

PREPARATION TIME **5** minutes

Quick summary
This clip shows a couple receiving a baby in a box through the post. They have to read the instructions in order to put him together. This demonstrates the importance of having a guide.

Equipment / resources needed
A copy of the film Robots, *Twentieth Century Fox Film Corporation, 2005. Certificate PG.*

▷ *Chapter 1: 0:01:08*　　☐ *Chapter 1: 0:03:25*

Projector and screen (or a TV), and a DVD player.

How to link to talk
- We all need instruction – not everything comes to us naturally. The Bible is like an instruction manual for life, given to us by God

- Because God created us, he knows what is best for us and he knows how we can get the best out of life. The Bible can correct us when we are living wrongly, and can show us how to live for God

OPTION 2

MAP/COMPASS

PREPARATION TIME **5** minutes

Quick summary
Using a map and a compass to illustrate your point, demonstrate how the Bible works better as a compass than it does as a map.

Equipment / resources needed
One local map.
One compass.

How it works
Explain the following:

- Because it is God's book, and because he is our Creator and our loving heavenly Father, the Bible can help show us how to live our lives in the best possible way (2 Timothy 3:15–17)

- You could say, 'But it is so old! It can't possibly help me with my life today'

- Let me illustrate how the Bible can still help to guide us

Spread the map out on the wall. Ask a volunteer to come up and use the map to find their way from a point 'A' to point 'B' (perhaps the route from their home to the place of your meeting). Then ask them how to get from point 'A' to a point 'B' that is not covered by the map (perhaps the route from their home to the Eiffel Tower or the Statue of Liberty). It is impossible.

- Maps are great inventions and we would be literally lost without them

- But, it is only useful if the map you are holding is being used in exactly the right place at exactly the right time

- If the Bible were like a map it would not be of much use to us today. It would only focus on the culture and customs of the Near East of 2,000 years ago. It wouldn't be useful in today's world

Now, bring out the compass and ask a volunteer to find North with it.

- Compasses don't give as much detailed information as maps

- However, the good thing about compasses is that they work anywhere at any time, and they can help us go in the right direction

How to link to talk
- God has designed the Bible to be much more like a compass than a map. This is why it is still useful today when showing us how best to live our lives. It provides us with principles that don't change with time, and that can help us to make all kinds of decisions *[you may want to give some illustrations that are relevant to your group]*

OPTION 3

PUZZLE COMPETITION

PREPARATION TIME **15** minutes

Quick summary
Teams must put together a jigsaw puzzle but not all of them will have everything they need. This shows how much we need the Bible for guidance.

NB: don't use this illustration if you played the Lego game earlier, they are very similar

Equipment / resources needed
Four identical jigsaw puzzles (two of them complete with the original puzzle picture).
Four envelopes (to put pieces in).
One picture from a different puzzle, to confuse one group.

How it works
Get hold of four identical puzzles and put the pieces into separate envelopes. Divide everyone in to four groups, and give each group an envelope. The teams must race to put their puzzle together, but there's a twist: not all the groups will have the same items. Group one should win!

Give:

- Group one – correct picture and all the pieces
- Group two – correct picture but missing some pieces
- Group three – wrong picture with all the pieces
- Group four – no picture with all the pieces

How to link to talk
- Only one group actually had the right picture and all the pieces!

- Some people go through life with the wrong picture or missing pieces. The Bible gives us the right picture and all the pieces to get through life

OPTION 4

BROKEN TELEPHONE GAME

PREPARATION TIME **0** minutes

Quick summary
A classic game of passing on a message through whispers. A spoken message can get confused, but God's word in the Bible is unchanging.

Equipment / resources needed
None.

How it works
Get the group to sit in a circle, or perhaps two circles if you have lots of people. Whisper a sentence into the ear of one person. They need to whisper what they heard into the ear of the person next to them. The message gets passed around the circle and the last person must

say out loud what they think they heard. Each person can only whisper the phrase once – no repeating! Hopefully you will get a very different sentence from the original!

You can make up any sentence you like, but the more likely it is to be mistaken the better.

Example: 'Mary ate banoffee pie in an apple tree in May.'

How to link to talk

- Although our message may have got confused here, God's word is unchanging – the Bible is his truth written down and it doesn't change

OPTION 5

NO RULES FOOTBALL

PREPARATION TIME **0**

minutes

Quick summary

The following analogy about kids playing football with no rules shows how Christians, just like children, need guidelines in order to feel free.

Equipment / resources needed

None.

How it works

Every Saturday, a group of eight year old boys played football in the park. They had a coach who put them in teams and refereed their games each week.

One Saturday, the coach didn't arrive on time, and one of the dads had to referee the game. This posed a problem: he didn't know the rules of football! He was already at a bit of a disadvantage: there was no pitch and there were no posts (usually, the boys used clothing to mark the sidelines and goals); he didn't have a whistle; the boys didn't have kits – they were just in their ordinary clothes; and he didn't know all of their names. The biggest problem, though, was that this dad didn't know the rules.

The match started as always. One boy shouted, 'The ball's out!' In reply, another boy shouted, 'No, that's not out!' The poor dad just didn't know, so he shouted, 'Play on!' One of the players made a really bad tackle, and a boy yelled, 'Hey, that's a foul!' Someone else said, 'That's not a foul!' The dad didn't know whether it was a foul or not, so he said, 'Play on', and they did. There were small boys lying hurt everywhere – the place looked like a battlefield! Eventually, to everyone's immense relief, the coach finally arrived. He had his whistle, he knew the boys' names and he put them in teams. Every time there was a foul or the ball went out, he blew the whistle, stopped the game, and imposed the rules.

How to link to talk

- Here's a question for you: were the players more free when the dad who didn't know the rules was refereeing? Or were they more free when there was someone in charge with a definite set of rules?

- God doesn't give us rules to make our lives restricted and dull

- The reason the Bible says, for example, 'Do not murder', isn't because murder is such fun! It is because not murdering others is the best way to live

- If God is our designer, our creator, then who better is there to listen to regarding how to live well?

POINT 2 – A WAY TO RELATIONSHIP

- If the Bible was just an instruction manual, it might seem a bit cold and boring: like a very big, very thick textbook

- Written communications can lead to real relationship. God speaks to us and builds a relationship with us primarily through the Bible. It is like a love letter, a text message (or several), and an email all rolled into one

- Before we become Christians, God speaks through the Bible in order to bring us to salvation through faith in Jesus (Romans 10:17; John 20:31)

- When we *are* Christians, God speaks through the Bible to help build our relationship with him

Choose one of the following 3 options:

OPTION 1

TEXT MESSAGE ILLUSTRATION PREPARATION TIME **5** minutes

Quick summary
Have a member of your team send you an encouraging text message. The Bible is God's encouragement to us.

Equipment / resources needed
Your mobile phone.
An encouraging text message sent to your phone.

How it works
Arrange for someone to text you at this point in the talk. A good message would be something like, 'I think you are great!' or some other encouragement.

How to link to talk
- The Bible is like a message from God – it is his encouragement to us and it tells us how much he loves us

CAR ILLUSTRATION

OPTION 2

PREPARATION TIME **0** minutes

Quick summary
This car manual analogy demonstrates the need for Christians to use the Bible to help them meet with God.

Equipment / resources needed
None.

How it works
Imagine that I've been given a brand new Porsche as a present.
I go outside to look at the car; I open the door and search the glove compartment until I find the owner's manual. It is a beautiful, glossy manual, and I think, 'Wow, that is fantastic!'
I take the manual indoors and start studying it. I get out my pen, and start underlining bits that look interesting. I learn the bits that I like off by heart and I even cut bits out of it and stick them on
my bathroom mirror so I can look at them while I brush my teeth!
I love this manual so much that I think, 'Well, maybe we could set some of this to music.' I ask a friend to compose a song and we sing bits of the Porsche manual!
Then I think, 'I wonder whether other people like the Porsche manual. Perhaps I'll join the Porsche Club. Or maybe I should learn German so I can study it in its original language!'
If I did all that, I would obviously have missed the point – the purpose of the manual is to help you drive the car

How to link to talk
* The Bible is a bit like that – it is a way to develop a relationship with God. If we only read the Bible and never meet with God, it's like having a manual for a car that you never drive – pointless!

VIDEO TESTIMONY

OPTION 3

PREPARATION TIME **5** minutes

Quick summary
This testimony gives us an example of how God can speak to people through the Bible.

Equipment / resources needed
The testimony video can be found online at youthalpha.org/lgmedia
You may want to use a projector and a screen in order to show the testimony to the whole group.

How to link to talk
* God wants to speak to us through the Bible! So how do we hear him?

POINT 3 – HOW DO WE HEAR GOD SPEAK THROUGH THE BIBLE?

Choose one of the following 4 options:

OPTION 1

BOLT
PREPARATION TIME 5 minutes

Quick summary
Still in his TV character, Bolt tries to send a message, via two troublesome cats, to the fictitious evil character 'The Green-Eyed Man'. The key message cannot be transmitted because of noise.

Equipment / resources needed
A copy of the film Bolt, *Disney's FastPlay, 2008. Certificate PG.*

▷ *Chapter 4: 0:16:16* ☐ *Chapter 4: 0:18:37*

Projector and screen (or a TV), and a DVD player.

How to link to talk
- Sometimes it's hard to hear God when there are lots of other voices shouting too

OPTION 2

RECEPTION ILLUSTRATION
PREPARATION TIME 0 minutes

Quick summary
Just as different locations can affect mobile phone reception, so the times and places where we try to hear God can affect our ability to listen.

Equipment / resources needed
Everyone's mobile phones.

How it works
Ask everyone to get out their mobile phones to see how much reception they have got. Sometimes reception is good, sometimes not so good – it depends on how close to a telecoms mast we are and what is getting in the way.

How to link to talk
- Sometimes certain things can interfere with reception and transmission. It is the same with hearing God. We sometimes need to go somewhere where it is easier or more quiet to get a 'better signal'

OPTION 3

SHEEP AND SHEPHERD GAME
PREPARATION TIME 0 minutes

Quick summary
A game to test voice recognition in a room full of noise.

Equipment / resources needed
Blindfolds – one for every pair.

How it works
Put everyone into pairs. In each pair, appoint one person as the sheep and the other as the shepherd. 'Sheep' must kneel on their hands and knees and should be blindfolded by their shepherd. On your word, the 'shepherds' must walk away and call their sheep's name. The first sheep to crawl back to their shepherd is the winner!

How to link to talk
- The more time we spend with God, the better we will get at recognising his voice among all the other noise

MIXING DESK

PREPARATION TIME **1–2** hours

Quick summary
Get the group to try and decipher three songs that have been mixed together – can they avoid the distraction of the mixed sound?

Equipment / resources needed
Equipment that will allow you to mix together three well-known songs to create just one track.

How it works
Play three well-known songs over the top of each other and see if anyone can identify them all. Give a prize to anyone who can.

How to link to talk
- Our world is so busy and full of noise, it can be hard to hear God speak to us

- The more we spend time with God, the better we will get at recognising his voice among all the other noise

- The right conditions are important in any form of communication

- There are various ways of achieving the right conditions to hear God speak through the Bible

- Choose a place where you are relaxed and where you won't be disturbed or get distracted (Mark 1:35)

- Begin by praying: ask God to speak to you through what you read

- Try not to switch off and let your mind wander – ask God for his help in this

- Ask yourself three key questions: what does this say? What does this mean? How should this affect me?

- Put what you have read and learned into practice (Matthew 7:24)

- Read it, learn from it, but most of all enjoy it!

CONCLUSION

'BIBLE' TESTIMONY

Finish by sharing a story (your own, or perhaps the story of someone else who is also running the course) about how God has spoken to you through the Bible.

- So, the Bible is God's main way of communicating with us

- It's a bit like an instruction manual for life, but it doesn't restrict our freedom, it enhances it

- The Bible can help deepen our relationship with God

- Let's all try to read the Bible at some point this week and see what God says to us

Choose one of the following 3 options:

OPTION 1

QUICK PRAYER TO CLOSE

PREPARATION TIME **0** minutes

Quick summary
Pray to end your session.

Equipment / resources needed
None.

How it works
- I am just going to say a short prayer to close

- Lord, thank you that you want to speak to us through the Bible. Please help us to read it, understand it, and hear your voice through it, in Jesus' name, Amen

How to link to talk
- Now we're going to have a quick break and then go into our small groups

- Thanks so much for coming to Youth Alpha today – see you next time!

OPTION 2

READ THE BIBLE

PREPARATION TIME **0** minutes

Quick summary
Give the group an opportunity to reflect on what they have heard in this session as well as a chance to flick through the Bible.

Equipment / resources needed
One Bible per person.
You may need a projector and a screen if you'd prefer the group to read a Bible passage chosen by you

How it works
Give everyone a Bible and give them time to look through it while worship music plays. You may want to encourage them to read a particular passage (eg: Psalm 23).
Alternatively, display a particular Bible passage on the screen and give the group time to read it.

- We are just going to take a moment to reflect on what we have heard today. Use this time to flick through the Bible you have been given/read the Bible verse that's on the screen

How to link to talk
- Now we're going to have a quick break and then go into our small groups

- Thanks so much for coming to Youth Alpha today – see you next time!

ALL ABOUT THE BIBLE
HAND OUT

PREPARATION TIME **5** minutes

Quick summary
Give everyone a copy of the 'All about the Bible' hand out.

Equipment / resources needed
You can find 'All about the Bible' on Sheet 5 at the end of this session, or online at youthalpha.org/lgmedia

How it works
Give everyone a copy of the 'All about the Bible' hand out.

How to link to talk
- Here is a hand out called 'All about the Bible'. You can take this away with you

- Now we're going to have a quick break and then go into our small groups

- Thanks so much for coming to Youth Alpha today – see you next time!

SESSION 5
WHY AND HOW SHOULD I READ THE BIBLE?
SMALL GROUP DISCUSSION QUESTIONS

[These can be combined at the end of the talk or interspersed after each teaching point. You can find an additional copy of this sheet online at youthalpha.org/lgmedia]

POINT 1 – AN INSTRUCTION MANUAL FOR LIFE

- Why do you think the Bible is so popular?

- Has anyone ever read the Bible before? How did you find it?

- Why do you think God bothered to give us the Bible?

- What do you think about the idea of the Bible being God's instruction manual for life?

- What do you think about the idea that the 'rules' that God gives us aren't there to stop us having fun? Do you agree?

POINT 2 – A WAY TO RELATIONSHIP

- Do you think that the Bible has anything helpful to say to you? Why/why not?

- Can it guide you in the way you live your life today?

- Has anyone ever read the Bible and felt God say something to them?

POINT 3 – HOW DO WE HEAR GOD SPEAK THROUGH THE BIBLE?

- How do you feel about the idea of reading the Bible regularly and asking God to speak?

- Will you give it a go this week?

You may like to include this optional extra, but it is not essential:

SESSION 5 BIBLE STUDY

Quick summary
This is an advanced option for small groups who may be ready for Bible study.

Equipment / resources needed
A Bible.

How it works
Read: Mark 4:1–8 and 13–20 – The parable of the sower

Then, in your small group, discuss the following questions:

- This is a parable. Jesus used stories like this to make points about how people live their lives. The key to understanding this parable is to realise that Jesus is not talking about different groups of people, but about the different ways we respond at different times in our lives

- How do you see yourself responding at this stage in your life?

- Have you ever known that God was talking to you but not done anything about it (v.15)?

- What kind of things distract you from God at different times in your life (vv.18–19)?

- What does Jesus promise to those who hear his words and actually do something about it (v.20)?

SHEET 5
ALL ABOUT THE BIBLE
HAND OUT

The Bible is really a whole library of short books slipped into one cover.

It is divided in two:

The Old Testament: covers the history of the Israelite people up until the birth of Jesus

The New Testament: covers the life of Jesus and his first followers who set up the church

If we combine both halves there are sixty-six books in total. Some of these books are like history books; others are full of poetry and love songs.

The Bible can be exciting reading: there is drama, war, love and murder. There are heroes and heroines, villains and evil kings.

Christians believe that the Bible was written through an amazing partnership between God and its human authors. It really is God's word, but it was also written by real people with their own ideas, words and stories to tell.

SESSION 6

HOW DOES GOD GUIDE US?

SESSION 6
HOW DOES GOD GUIDE US?

SUMMARY

AIMS OF THIS SESSION

- To encourage the group to know that God wants to guide our lives

- To explain that God's plan is the best for us

- To explore the different ways that God guides us

NOTES

- If your Youth Alpha Weekend/Day is coming up soon, you may want to go through the final details. Encourage anyone who hasn't already booked to do so as soon as possible

- Remember to collect permission forms from the group

- If you have had your Weekend/Day, ask people to feed back from it

- Suggest that any small groups who haven't yet had a go at praying together might try at the end of this session

SESSION OVERVIEW

- Food
- Welcome
- Ice breaker game
- Worship *(if applicable)*
- Talk
    - Introduction
    - Point 1 – Through the Bible (Commanding Scripture)
    - Point 2 – By the Holy Spirit (Compelling Spirit)
    - Point 3 – Common sense
    - Point 4 – Advice from others (Counsel of the Saints)
    - Point 5 – Random signs (Circumstantial Signs)
    - Conclusion
- Small groups

WELCOME

- Welcome back to Youth Alpha!

- It's great to have you here with us

- Before we get going, let's start with an ice breaker game as usual

ICE BREAKER GAME

Choose one of the following 3 options:

BEAN BLITZ

PREPARATION TIME 30 minutes

Quick summary
Jelly beans are at stake in this guessing game!

Equipment / resources needed
One envelope/bag per person, containing at least ten jelly beans.

How it works
Give everyone their bag of jelly beans. Explain to the group that the object of the game is to get as many beans as they can.
The game is played by approaching someone with a certain number of beans in your closed hand. You say to the person, 'Odd or even?' They then have the opportunity to guess whether you have an odd or even number of beans in your hand (but they can choose not to guess at all). If they guess correctly, you must give them the beans in your hand. If they guess incorrectly, you may take from them the number of beans that you have in your hand. If you run out of beans, you are out of the game.
The person with the most beans at the end is the winner. Their prize is the jelly beans.

WATER PISTOL GAME

PREPARATION TIME 5 minutes

Quick summary
Teams help volunteers to try to find a water pistol and squirt everyone!

NB: this game can be used as an ice breaker, or for Point 1 of the teaching.

Equipment / resources needed
One water pistol (full).
Two blindfolds.

How it works
The aim of this game is to get as many people wet as possible!
Ask for two volunteers and blindfold them both. Divide the rest of the group into two, and assign each 'team' a volunteer to cheer for.
Tell the volunteers that this is a two-part game. In part one, you are

going to hide an object – a fully-loaded water pistol – somewhere in the room (let everyone else see where you put it) and the teams will shout instructions to help the blindfolded players find it. Encourage them to shout loudly as they are not allowed to touch their player.

The first person to find the water pistol wins part one. At this point, stop the game.

Get them to keep their blindfolds on and explain part two. Tell them that the object they were looking for was a water pistol.

In part two, the player with the water pistol must try to squirt the other volunteer with water – when they do, the game is over. The player without the water pistol must try to avoid getting hit by water. Again, the players must be directed by their teams.

Once the second volunteer has been squirted (or at least when they are wet enough for your liking), stop the game. Ask each player how easy/ difficult they found it to hear their team guiding them.

We suggest you spend no longer than five minutes on this game.

SMALL GROUPS (ADVANCED)

PREPARATION TIME 0 minutes

Quick summary
In your small groups, get everyone thinking about the future and how they will achieve their goals.

NB: this option is for advanced groups.

Equipment / resources needed
One sheet of paper per person.
One pen per person.

How it works
Hand out pens and paper to the group. Ask them:

- Where do you think you'll be when you are thirty?

- For example: Who will your friends be? What kind of career will you have? What kind of life will you lead? Will you be happy? Where will you live? Who will you be living with? What will your ambitions be?

- On the piece of paper write or draw your life at the age of thirty

After a few minutes, give each person a moment to talk about their piece of paper.

- Let's make a list of the decisions you will have to make to get you from where you are now to where you want to be when you are thirty

- What will be your main sources of guidance in making those decisions?

We suggest you spend no longer than ten minutes on this activity.

INTRODUCTION

- Welcome to week six of Youth Alpha

- Last week, we talked about how the Bible is the main way in which God communicates with us. The week before that, we looked at how prayer plays a major role in our communication with God

- This week we're looking at the question of how God guides us? How can we figure out what God is saying to us?

Choose one of the following 3 options:

MISSION IMPOSSIBLE III

PREPARATION TIME **5** minutes

Quick summary
In this clip, we see a clear example of guidance as Ethan is led by Benji through the streets to find his wife.

Equipment / resources needed
A copy of the film Mission Impossible III, *Paramount Pictures, 2006. Certificate 12.*

▷ *Chapter 17: 1:38:31*   ☐ *Chapter 17: 1:42:07*

Projector and screen (or a TV), and a DVD player.

How to link to talk
- If only being guided by God was as easy as that!

WATER PISTOL GAME

PREPARATION TIME **5** minutes

Quick summary
Teams help volunteers to try to find a water pistol and squirt everyone!

NB: if you used this game as an icebreaker, do not repeat it now.

Equipment / resources needed
One water pistol (full).
Two blindfolds.

How it works
The aim of this game is to get as many people wet as possible!
Ask for two volunteers and blindfold them both. Divide the rest of the group into two, and assign each 'team' a volunteer to cheer for.
Tell the volunteers that this is a two-part game. In part one, you are going to hide an object – a fully-loaded water pistol – somewhere in the room (let everyone else see where you put it) and the teams will shout instructions to help the blindfolded players find it. Encourage them to

shout loudly as they are not allowed to touch their player.
The first person to find the water pistol wins part one. At this point,
stop the game.
Get them to keep their blindfolds on and explain part two. Tell them
that the object they were looking for was a water pistol.
In part two, the player with the water pistol must try to squirt the other
volunteer with water – when they do, the game is over. The player
without the water pistol must try to avoid getting hit by water. Again,
the players must be directed by their teams.
Once the second volunteer has been squirted (or at least when they are
wet enough for your liking), stop the game. Ask each player how easy/
difficult they found it to hear their team guiding them.
We suggest you spend no longer than five minutes on this game.

How to link to talk
- There are so many voices shouting at us, vying for our attention
  all the time. As Christians, we really want to hear God's voice,
  but all the noise around us can make it hard

- Guidance is about figuring out what God is saying to us and
  following his instructions

OPTION 3

LEGO CHALLENGE

PREPARATION TIME **5** minutes

Quick summary
How fast can a blindfolded person, guided only by their team,
assemble a Lego kit?

Equipment / resources needed
One small Lego kit per group (the same as you may have used in the
session on the Bible).
One blindfold per group.

How it works
Ask everyone to move into their small groups. Blindfold one member of
each group, and give them a small Lego kit. Explain that the blindfolded
member is the only person allowed to touch the Lego set; the rest of
the team must direct them on how to put the pieces together. It will be
difficult, but, given time, perhaps one group might finish the task.

How to link to talk
- There are so many voices shouting at us, vying for our attention
  all the time. As Christians, we really want to hear God's voice,
  but all the noise around us can make it hard

- Guidance is about figuring out what God is saying to us and
  following his instructions

- Learning to receive guidance is a vital part of life. We all need guidance in many different areas – from directions on how to get to a friend's house, to advice on which subjects we should continue to study at school

- Jesus says, 'My sheep listen to my voice; I know them, and they follow me' (John 10:27). Christians follow the guidance of God

- Typically, guidance is more of a process – God promises to guide us when we ask him

- God has a good plan for each of us (Psalm 32:8; John 10:3–4; Jeremiah 29:11; Romans 12:2)

- God's guidance is not like a set of rules or directions yelled out to us. Instead, it comes out of the relationship that we have with him

- It is wise to involve God in all of our big decisions (Isaiah 30:1–2)

- Without God we are likely to get into a mess

- God guides us in many different ways

- We're going to look at five ways that God guides us

NB: the titles of the points all have the option to begin with the letters 'C' and 'S'. If you think that would be helpful for your group, do use these versions of the titles.

POINT 1 – THROUGH THE BIBLE (COMMANDING SCRIPTURE)

- The Bible is full of general guidelines about how we should live our lives and we should always follow these

- For example, if you are wondering about whether or not to murder someone, you don't have to pray about it – God has already said 'do not murder'! Some answers are clearly laid out in the Bible

- God also speaks to us about specific situations through the Bible

- If we make a habit of studying the Bible regularly, then God will often bring a particular verse to light at just the right time to help guide us in a decision (Psalm 119:105; Psalm 119:130–133)

Choose one of the following 3 options:

OPTION 1

EVAN ALMIGHTY

PREPARATION TIME 5 minutes

Quick summary
In this clip, Evan is led to the Bible and it instructs him on what to do: in Genesis 6:13–15, he reads that he must make an ark out of gopher wood. We see that printed words can be a source of instruction.

Equipment / resources needed

A copy of the film Evan Almighty, *Universal Studios, 2007. Certificate PG.*

▷ *Chapter 4: 0:14:39*　　☐ *Chapter 4: 0:15:35*

Projector and screen (or a TV), and a DVD player.

How to link to talk

- Just as Evan was led to the Bible to receive instruction, so God also speaks to us through his printed word. Sometimes when we are reading the Bible, a particularly relevant part might jump out and speak to us directly

OPTION 2

HOW NOT TO BE GUIDED BY THE BIBLE

PREPARATION TIME ⬤ **0** minutes

Quick summary

This story, of a man randomly selecting Bible passages to instruct him, demonstrates how not to be guided by the Bible.

Equipment / resources needed

None.

How it works

There was a man who decided he would let God guide him by opening the Bible at random and pointing to a spot on the page. He figured he would do whatever that verse said. So he tried it.

He said, 'Lord, what shall I do?' He opened his Bible at random, and landed on Matthew 27:5, which says: 'Then Judas went and hanged himself.' So he thought, 'Oh well, maybe second time lucky?' and he tried again. This time his finger was pointing at

Luke 10:37, which reads: 'Go and do thou likewise.' He thought, 'Oh dear!' He tried a third time, and got John 13:27, which says: 'What you're about to do, do quickly.'

How to link to talk

- Perhaps reading the Bible randomly like that isn't the best way to go. But God *does* use the Bible to guide us. Sometimes when we are reading the Bible, a particularly relevant part might jump out and speak to us directly

OPTION 3

'GUIDED BY THE BIBLE' TESTIMONY

Share a story (your own, or perhaps the story of someone else who is also running the course) about a time in your life when the Bible spoke clearly and directly into a specific situation.

POINT 2 – BY THE HOLY SPIRIT (COMPELLING SPIRIT)

- The Holy Spirit helps us to recognise God's voice (John 10:3–4; Acts 16:7)

- God speaks to us as we pray (Acts 13:1–3)

- Sometimes he speaks to us by putting strong feelings that we just cannot get rid of in our hearts and minds (Philippians 2:13)

- Sometimes he speaks in more extraordinary ways: prophecy (Acts 11:27), dreams (Matthew 1:20), visions (Acts 16:10), angels (Genesis 18:1–15), audible voices (1 Samuel 3:4–14)

Choose one of the following 4 options:

OPTION 1

AUDIO RECORDING

PREPARATION TIME **30** minutes

Quick summary
See if the group can guess the well known voices. We can learn to recognise the voices of famous people, and, through the Holy Spirit, we can also learn to recognise the voice of God.

Equipment / resources needed
Some recordings of well known voices.

How it works
Make some sound recordings of famous people who are well known by the group. (It could be a radio DJ, a TV personality or an actor/actress.) Play the recordings to the group, and ask them to identify the voices. Play as many different voices as you think best.

How to link to talk
- We can learn to recognise the voices of famous people, but we all know the voices of those we love. They are the people who can genuinely get away with just saying, 'It's me!' when they phone you

- In the same way, we can recognise the voice of God through the Holy Spirit. We can learn to recognise his gentle whisper

OPTION 2

CORNFLAKE OBSTACLE COURSE

PREPARATION TIME **5** minutes

Quick summary
A volunteer must be led through an obstacle course made of cornflakes, while the rest of the group try to distract them. This game shows how hard it can be to focus on God's guidance and ignore the rest of the noise.

Equipment / resources needed

One box of cornflakes.
One blindfold.

How it works

Ask for a volunteer and get them to leave the room. While they are out, put small piles of cornflakes all around the room.
Choose someone to be a guide. Ask the guide to go out and blindfold the volunteer and bring them back into the room. The guide is allowed to speak to the volunteer, but cannot touch them.
Explain that the room is booby-trapped (but don't say what with), and the volunteer's mission is to get from one end of the room to the other without running into the traps! Ask the rest of the group to try and distract the volunteer by shouting, etc. Hopefully, having one constant voice next to them throughout will enable them to navigate their way through the course. At the end of the game, ask the volunteer how they found the experience: what made it possible/impossible.

> #### Suggested tip
> *Asking the volunteer to go barefoot makes it more fun for everyone!*

How to link to talk

- There are so many voices shouting at us, vying for our attention all the time. As Christians, we really want to hear God's voice, but all the noise around us can make it hard

- God's Holy Spirit speaks to us in whispers, and he comes alongside us to guide us through life

PRAYER IS TWO-WAY

PREPARATION TIME **0** minutes

Quick summary

This analogy shows the group that prayer needs to be a two-way conversation between ourselves and God.

Equipment / resources needed

None.

How it works

Let's imagine I go to the doctor and I say, 'Hello, doctor! I've got a number of problems today. I've got fungus growing under my toenails, and I've got a problem with my knee. I think I'm getting a bit of arthritis in my hips, I have tennis elbow and I think I'm beginning to develop flu symptoms. I also have problems sleeping at night.' Imagine I pour out all my problems, and then I say, 'It's been very nice to see you, doctor. Goodbye!' In this situation, the doctor might say, 'Hang on a second, do you want to hear what *I* have to say?'

How to link to talk

- Sometimes I think God says to us, 'Do you want to hear what I have to say?'
- We need to make time and space to listen to God's voice

OPTION 4

'GUIDED BY THE HOLY SPIRIT' TESTIMONY

Share a story (your own, or perhaps the story of someone else who is also running the course) about a time in your life when you sensed the Holy Spirit guiding you.

POINT 3 – COMMON SENSE

- God has given us a conscience and a brain, and he wants us to use them! If something seems like a stupid idea, then it probably is ... enough said

Choose one of the following 2 options:

OPTION 1

STUNTS CLIP

PREPARATION TIME **5** minutes

Quick summary
An Alpha advertisement showing clips of people doing stupid things. God gave us common sense so we could tell which things are good ideas and which things are not.

Equipment / resources needed
The link to this video can be found online at youthalpha.org/lgmedia
You may want to use a projector and screen in order to show the clip to the whole group.

How to link to talk
- Some things in life are just bad ideas! God gave us a brain. Our common sense is a gift

OPTION 2

JENGA WORLD RECORD

PREPARATION TIME **5** minutes

Quick summary
Some people don't have any common sense. In this clip, a reporter interviews a man who has made a replica 'Leaning Tower of Pisa' using Jenga blocks, but forgets that it isn't sensible to trail a microphone lead around it ...

Equipment / resources needed
To find the link for this clip, please visit youthalpha.org/lgmedia
You may want to use a projector and a screen in order to show the clip to the whole group.

How to link to talk

- God gave us a brain (trailing a microphone lead around a Jenga tower isn't a great way of using it). Our common sense is a gift

POINT 4 – ADVICE FROM OTHERS (COUNSEL OF THE SAINTS)

- The wiser you are, the more aware you will be that you need help to make the most of life

- Proverbs 15:22 says: 'Plans fail for lack of counsel, but with many advisers they succeed'

- Proverbs 20:18: 'Make plans by seeking advice'

Choose one of the following 3 options:

OPTION 1

FINDING NEMO

PREPARATION TIME **5** minutes

Quick summary
In this clip, the fish warn Dory to go through the trench, not over it, in order to avoid danger. She looks to her friends for guidance.

Equipment / resources needed
A copy of the film Finding Nemo, *Disney/Pixar, 2003. Certificate U.*

▷ *Chapter 13: 0:38:23* ☐ *Chapter 13: 0:42:16*

Projector and screen (or a TV), and a DVD player.

How to link to talk

- Just as Dory gets advice in that clip, so God has given us friends and family to help us make important decisions. We should weigh up their advice

OPTION 2

GROUP DISCUSSION

PREPARATION TIME **5** minutes

Quick summary
Give each group a copy of the 'Who is going to guide you?' hand out.

Equipment / resources needed
A copy of the 'Who is going to guide you?' hand out for each person.

How it works
Give everyone a copy of the 'Who is going to guide you?' hand out. This can be found on Sheet 6 at the end of this session, or online at youthalpha.org/lgmedia
Have the group place the following sources of guidance (see list) in order of usefulness, with the most useful at the top and the least useful at the bottom.

How to link to talk

- Here is a hand out called 'Who is going to guide you?' Let's discuss it now, and you can take it away with you when you leave

Discuss in your small groups:

- Is there anything on this list that you think God would never use to guide us? Why/why not?

- Which sources of guidance would you feel most and least comfortable with?

'ADVICE OF FRIENDS' TESTIMONY

Share a story (your own, or perhaps the story of someone else who is also running the course) about a time in your life when you were led by God through the advice of friends.

POINT 5 – RANDOM SIGNS (CIRCUMSTANTIAL SIGNS)

- Circumstances – our eyes should be open to opportunities and to closed doors

- Sometimes God engineers 'coincidences'!

- But sometimes we need to keep going in spite of difficulty (Acts 16:7; 1 Corinthians 16:9)

Choose one of the following 3 options:

BRUCE ALMIGHTY

PREPARATION TIME **5** minutes

Quick summary
In this clip, Bruce asks God for a sign and gets lots of them! Even random, coincidental events can be used by God to guide us.

Equipment / resources needed
A copy of the film Bruce Almighty, *Buena Vista Home Entertainment, Inc, 2003. Certificate 12.*

▷ *Chapter 5: 0:21:08* ☐ *Chapter 6: 0:23:06*
Projector and screen (or a TV), and a DVD player.

How to link to talk

- Like Bruce following that truck, God sometimes uses coincidences and random stuff to speak to us

THE SAMARITANS

PREPARATION TIME **0** minutes

Quick summary

This true story about the man who set up the Samaritans hotline shows that even random, coincidental events can be used by God to guide us.

Equipment / resources needed

None.

How it works

A man called Reverend Chad Varah founded the Samaritans: a telephone hotline which helps and supports people who are in despair or even suicidal. Somebody calls the Samaritans every twenty seconds. In the early 1950s Reverend Varah was the vicar of a very busy church near Clapham Junction in London. Although he had this idea of a telephone hotline, he didn't think he was the right person to get it started, because he was so busy. So he said to the Lord, 'I'm not the person to do this. I think you need someone from a church in the City' (London's financial district). Churches in the City have very few parishioners, and therefore the vicars have more time available.

A few days later, he was invited to become the vicar of a church exactly like that: the Church of St Stephen's, Walbrook, in the City of London. When he saw the patrons of the church and they asked him what he'd do once he was appointed, he said, 'Well, I'd set up a telephone hotline.' They thought it was a great idea.

On his way to the church, Reverend Varah was thinking: 'What would be the best number for this hotline?' He wanted something that could be easily memorised. He knew that the first three characters would be letters (that was how phone numbers worked back then), so, as the local area was Mansion House, the letters would be M-A-N. He wondered, 'What could the numbers be, in order to give it a hint of emergency? Something like 999.' He decided that the perfect number would be 'MAN 9000' – easily memorable, with a hint of emergency.

He found the church telephone buried under some rubble in the vestry. Once he salvaged it, he dialled the operator and tried to persuade her to give him the phone number 'MAN 9000'.

He asked if it might be possible to change the church's number to 'MAN 9000'. She explained that it was very unlikely: 'Someone with a number as memorable as that wouldn't change it for love nor money.' Reverend Varah said, 'I have no money, but I have plenty of love! Would you tell me who the number "MAN 9000" belongs to so I can contact them myself?' The operator asked him where he was calling from, and he realised he didn't even know the church's number. He wiped the dust from the phone handset and saw, in clear print, 'MAN 9000'!

After explaining this coincidence to the operator, Reverend Varah said to God, 'I get the message! You had this planned even before the telephone was installed. Now please stop with the coincidences, because it's getting weird!'

How to link to talk
- Just as Reverend Varah found he already had the phone number he needed, so God sometimes uses coincidences and random stuff to speak to us

'COINCIDENCES' TESTIMONY

Share a story (your own, or perhaps the story of someone else who is also running the course) about a time in your life when God used 'coincidences' to guide you.

CONCLUSION

- Don't rush decisions – sometimes we have to wait

- Remember that we all make mistakes – but God forgives (Psalm 103:12)

- Let God guide you and watch your life take off

Choose one of the following 2 options:

QUICK PRAYER TO CLOSE

PREPARATION TIME **0** minutes

Quick summary
Pray to end your session.

Equipment / resources needed
None.

How it works
- I am just going to say a short prayer to close

- Lord, thank you that you promise to lead those who ask you. Please help us to hear your voice. I pray that you would lead each of us and help us to figure out what you are saying to us. In Jesus' name, Amen

How to link to talk
- Now we're going to have a quick break and then go into our small groups

- Thanks so much for coming to Youth Alpha today – see you next time!

OPTION 2

LISTEN TO A SONG

PREPARATION TIME **5** minutes

Quick summary
Play a worship song and invite the group to close their eyes and ask God to speak to them as they listen.

Equipment / resources needed
An appropriate song to play.
A CD player/iPod with speakers.

How it works
Encourage the group to close their eyes, listen to the words of the song, and ask God to speak to them as they listen.

- We are going to have some time to reflect upon what we've heard today, while listening to a relevant song

How to link to talk

- Now we're going to have a quick break and then go into our small groups

- Thanks so much for coming to Youth Alpha today – see you next time!

SESSION 6
HOW DOES GOD GUIDE US?
SMALL GROUP DISCUSSION QUESTIONS

[These can be combined at the end of the talk or interspersed after each teaching point. You can find an additional copy of this sheet online at youthalpha.org/lgmedia]

POINT 1 – THROUGH THE BIBLE (COMMANDING SCRIPTURE)
- Do you believe God speaks to people through the Bible?
- Have you ever had a time in your life when this was true?

POINT 2 – BY THE HOLY SPIRIT (COMPELLING SPIRIT)
- Do you believe God speaks to people by the Holy Spirit?
- Have you ever had a time in your life when this was true?

POINT 3 – COMMON SENSE
- Do you believe God speaks to people through their common sense?
- Have you ever had a time in your life when this was true?

POINT 4 – ADVICE FROM OTHERS (COUNSEL OF THE SAINTS)
- Do you believe God speaks to people through advice from others?
- Have you ever had a time in your life when this was true?

POINT 5 – RANDOM SIGNS (CIRCUMSTANTIAL SIGNS)
- Do you believe God speaks to people through random signs?
- Have you ever had a time in your life when this was true?

GENERAL DISCUSSION POINTS
- How do you feel about the idea of being guided by God?
- Do you think you are on course to make the best of your life?
- In the last few weeks, has anyone had a sense that God might have been guiding them? If so, what was the experience?
- Which sources of guidance would you feel most and least comfortable with?
- Are some sources of more use in certain areas? If so, which ones in which areas?
- Are you willing to ask God for his guidance?

You may like to include this optional extra, but it is not essential:

OPTIONAL EXTRA – GOING DEEPER

SESSION 6 BIBLE STUDY

Quick summary
This is an advanced option for small groups who may be ready for Bible study.

Equipment / resources needed
A Bible.

How it works
Read: Proverbs 16:1–9 – Commit to the Lord whatever you do

Then, in your small group, discuss the following questions:

- What must we do if we want God to guide us? (vv.3, 5 and 7)

- What does God promise to those that try to live according to his plans? (vv.6–8)

- Do any of you have examples that show that things go better when we live God's way?

- Can anyone give examples of God's blessing?

SHEET 6
WHO IS GOING TO GUIDE YOU?
HAND OUT

WHOSE ADVICE WOULD YOU LISTEN TO FIRST?

- Friends
- Research from books or the internet
- Magazine 'problem page'
- Teachers
- A priest/minister/pastor
- TV
- Parents
- Doctor
- Youth worker
- Horoscopes
- A politician
- Celebrities on TV
- Guidance counsellor

WEEKEND

SESSION 1

WHAT ABOUT THE HOLY SPIRIT?

WEEKEND SESSION 1
WHAT ABOUT THE HOLY SPIRIT?

SUMMARY

AIMS OF THIS SESSION

- To encourage the group to understand that the Holy Spirit is in all Christians and is not a new concept!

- To explain that we also need to be filled with the Spirit

- To explore the idea of spiritual gifts together

NOTES

- Encourage your leaders to use the 'Optional Extra – Going deeper' Bible study during their small group time, so that groups have a chance to look at the passage on 'spiritual gifts' together

- Ask group leaders to explain that in the second session, everyone will have an opportunity to receive prayer, during which they may be filled with the Spirit. Ask leaders to discuss with their groups how people feel about that

SESSION OVERVIEW

- Welcome
- Ice breaker game
- Worship
- Talk
    - Introduction
    - Point 1 – The Holy Spirit throughout the Bible
    - Point 2 – The Holy Spirit makes us part of God's family
    - Point 3 – The Holy Spirit gives us gifts
    - Conclusion
- Small groups

WELCOME

- Welcome to the Youth Alpha Weekend/Day!

- It's great to have you here with us

- Before we get going, let's start with an ice breaker game

ICE BREAKER GAME

Choose one of the following 3 options:

OPTION 1

NAME BINGO

PREPARATION TIME 30 minutes

Quick summary
Bingo with a twist!

Equipment / resources needed
One sheet of paper for each person with 'bingo' grid drawn on.
One pen for each person.
An additional small piece of paper per person.
One hat or bowl.

How it works
As the group enters the room, give each person one small piece of paper, one larger piece of paper with a 'bingo' grid on it (we suggest either 4x4 or 5x5 sized grid) and a pen. Ask each person to write their name on the smaller piece of paper and to give it back to you right away. Put all the names in a bowl or a hat. Give the group three minutes to walk around the room and get a different person to write their name in each empty box of their grid, until everyone's grid is filled.
Once this is complete, pull one name out of the hat at a time and announce it – if someone has this name on their sheet, they should put an 'X' through the corresponding box on their paper. The winner is the first person to mark a whole row either horizontally, vertically, or diagonally.

OPTION 2

CHOCOLATE MOUSSE GAME

PREPARATION TIME 10 minutes

Quick summary
A messy game where volunteers have to eat chocolate mousse through a pair of tights.

Equipment / resources needed
One table.
Between three and five pairs of cheap tights (you can buy these at a supermarket).
Between three and five bowls of chocolate mousse (or yoghurt).
Baby wipes (or similar) for cleaning up afterwards.

How it works
Set up a table at the front with three (or more) bowls of chocolate mousse/yoghurt in them. Ask for three volunteers who don't mind a bit of mess and who like chocolate/yoghurt. Give each of them a pair of tights and tell them to put these over their heads. On your word, they must put their hands behind their backs and try to eat as much chocolate mousse as they can through the tights. Give them one minute to do this. The person who has eaten the most wins.

BISCUIT GAME

PREPARATION TIME **0** minutes

Quick summary
A game in which volunteers must eat a dry biscuit and try to whistle at the same time.

Equipment / resources needed
Three dry biscuits/Weetabix/cream crackers – any sort of very dry biscuit.

How it works
Ask for three volunteers (who can both whistle and are allowed to eat wheat!). Give each of them a biscuit and tell them that the aim of the game is to eat the whole thing as fast as they can. The winner is the first person to completely eat their biscuit (so their mouth is empty) and then whistle. Whistling is harder than you think with a dry mouth!

INTRODUCTION

- Welcome to the Youth Alpha Weekend (or Day). It's so cool that you are here

- The theme for this weekend is the third person of 'the Trinity'. Remember we chatted about that earlier in the course? There's God the Father, who we've talked about quite a bit; God the Son – Jesus – who we've chatted about a lot; and the third person in the Trinity, God the Holy Spirit. We haven't chatted about him very much yet, so this weekend/day is all about the Holy Spirit

Choose one of the following 2 options:

GUESS WHO?

PREPARATION TIME **1–2** hours

Quick summary
This option demonstrates how unmasking familiar faces makes everything seem clearer. This is what we need to do when we're trying to understand the Holy Spirit.

Equipment / resources needed
Pictures of people in your group, or famous celebrities.

A computer.

You may want to use a projector and a screen in order to show the pictures to the whole group.

How it works

If you are very organised, you could take some photos of your group prior to the weekend. Try to get close-up shots of their faces only. If this isn't possible, you can use pictures of well-known celebrities (you can find these online). Using Powerpoint (or a similar programme), cover the pictures up using several pieces, so that you cannot tell who the people are. Piece by piece, unveil one face at a time and ask the group to guess who each person is. You could give out prizes (or respect points).

> **Suggested tip**
>
> *For a low-tech version of this option, you could use large photos with paper over the top to cover them. Reveal a small part of each photo at a time.*

How to link to talk

- The Holy Spirit has remained masked and misunderstood for too long, or perhaps we've just never had the chance to see all that he is. In part, this may be because some older versions of the Bible call him the 'Holy Ghost', which sounds a little scary

- Actually, he is not a 'ghost' at all – he is the third person of the Trinity of God – Father, Son and *Holy Spirit*

THE SIMPSONS

PREPARATION TIME **5**

minutes

Quick summary

In this Simpson's clip, we see the faith healer come to town. He is showy and does a rap, while Bart 'heals' Homer of having a bucket on his head! This is an example of how the Holy Spirit can be incorrectly portrayed.

Equipment / resources needed

A copy of The Simpsons: *'Faith Off', (season 11, episode 11), Twentieth Century Fox Film Corporation, 2000. Certificate PG.*

▷ *Chapter 4: 0:08:48* ☐ *Chapter 4: 0:09:34*

Projector and screen (or a TV), and a DVD player.

How to link to talk

- The Holy Spirit has remained masked and misunderstood for too long, or perhaps we've just never had the chance to see all that he is. In part, this may be because some older versions of the Bible call him the 'Holy Ghost', which sounds a little scary

- Actually, he is not a 'ghost' at all – he is the third person of the Trinity of God – Father, Son and *Holy Spirit*

- In this session we're going to look at who the Holy Spirit is and what he does

- To do this, we are going to take a quick tour through the Bible, starting at the very beginning. Let's start with a quick illustration

POINT 1 – THE HOLY SPIRIT THROUGHOUT THE BIBLE

Choose one of the following 3 options:

CONTACT

PREPARATION TIME **5** minutes

Quick summary
This clip shows an amazing sequence as the camera speeds through the entire cosmos. This shows us the grandeur and beauty of creation.

Equipment / resources needed
A copy of the film Contact, *Warner Bros, 1997. Certificate PG*

▷ *Chapter 1: 0:00:32* ☐ *Chapter 1: 0:03:28*

Projector and screen (or a TV), and a DVD player.

How to link to talk
- The Holy Spirit was involved in creating everything that we see, and even all of the galaxies we can't see – amazing!

POWERS OF TEN

PREPARATION TIME **5** minutes

Quick summary
This clip begins in deep space, before zooming into a shot of our galaxy. This is followed by a shot of earth, and the clip eventually ends once it has shown the inside of a cell. This shows us the grandeur and beauty of creation.

Equipment / resources needed
To find the link for this clip, please visit youthalpha.org/lgmedia
You may want to use a projector and a screen in order to show the clip to the whole group.

How to link to talk
- The Holy Spirit was involved in creating everything that we see, and even all of the galaxies we can't see – amazing!

BREATH TEST GAME

PREPARATION TIME 10
minutes

Quick summary
The Holy Spirit is described in the Bible as God's breath, but can members of your group identify different smells from the breath of others?

Equipment / resources needed
Foods that will emit a strong smell. For example: a clove of garlic, coffee, salami, curry sauce, a strong mint, banana.

How it works
Ask for four or five volunteers who are willing to eat or suck something strong-tasting. Ensure that the rest of the group don't see what the volunteers are eating (you may want them to eat in another room). Once the volunteers have finished eating, get the rest of the group to parade past them and, by smelling their breath, try to guess what they have just eaten.

How to link to talk
- The Hebrew word for Holy Spirit is 'ruach' which means 'breath'. In Genesis, The Holy Spirit is described as God's breath. He breathes life into things, including us!

- Now we're going to race through the whole Bible in order to see the places where the Holy Spirit was at work

CREATION

- The Holy Spirit was involved in the creation of the universe. In Genesis 1:2, we see that 'the earth was formless and empty, darkness was over the surface of the deep, and the Spirit of God was hovering over the waters'. The Holy Spirit was there at the beginning. It says he was 'hovering', waiting to bring new things into being. In the same way, he is waiting to bring new things in each of our lives into being today

- The Holy Spirit is known as the breath of God. The Holy Spirit breathed life into humans (Genesis 2:7)

- If we go through the Bible cover to cover, we see the Holy Spirit moving throughout

OLD TESTAMENT

- In the Old Testament, God gave his Holy Spirit to particular people at particular times to do particular jobs. Not everyone was filled with the Spirit – only a few people, including those who needed:

    - to express themselves in art: Bezalel (Exodus 31:1–5)

    - to lead: Gideon (Judges 6:14–16, 34)

    - to perform feats of great strength: Samson (Judges 15:14–15)

    - to prophesy: Isaiah (61:1–3)

- God promised that at the right time the Holy Spirit would come in a new way (Ezekiel 36:26–27) – that he would fill all believers, both young and old, all of the time (Joel 2:28–29)

Choose one of the following 3 options:

BACKPACK PRESS-UP

PREPARATION TIME **5** minutes

Quick summary
This practical example shows us that God's laws were a burden upon us because they weren't in our hearts, just like the heavy backpack is a burden when it has the energy drinks inside it.

Equipment / resources needed
Lots of bottles of water and/or energy drinks.
One rucksack.

How it works
Before the session starts, fill a backpack with bottled energy drinks or water (tip: use lots of bottles, or it will be too easy!). Ask a volunteer to do a few normal press-ups before putting the heavy rucksack on their back and asking them to try a few more. Next, take the bottles out of the rucksack and show the volunteer, and the rest of the group, what was in there. Give the volunteer one of the bottles and ask them to drink some of the energy drink/water. Once they've done this, ask them to do some more press-ups with the empty rucksack on their back. Following this, ask them which part of the demonstration was easiest: the press-ups with the empty rucksack, or the press-ups with the full rucksack?

NB: you may want to give the remaining drinks out to the rest of the group. Tell them they are free gifts, just like the gifts of the Holy Spirit!

How to link to talk
- When God's law was a set of rules that were written down, it was hard to follow. The rules were a burden upon us because they weren't in our hearts. However, God wanted to put his laws in our hearts. Just like in this example, the stuff that was so heavy to carry on the outside (the bottles in the backpack) was actually helpful and refreshing when it was on the inside

PACMAN ONLINE

PREPARATION TIME **5** minutes

Quick summary
Show the group 'Pacman', an online version of an old school computer game in which the player's character (Pacman) becomes invincible when he eats special food. During these times he can eat the ghosts; however, his super-power fades after a short period of time.

Equipment / resources needed

A computer on which to play the game. You can find the link to Pacman online at youthalpha.org/lgmedia

How to link to talk

- Pacman's invincibility works in a similar way to God's Spirit in the Old Testament – he came upon certain people at certain times, but only for a particular task. This is great, but wouldn't it be even better to have the Holy Spirit permanently?

ELECTRIC PLUG

PREPARATION TIME **10** minutes

Quick summary

Can one of your group members rewire a plug? Even if they can, what is the use of a plug on its own? Every plug needs a power source, and God's Spirit is our power source.

Equipment / resources needed

One electrical plug, taken apart.
One screwdriver.

How it works

Get an electrical plug and take it apart. Ask for a volunteer and give them a screwdriver. Tell them they have thirty seconds to put the plug back together. As the volunteer is struggling to get all the wires correctly fixed in the right places, explain the point below.

How to link to talk

- Even if *[insert volunteer's name]* manages to wire this, a plug on its own is fairly useless, isn't it? In order for us to use this plug, it needs to be connected to a power source

- God's Spirit is the power source that we, as Christians, can connect to, and not just as a one-off, but all the time

OLD TESTAMENT CONTINUED

- In the Old Testament the covenant (or agreement) between God and his people was an external (outside) one. They had to keep lots of rules and sacrifice lots of animals – it was a burden on them: they couldn't manage it

- But God promised that the time would come when the agreement would be an internal one – in their hearts – and that to help them keep, it the Holy Spirit would come to everyone (Ezekiel 36:26–27; Joel 2:28–29)

- Then we get to the New Testament …

JESUS

- John the Baptist announced that someone was coming who would baptise people, not only with water, but also with the Holy Spirit (Luke 3:16). Eventually, Jesus was born

- When Jesus was baptised, the Holy Spirit came down on him and he received power (Luke 3:22; 4:1)

- After Jesus' resurrection, he promised that his disciples would receive the Holy Spirit, but they still had to wait (John 7:37–39)

PENTECOST/THE EARLY CHURCH

- After Jesus' death, resurrection and ascension into heaven, the Holy Spirit finally arrived

- On the day of Pentecost, the disciples were praying together and suddenly the Holy Spirit came and filled them in a completely new way (Acts 2:1–2)

- The disciples spoke in new languages, received new boldness and new power (Acts 2:3–4)

- From there they went out and literally changed the world!

TODAY

- The great news is that the same Holy Spirit is available to all of us (Acts 2:38–39)

- Now let's look at what the Holy Spirit does

POINT 2 – THE HOLY SPIRIT MAKES US PART OF GOD'S FAMILY

- Like it or loathe it, we were all born into some kind of a human family

- When we become a Christian, the Holy Spirit gives us a new birth into God's family

- In John 3:3–5 Jesus talks to a priest called Nicodemus about the kingdom of God. 'Jesus declared, "I tell you the truth, no one can see the kingdom of God unless he is born again." "How can a man be born when he is old?" Nicodemus asked. "Surely he cannot enter a second time into his mother's womb to be born!" [He's right, that would just be weird.] Jesus answered, "I tell you the truth, no one can enter the kingdom of God unless he is born of water and the Spirit" '

- That expression 'born again' can have negative connotations these days, can't it? What Jesus is saying is that when we become Christians, we start a new spiritual life

- Romans 8:1–2 says: 'Therefore, there is now no condemnation for those who are in Christ Jesus, because through Christ Jesus the law of the Spirit of life set me free from the law of sin and death'

- When we become Christians we are forgiven by God, and he gives us new life. Living by the Spirit means we are set free from the old law of sin and death. That same chapter, Romans 8, goes on to say: 'Those who are led by the Spirit of God are children of God. For you did not receive a spirit that makes you a slave again to fear, but you received the Spirit of adoption. And by him we cry, "Abba, Father." The Spirit himself testifies with our spirit that we're God's children. And if we're children, then we're heirs – heirs of God and co-heirs with Christ, if indeed we share in his sufferings in order that we may also share in his glory'

- We are children of the King of Kings, so we can call God 'Father'. We are his heirs – we inherit his kingdom

Choose one of the following 4 options:

OPTION 1

FAMOUS FAMILIES

PREPARATION TIME **30** minutes

Quick summary
In this game, each member of the group randomly becomes a 'member' of a famous family, and must try to find their other family 'members' without speaking to anyone. When we become Christians, we become members of God's family.

Equipment / resources needed
Lots of small pieces of paper (one per person).
One balloon for each person.

How it works
Think of several famous families, each with four or five well-known people in it, for example: Homer, Marge, Bart, Lisa and Maggie Simpson; Barack, Michelle, Sasha and Malia Obama, etc. Be sure to choose families that your group will know, and make sure that there is one character for every person in your group. Write the name of each family member down on a separate piece of paper, place each name inside its own balloon and blow the balloons up.
Throw all of the balloons in the air and get each member of the group to grab one and burst it. Once they've found the name of a family member inside it, they must try to find the other members of their 'family' – without speaking!

> ### Suggested tip
> *If you have time, you could do more in these 'family' groups. For example, you could tape each group together and ask them to perform an activity such as tying each other's shoelaces or walking around an obstacle course, etc.*

How to link to talk
- The Holy Spirit makes us part of God's family

OPTION 2

ABRAHAM LINCOLN'S SON

PREPARATION TIME **0** minutes

Quick summary

This story about Abraham Lincoln's son bringing a man directly to the President gives us an idea of how we can get to God through his son Jesus.

Equipment / resources needed

None.

How it works

A young soldier was fighting for the Union army in the American Civil War. His older brother and father had both died while fighting. He went to Washington, DC to ask President Abraham Lincoln for exemption from military service, so that he could go back and help his sister and mother with the spring planting on the family farm. When he arrived in Washington, he went to the White House, approached the doors, and asked to see the president.

He was told, 'You can't see the president! Don't you know there's a war on? The president's a very busy man. Now go away, son! Get back out there and fight like you're supposed to.' So he left, very disheartened. He was sitting on a park bench, not far from the White House, when a little boy came up to him. The young boy said, 'You look unhappy. What's wrong?' The soldier looked at the young boy and began to spill his heart out. He told the child that since his father and brother had been killed in the war, he was the only male left in the family, and he was desperately needed back at the farm.

The little boy took the soldier by the hand and led him around to the back of the White House. They went through the back door, past the guards, past all the generals and the high ranking government officials until they got to the president's office. The little boy didn't even knock on the door, but just opened it and walked in. There was President Lincoln with his secretary of state, looking over battle plans on the desk. President Lincoln looked up and said, 'What can I do for you, Todd?' Todd said, 'Daddy, this soldier needs to talk to you.' The soldier had a chance to plead his case to President Lincoln, and was excused from the war due to his circumstances.

[James S. Hewett, Illustrations Unlimited *(Tyndale House Publishers Inc., 1988), pp.72–73.]*

How to link to talk

- In the same way, we are now part of God's family – it's as if Jesus himself has walked us past the security and right into God's throne room. We have access to the Father through Jesus

- The amazing thing is that the more time we spend with God, the more we become like him

DOGS AND THEIR OWNERS

PREPARATION TIME 5 minutes

Quick summary
Show some funny pictures of dogs that look like their owners in order to demonstrate that once we are part of God's family, we begin to become more like God – there is a family likeness.

Equipment / resources needed
To find the link for these images, please visit youthalpha.org/lgmedia
You may want to use a projector and a screen in order to show the pictures to the whole group.

How to link to talk
- Isn't it strange how some dogs look like their owners? (Or do the owners look like their dogs?)
- The Holy Spirit makes us part of God's family, and a family likeness begins to show. As we spend time with God we become more like him

DRAWING THE FAMILY LIKENESS

PREPARATION TIME 0 minutes

Quick summary
In small groups, ask each person to consider what is unique about their family.

Equipment / resources needed
One pen per person.
One sheet of paper per person.

How it works
Part 1
Hand out the pens and paper and encourage the group to draw or write down the characteristics that their family share – the things that make up their family likeness. These do not have to be physical things, like hair colour or face shape, they could also be personality traits, such as being quick to get angry or quick to laugh, or personal tastes. For example: we all like watching sport or eating kebabs. When they have finished, the groups should take a few minutes to discuss what they have each put down. (Leaders must ensure sensitivity – if people are sharing honestly we must make sure no one feels teased, especially if they are sharing negative qualities about themselves.)

Part 2
Now get leaders to ask their groups what they think are the characteristics of Christians. Allow the groups to be totally honest, and let them know that the characteristics do not have to be positive. Ask

one person in each group to write down/draw what the others say. Each group should end this section by talking about which characteristics are good and which are not. Which attributes should they try to imitate, and which should they try to change in order to encourage a more positive perception of the church?

How to link to talk
- The Holy Spirit makes us part of God's family, and a family likeness begins to show. As we spend time with God we become more like him

- We may not necessarily begin to physically look like God, but we will grow like him in terms of how we act and live. Galatians 5:22–23 says this: 'The fruit of the Spirit is love, joy, peace, patience, kindness, goodness, faithfulness, gentleness and self-control. Against such things there is no law.' These are the characteristics of God's family and the Holy Spirit helps to grow this 'fruit' inside our own lives. He helps us to become more like Jesus

- We are all one big family, and with the help of the Holy Spirit we can learn to work together

POINT 3 – THE HOLY SPIRIT GIVES US GIFTS

- So what does the Holy Spirit do? Well, he makes us part of God's family. He also helps us to understand God, helps us to pray and helps us to understand the Bible. He gives us the power to live for Jesus and gives us the courage to tell others so that they can join the family too. It is the Holy Spirit who is responsible for making God's family grow

- The other important thing to tell you about the Holy Spirit is that, just like our human parents, God loves to give gifts to his children. Only these are 'spiritual' gifts rather than physical presents

Choose one of the following 2 options:

OPTION 1

SCHOOL OF ROCK

PREPARATION TIME **5**
minutes

Quick summary
In this clip, we see Duey giving out different roles to each of the children, and we discover that each one of them has a particular gift to offer the team. The same is true of God's family – we all have something different to bring.

Equipment / resources needed
A copy of the film School of Rock, *Paramount Pictures, 2004. Certificate PG.*

▷ *Chapter 6: 0:28:12* ☐ *Chapter 6: 0:29:50*

Projector and screen (or a TV), and a DVD player.

How to link to talk
- In that clip we see Duey giving everyone a role to play according to their gifts

- In a similar way, the Holy Spirit gives each of us different gifts to help us play our part

THE ONE-MAN CHURCH

PREPARATION TIME **0** minutes

Quick summary
This story shows how easy it can be to leave our responsibilities to someone else. God wants every one of us to be involved in his church; that's why he gives us individual gifts that will help us work together.

Equipment / resources needed
None.

How it works
A pastor received this letter:

'Dear Pastor, there are 566 people in our church. 100 are frail and elderly – so that leaves 466 to do all the work. 80 of these are young people who are busy at school or college, so that leaves 386 to do all the work. 150 of these are tired businesspeople – they have no time, so that leaves 236 to do all the work. 150 of these are tied up with children, which leaves 86 to do all the work. 15 people live too far away to come here regularly, so that leaves 71 to do all the work. 69 people say they've already done their bit for the church, so that leaves you and me. But I'm exhausted, so good luck to you.'

How to link to talk
- God wants us all to be involved in his church; that's why he gives us different gifts that will help us work together

---

- In 1 Corinthians 12, the Bible tells us about these spiritual gifts. Verse 4 says that 'there are different kinds of gifts, but the same Spirit'. God gives different gifts to each of us, but they are all given by the same Spirit. We need to understand this in order to prevent ourselves from feeling jealous of other people's gifts; it is God who gives them

- Verses 7–11 say: 'Now to each one the manifestation of the Spirit is given for the common good. To one there is given through the Spirit the message of wisdom, to another the message of knowledge by means of the same Spirit, to another faith by the same Spirit, to another gifts of healing by that one Spirit, to another miraculous powers, to another prophecy, to another distinguishing between spirits, to another speaking in different kinds of tongues, and to still another the interpretation of tongues. All these are the work of one and the same Spirit, and he gives them to each one, just as he determines'

- This isn't a definitive list of all of God's gifts, this is just a few of them. The thing to remember is that the gifts are from God, and he decides what to give and when

CONCLUSION

- So we've seen that the Holy Spirit has been present since creation and has remained present throughout the Bible. The Holy Spirit isn't just a concept recently invented by the church

- The Holy Spirit makes us part of God's family and gives us spiritual gifts

- Every Christian has the Holy Spirit living *in* them, but not every Christian is *filled* with the Holy Spirit

- The Bible says, 'Be filled with the Spirit' (Ephesians 5:18–20). That is what we are going to talk about in the next session

- Let's pray as we close

QUICK PRAYER TO CLOSE

PREPARATION TIME **0** minutes

Quick summary
Pray to end your session.

Equipment / resources needed
None.

How it works
- I am now going to say a short prayer to close

- Lord, we thank you that you have given us your Holy Spirit. I pray that when we meet up later you might fill each of us with your Spirit. Please help us with our discussion now. In Jesus' name, Amen

How to link to talk
- We're finished for now – we'll continue later today with the next session, which is called, 'How Can I Be Filled with the Holy Spirit?'

WEEKEND SESSION 1
WHAT ABOUT THE HOLY SPIRIT?
SMALL GROUP DISCUSSION QUESTIONS

[These can be combined at the end of the talk or interspersed after each teaching point. You can find an additional copy of this sheet online at youthalpha.org/lgmedia]

NOTE

On the Alpha Course this is often the point when the gift of tongues is discussed at some length. This is done for the sake of clarity, and to reassure the members of the group about what might take place during the ministry time at the end of the next session. You might like to bear this in mind if you intend to speak about the gift of tongues later, and should encourage your group leaders to discuss it in their small groups.

POINT 1 – THE HOLY SPIRIT THROUGHOUT THE BIBLE

- Which of these words would best have described your view of the Holy Spirit before this weekend/day? Ghost, God, ghoul, spiritual presence, comforter, helper, myth, power

- Are there any other words you would have used?

- What do you think about the idea that the Holy Spirit has been around since creation?

- Does the idea of the Holy Spirit seem positive to you?

POINT 2 – THE HOLY SPIRIT MAKES US PART OF GOD'S FAMILY

- How do you feel about the idea of being part of God's family?

- How do you feel about having direct access to God through the Holy Spirit?

- Do you see a 'family likeness' in the Christians you know?

- What are the characteristics that you most associate with Christians?

POINT 3 – THE HOLY SPIRIT GIVES US GIFTS

- How do you feel about the idea of being filled with the Holy Spirit? Does it sound great, normal, or a bit scary?

- How do you feel about the idea of God giving us all spiritual gifts? *[We suggest you move from here on to the optional Bible study if appropriate]*

- How do you feel/what do you think about the Holy Spirit after this morning's talk?

You may like to include this optional extra, but it is not essential:

WEEKEND SESSION 1 BIBLE STUDY

Quick summary
This is an advanced option for small groups who may be ready for Bible study.

Equipment / resources needed
A Bible.

How it works
Read: 1 Corinthians 12:1–11 – Spiritual gifts

Then, in your small group, discuss the following questions:

- Has anyone in the group heard of or had any experience of spiritual gifts?

- What gifts are listed in this passage? (vv.8–10)

- Take some time to talk through the various gifts listed

- Are you excited by the idea of God giving people supernatural gifts?

- Why or why not?

- Why does God give these gifts to people? (v.7)

youthalpha.

WEEKEND SESSION 2

HOW CAN I BE FILLED WITH THE HOLY SPIRIT?

WEEKEND SESSION 2
HOW CAN I BE FILLED WITH THE HOLY SPIRIT?

SUMMARY

AIMS OF THIS SESSION

- To encourage the group that God wants to fill us with his Holy Spirit

- To explain that we need to go on being filled with the Spirit – this is not a one-off thing

- To explore this practically by praying for each other and asking him to fill us

NOTES

- Remind your team to sit with their groups during this session so they are ready to pray at the end of the talk

- Encourage them to offer prayer to each person, rather than waiting to be asked

- You might want to do a very quick prayer ministry training refresher with your team before the session

- Pray, and trust that God will do what he wants to do

SESSION OVERVIEW

- Welcome
- Ice breaker game
- Worship
- Talk
    - Introduction
    - Point 1 – What happens when people experience the Holy Spirit?
    - Point 2 – Can anything stop us from being filled?
    - Conclusion
- Prayer ministry time

WELCOME

- Welcome to the second session of the Youth Alpha Weekend/Day!

- Before we get going, let's start with an ice breaker game

ICE BREAKER GAME

Choose one of the following 3 options:

BALLOON STOMPING

PREPARATION TIME **0** minutes

Quick summary
The aim of this game is to try and pop everyone else's balloon, while keeping your own intact.

Equipment / resources needed
One balloon for each person (plus a few spares).
One piece of string (approximately forty centimetres) per person.

How it works
Give everyone a balloon and a piece of string. Tell them to blow up the balloon and tie it to their ankle with the piece of string (but not too tightly!). When everyone is ready, tell the group that the aim of the game is to try to burst everyone else's balloons by jumping on them – if, however, their own balloon gets burst, they are out. The last person with their balloon intact wins! We suggest you spend no longer than five minutes on this game.

FIND THE MARBLES

PREPARATION TIME **5** minutes

Quick summary
This is a very messy game in which volunteers must use their feet to find marbles/stones that are hidden in a bucket of baked beans!

Equipment / resources needed
Between two and three buckets or tubs.
Between six and twelve cans of baked beans.
Fifteen marbles or stones.
Three chairs.
Plastic sheet to prevent mess.
Baby wipes, water and towels to clean up with.

How it works
Set up two or three tubs/buckets and fill each with between two and four tins of baked beans. Put five marbles (or stones) into each tub and make sure they cannot be seen. Ask for two volunteers who are happy

*to get their feet dirty. Tell them to take their socks and shoes off, give
them each a chair to sit on and blindfold them. Tell them that the first
person to remove five marbles/stones from the tub of beans using only
their feet will be the winner. We suggest you either do this outside or put
a plastic sheet down in order to avoid mess. We suggest you spend no
longer than five minutes on this game.*
*Have lots of wet wipes and a bowl of water ready for the volunteers to
wash their feet with once they've finished.*

NB: This game will get very messy!

OPTION 3

HUMAN PYRAMID

PREPARATION TIME **0** minutes

Quick summary
A competition in which teams must try to make the tallest human pyramid.

Equipment / resources needed
None! Just bodies.

How it works
*Split your group into teams of between eight and ten people (you need
at least six people per group) and tell them their aim is to make the
tallest human pyramid in one minute or less. The team with the tallest
pyramid wins!*

*NB: remind groups that bigger/stronger people should go on the bottom of
the pyramid.*

INTRODUCTION

- This session is all about how we can be filled with the Holy Spirit

Choose one of the following 4 options:

OPTION 1

VACUUM EXPERIMENT

PREPARATION TIME **5** minutes

Quick summary
*This experiment shows that a full bottle won't be harmed in hot/cold
conditions, whereas an empty bottle should totally collapse. This helps
to illustrate the point that when Christians are filled with the Holy Spirit,
they are stronger.*

Equipment / resources needed
Two large soft drink bottles – one must be full, brand new and

unopened, the other should be empty (with the lid screwed on tight).
Two large buckets/bowls (must be big enough to submerge bottles fully).
Hot/boiling water for one bucket.
Cold water for the other.

How it works

Submerge the full bottle (with its lid on) in the bowl of hot water for a couple of minutes. Take it out and then plunge it immediately into the bowl of cold water. Hold it there for a couple of minutes. Nothing will happen. Repeat the process with the empty bottle (with its lid on) and after a couple of minutes in the cold water, the bottle should collapse/ crumple in on itself. See if the scientists in your group can give an explanation for this.

How to link to talk

- The bottle that was filled with liquid was strong, whereas the bottle that was empty wasn't. This helps us to understand the importance of being filled with the Holy Spirit: when Christians are filled, they are stronger

CAN EXPERIMENT

PREPARATION TIME **0**
minutes

Quick summary

If a can is full and unopened, it should be able to carry a person's weight, but an empty can will crumple. This helps to illustrate the point that when Christians are filled with the Holy Spirit, they are stronger.

Equipment / resources needed

Two cans of soft drink – one empty, the other unopened.

How it works

Ask for a volunteer to balance on the unopened, full can using only one leg. Flick the side of the can and nothing will happen. Then ask the volunteer to do the same with the empty can. They should be able to do it without it collapsing immediately, but flick the side and it should crumple and get squashed.

NB: be very careful you don't hurt your fingers – it may be worth practicing first!

How to link to talk

- The can that was filled was strong, whereas the can that was empty wasn't. This helps us to understand the importance of being filled with the Holy Spirit: when Christians are filled, they are stronger

MENTOS EXPERIMENT

PREPARATION TIME **5** minutes

Quick summary
When you put Mentos into a bottle of Diet Coke, you get an amazing explosion. This helps to illustrate the power that is created when a Christian is filled with the Holy Spirit.

Equipment / resources needed
One packet of Mentos sweets.
One large bottle of Diet Coke.

How it works
Practice this before the session to make sure it works!
Open a large bottle of Diet Coke and drop between one and three Mentos into the liquid, then stand back and watch it create a big fountain.

NB: this demonstration is best done outdoors.

> Suggested tip
> *For an alternative way of demonstrating this explosion, get some volunteers to hold a Mento sweet in their mouth and take a sip of Diet Coke. The last person to open their mouth wins!*

How to link to talk
- In a similar way, when you combine a person – for example, you – and the Holy Spirit, there is power

MENTOS AND DIET COKE VIDEO

PREPARATION TIME **5** minutes

Quick summary
A clip showing what can happen when you combine Mentos and Diet Coke – basically a fireworks display without the fireworks. This helps to illustrate the power that is created when a Christian is filled with the Holy Spirit.

Equipment / resources needed
To find the link for this clip, please visit youthalpha.org/lgmedia
You may want to use a projector and a screen in order to show the clip to the whole group.

How to link to talk
- In a similar way, when you combine a person – for example, you – and the Holy Spirit, there is power

- To be strong Christians we need to be filled with the Holy Spirit

- We are going to talk now about how we can do just that

POINT 1 – WHAT HAPPENS WHEN PEOPLE EXPERIENCE THE HOLY SPIRIT?

- The Book of Acts tells the story of the Christian church's beginnings, and it is filled with amazing instances of people being filled with the Holy Spirit

Choose one of the following 3 options:

SMALLVILLE

PREPARATION TIME **5** minutes

Quick summary
In this Smallville clip, Superman's transfers his powers onto Lana. Although we can't actually see the powers, and although we can't see them being transferred, we can see that this has a powerful impact on Lana. Similarly, we can't see the Holy Spirit, but when people are filled by him, we see powerful results.

Equipment / resources needed
A copy of Smallville, *season 7, episode 7, Warner Bros Entertainment Inc., 2007. Certificate 15.*

▷ *Chapter 1: 0:02:21* ☐ *Chapter 1: 0:03:17*

Projector and screen (or a TV), and a DVD player.

How to link to talk
- We can't actually see the powers in this clip, but we can see the effect they have on Lana. The same is true of the Holy Spirit: we can't see him, but when he moves powerfully (as in the book of Acts), we can certainly see the results

FIZZY WATER

PREPARATION TIME **0** minutes

Quick summary
This demonstration offers a fun way of explaining God's power while getting others wet.

Equipment / resources needed
One bottle of fizzy water.

How it works
Shake the bottle of fizzy water before asking for a volunteer. Tell the volunteer that for the rest of the talk, every time you say the words 'Holy Spirit', they have to open the bottle briefly and spray everyone!

How to link to talk
- We can't actually see what is making the water spray out of the bottle, but we can see the effects of it when *[insert name of volunteer]* opens the bottle. The same is true of the Holy Spirit: we

can't see him, but when he moves powerfully (as in the book of Acts), we can certainly see the results

CANDLE ILLUSTRATION

PREPARATION TIME **5** minutes

Quick summary
In this illustration, trick a volunteer into blowing into a big pile of flour. Just as we can't see the volunteer's breath, the effects of blowing into the flour will be obvious, so we can see the powerful results of the Holy Spirit when he fills us, even though we can't see him.

Equipment / resources needed
One blindfold.
One candle.
Lighter/matches.
One plate of flour.

How it works
Ask for a volunteer and blindfold them. Explain that you are going to put a candle in front of them, and in order to put it out, they have to blow really hard. Put the lit candle about ten centimetres (a safe distance) from the volunteer's mouth and tell them to blow. Next, explain that you are going to move the candle a bit further away; move it back slightly and get them to blow it out again. Then, tell them that the candle is going to be moved even further away, and explain that in order to put it out, they'll have to blow really hard. At this point, put a plate of flour near the volunteer's face, but not so close that they get suspicious. Tell them to blow really hard, and watch their face get covered in flour!

How to link to talk
- We can't actually see *[insert volunteer's name]*'s breath, but we did see the effect of it when he/she blew on the candle/flour. The same is true of the Holy Spirit: we can't see him, but when he moves powerfully (as in the book of Acts), we can certainly see the results

- Some of you might be wondering what it means to be 'full' of the Holy Spirit? Is it the same as becoming a Christian? Let me give you an example

Choose one of the following 4 options:

GAS LANTERN

PREPARATION TIME **0** minutes

Quick summary
This illustration allows you to demonstrate the difference between having the Holy Spirit in you (the light is on, but it isn't filling the darkness

completely) and being filled with the Holy Spirit (the light is turned up as high as possible, filling the darkness).

Equipment / resources needed
One gas lantern/camper's stove.

How it works
Turn off the lights/darken the room as much as you can. Start with the gas lantern turned down low.

- As we have said before, all Christians have the Holy Spirit in them

- The question is, how much will we allow the Holy Spirit to fill us?

Open the valve on the lantern, allowing more and more gas to flow until the room becomes as bright as it can be.

How to link to talk
- All Christians have the Holy Spirit *in* them, but not all Christians are *filled* with the Holy Spirit

- God doesn't want us to just have a little bit of his Spirit; he wants us to be filled so that we burn brightly, giving off heat and light to those around us

PILOT LIGHT

PREPARATION TIME   **0**   minutes

Quick summary
This analogy explains the difference between having the Holy Spirit in you and being filled with the Spirit.

Equipment / resources needed
None.

How it works
Have you ever seen an old fashioned gas oven? They have a little pilot light that is always on. In a way, that's like every Christian: we always have the Spirit of God living within us. Some people live their whole lives with their pilot light on, but they never go further than that. In contrast, when you turn the gas on, the pilot light suddenly catches alight with a 'whoosh' and gets very hot, very quickly. Some Christians are like regular pilot lights, and some Christians are lit pilot lights – firing on all cylinders!

How to link to talk
- All Christians have the Holy Spirit *in* them, but not all Christians are *filled* with the Holy Spirit

BALLOON ILLUSTRATION

PREPARATION TIME 0 minutes

Quick summary
This illustration allows you to demonstrate the difference between having the Holy Spirit in you (the balloon is filled with air, but there is room for more) and being filled with the Holy Spirit (the balloon has so much air in it, it bursts!).

Equipment / resources needed
One balloon.

How it works
Blow up the balloon, but only a little.

- Does this balloon have air in it? Yes – but it is not as full as it is designed to be

- All Christians have the Holy Spirit living in them – we have said this – but being filled with the Holy Spirit is a bit like this:

Blow up the balloon until it is quite big.

- Is this balloon full of air? Yes – and the great thing about the Holy Spirit is that you can be filled, but you can always have more!

Keep blowing up the balloon – until it bursts!

How to link to talk
- No analogy is perfect – thankfully, being filled with the Holy Spirit won't make us pop! The point is that you can always have more of the Spirit

- All Christians have the Holy Spirit *in* them, but not all Christians are *filled* with the Holy Spirit

POPCORN MACHINE

PREPARATION TIME 5 minutes

Quick summary
A popcorn machine can have corn kernels in it (a Christian can have the Holy Spirit in them), but the kernels will not 'pop' until you turn the machine on (until the Christian is filled with the Spirit).

Equipment / resources needed
One popcorn machine.
Popping corn/corn kernels.

How it works
Plug in the popcorn machine at the front of the room. Explain that:

- The popcorn maker represents us. When we become a Christian the Holy Spirit comes to live inside us

Pour a number of unpopped kernels into popcorn maker.

- We have a choice at this point: leave the popcorn as it is, or ask for God's power to fill us. If we choose to ask him to fill us, watch what happens!

Turn on the power button and as you keep talking, the popcorn will begin to pop and spill over. This demonstrates that what was once so easily held inside can no longer be contained. Leave the corn to continue popping to show that we can go on being filled.

How to link to talk

- All Christians have the Holy Spirit *in* them, but not all Christians are *filled* with the Holy Spirit

---

- In the New Testament, Paul writes to the Ephesians saying, 'Be filled with the Holy Spirit' (Ephesians 5:18). The translation of this means 'go on being filled', so being filled with the Spirit shouldn't just be a one-off experience. Paul wanted everyone to be constantly filled and refilled

- In book of Acts, we see that things happen when people are filled with the Spirit

- Here is what happened to Cornelius and his family when they were filled:

  - **power**: they experienced something physical; a sort of power went through them. Sometimes we can see something happening when people are filled with the Spirit (Acts 10:44–45), although this isn't always the case. If we do not feel anything physically, it doesn't mean we haven't been filled

  - **praise**: they found exciting new ways of praising God (Acts 10:46). Their encounter with the Spirit made them fall more in love with God

  - **prayer**: in a new language, sometimes called the gift of tongues. This is another way of praying to God, but in a language that we don't normally understand. This can help us to communicate directly to God – it allows our spirit to speak directly to his (Acts 10:46). Not every Christian prays in tongues, though, and it isn't the only mark of having been filled with the Spirit. It can be a great gift, especially when we don't know how or what to pray (1 Corinthians 14). *[You may wish to explain more about the gift of tongues]*

- Ultimately, what the Spirit does is lead us deeper into relationship with Jesus. He helps us fall in love with Jesus and all of us need to experience love

- Love nearly always involves emotion, and it's okay to express our feelings about God

ROBBIE WILLIAMS

PREPARATION TIME **5** minutes

Quick summary
In this clip, we see Robbie Williams break down in tears at the end of his song 'Feel'. We all need to feel love, and that is what happens when we are filled with the Spirit: we feel loved.

Equipment / resources needed
A copy of Robbie Williams: What we did last summer – live at Knebworth, *The In Good Company Co Ltd, 2003. Certificate N/A.*

▶ *Chapter 17: 1:31:26*   ☐ *Chapter 17: 1:34:47*

Projector and screen (or a TV), and a DVD player.

How to link to talk
- It's interesting that it was just as he sang 'I just wanna feel real love' that Robbie Williams broke down. There's truth in that – all of us need to feel love. *Love* is what we need most; all of us need to feel love. And *that's* the experience of the Spirit. Being filled is about having a relationship with Jesus, it is not an 'end' in itself

ARGUING COUPLE

PREPARATION TIME **0** minutes

Quick summary
This story helps to explain the importance of focussing on the Spirit's role in our relationship with Jesus, rather than on the physical manifestations of being filled. The old lady in this story doesn't just need to be kissed, she needs to feel loved.

Equipment / resources needed
None.

How it works
Let me tell you a story about an unusual married couple. Although they had been married for fifty years, they had argued throughout their married life. From the very start of their marriage they argued day in, day out, for every week of every month of every year! When their fiftieth wedding anniversary arrived, the whole family got together to choose an appropriate golden wedding present. Finally, they decided that the best gift they could give was an all expenses paid visit to a top psychiatrist.

The couple argued about whether or not they should accept this gift, they argued on the way to their appointment, and as they walked into the psychiatrist's office they were still arguing. The psychiatrist asked them a question, and immediately they started arguing. The psychiatrist, thought he had better do something, and quick. 'Stop!' he said. 'Look, I'm going to do something I have never done before in my entire professional career.' He got up from his desk, walked over to the couple, took the little old lady in his arms and kissed her, on the lips, for a very long time! Then he said

to the man, 'That is what this woman needs – three times a week.' The old man scratched his head and said, 'Okay, doctor, if that's what you recommend. I'll bring her in Mondays, Wednesdays and Fridays.'

How to link to talk
- *Love* is what we need most; all of us need to feel love. And *that's* the experience of the Spirit. Being filled is about having a relationship with Jesus, it is not an 'end' in itself

FALLING IN LOVE

PREPARATION TIME **0**

minutes

Quick summary
This analogy explains the importance of focussing on the Spirit's role in our relationship with Jesus, rather than on the physical manifestations of being filled. When we fall in love, it isn't the feelings we experience that matter, it's the person we love that counts.

Equipment / resources needed
None.

How it works
Have you ever fallen in love? All of us behave differently when it happens. When some people fall in love, they say they feel no emotion. When other people fall in love, they get tingles up and down their spine, and their heart starts thumping! Now, these physical feelings (what we sometimes call 'manifestations') are not what matters; it's the falling in love that counts. It would be crazy to focus on the physical effects of falling in love rather than on the actual person we've fallen in love with, wouldn't it? In the same way, when we are filled with the Spirit, we should focus on Jesus and not just on any physical manifestations we may experience.

How to link to talk
- *Love* is what we need most; all of us need to feel love. And *that's* the experience of the Spirit. Being filled is about having a relationship with Jesus, it is not an 'end' in itself

POINT 2 – CAN ANYTHING STOP US FROM BEING FILLED?

- God wants to fill all his children with his Holy Spirit, but sometimes we put up barriers that make it difficult for this to happen

THE MATRIX

PREPARATION TIME 5 minutes

Quick summary
In this clip we see the 'blue pill/red pill' scene, in which Neo gets to choose which pill to take. And so it is with the Holy Spirit – if we want him to, God will fill us with his Spirit.

Equipment / resources needed
A copy of the film The Matrix, *Village Roadshow Films (BVI) Limited, 1999. Certificate 15.*

▷ *Chapter 8: 0:24:07* ☐ *Chapter 8: 0:28:38*

Projector and screen (or a TV), and a DVD player.

How to link to talk
- In that scene Neo got to choose whether to take the red pill or the blue pill

- In a similar way, God won't force himself on us – it is our decision to let him in

- You've heard about the Holy Spirit – now is the time to decide whether you want to ask him to fill you or not

SPONGE ILLUSTRATION

PREPARATION TIME 5 minutes

Quick summary
A hard, dry cloth is transformed when water is sprinkled on it. Similarly, our hearts can be hard until we believe that we can receive God's spirit.

Equipment / resources needed
One sponge cloth – cut into a heart shape if possible. Make sure it is as dry as it can be.
One bowl of water.

How it works
Hold up the sponge.

- We can be like this sponge – it is designed to be filled with water, but is hard and resistant. Our hearts can become hard and resist God

- When we believe that God wants us to have such a good gift (his Spirit), it is like water softening this sponge

Sprinkle water on the sponge until it becomes soft.

- When our hearts are soft, we are ready to be filled with the Holy Spirit

Place the sponge in the bowl of water until it is so full, water pours out of it when you lift it up.

How to link to talk
- That is how we are meant to live as Christians – overflowing with God's love; so much so that we 'drip' it everywhere we go!

PRESENTS FOR CHILDREN

PREPARATION TIME **0** minutes

Quick summary
This analogy will help the group to understand that God only wants to give us, his children, good gifts. If a human father wouldn't give his child a bad gift, God certainly wouldn't do that.

Equipment / resources needed
None.

How it works
One day, Jesus said to his disciples, 'Look, some of you are fathers. Suppose your child comes to you at lunchtime and says, "I'd love some fish and chips for lunch, Dad," and you say, "Great, there's a good fish and chip shop down the road, I'll go and get you some," but, instead of going to the fish and chip shop, you go to the pet shop and you get a snake. Would you then give the snake to your child instead of the fish and chips they asked for?'

Jesus' actual words were these: 'Which of you fathers, if your children ask for a fish *[he forgot to mention the chips!]*, will give him a snake instead? Or if he asked for an egg, will give him a scorpion? If you then, though you are evil *[he basically says, 'You're an evil bunch']*, know how to give good gifts to your children, how much more will your Father in heaven give the Holy Spirit to those who ask him!' (Luke 11:11–13).

How to link to talk
- Sometimes it's fear, that puts a barrier up between us and God; but he isn't going to give you something terrible – he's going to give you the Holy Spirit!

So what can hold us back from being filled?

- Sometimes it's doubt – we doubt that God will give us his Spirit if we ask – but the Bible says 'everyone who asks shall receive' – and everyone means *everyone*, including you and me (Luke 11:9–10)

- Sometimes we get scared that it might not be a good thing – but God is our father and wants to give us good gifts (Luke 11:11–13)

- Sometimes we doubt that we're worthy of the gift – we might think, 'God knows what I'm really like, I'm not holy enough.' But Jesus doesn't say, 'How much more will your Father in heaven give the Holy Spirit to really holy people who've been Christians for a very long time and deserve it.' He says: 'How much more will your Father in heaven give the Holy Spirit to those who ask him!' (Luke 11:13). All we have to do is ask him

CONCLUSION

- It is not good enough to just talk about being filled with God's Holy Spirit, we need to give God the chance to fill us

- Let's ask him now

PRAYER – ASK TO BE FILLED WITH THE SPIRIT

PREPARATION TIME **0** minutes

Quick summary
Say a prayer asking God to fill the group with his Holy Spirit. Follow this prayer by ministry time.

Equipment / resources needed
None.

How it works

- Lord, today we've talked about your Holy Spirit, but we don't want to just talk about it. We want you to come and fill us with your Spirit. So we pray the prayer that the church has prayed for the past 2,000 years. We say, 'Come, Holy Spirit!' Would you please come and fill us. Now let's wait on him

For guidance on leading this time of prayer ministry, please refer to the article called 'How to pray for each other on Youth Alpha', which can be found on page 343, or see the team training session on page 388.

There are no small group questions for this talk, as we usually go into ministry time after this session.

WEEKEND SESSION 3

HOW CAN I MAKE THE MOST OF THE REST OF MY LIFE?

WEEKEND SESSION 3
HOW CAN I MAKE THE MOST OF THE REST OF MY LIFE?

SUMMARY

AIMS OF THIS SESSION

- To encourage the group to understand that true worship is offering our lives to God

- To explain that following Jesus is counter-cultural and our lives will look different to how they did before

- To explore how to live differently

NOTES

- We suggest that you meet in small groups at the start of this session and talk about what happened in the ministry time at the end of the second Weekend/Day session. (NB: there are no suggested small group questions for this session)

- At the end of this talk you should have another time of prayer ministry, and ask God to fill everyone with his Holy Spirit

- Again, remind your team to sit with their groups during this session so they are near enough to pray easily

- Encourage them to offer to pray for each person rather than waiting to be asked

SESSION OVERVIEW

- Small groups
- Welcome
- Ice breaker game
- Worship
- Talk
    - Introduction
    - Point 1 – What should we do?
    - Point 2 – How do we do it?
    - Point 3 – Why should we offer our lives to God?
    - Conclusion
- Prayer ministry time

WELCOME

- Welcome to the final session of the Youth Alpha Weekend/Day!

- Before we get going, let's start with an ice breaker game

ICE BREAKER GAME

Choose one of the following 3 options:

OPTION 1

EX-STRAW-DINARY

PREPARATION TIME **0** minutes

Quick summary
Can each member of the group turn a straw around using only their tongue?

Equipment / resources needed
One straw per person.

How it works
Each person should put one end of a straw in their mouth. Using only their lips and tongue, they must turn it around totally, so they end up with the opposite end of the straw in their mouth. The first person to achieve this wins. We suggest you spend no longer than five minutes on this game.

OPTION 2

LAUGHTER EIGHTS

PREPARATION TIME **0** minutes

Quick summary
Can each member of the group manoeuvre a chocolate mint from their forehead into their mouth?

Equipment / resources needed
One 'After Eight' (chocolate mint) per person.

How it works
Give each person an After Eight (chocolate mint) and tell them to place it on their forehead. Using only gravity and their facial muscles, they must get the After Eight into their mouth. By the time they have finished, a chocolate trail should remain on their face – a result of the After Eight melting en route. This can be done as a competition between individuals or as a team relay. We suggest you spend no longer than five minutes on this game.

MALTESER RELAY

PREPARATION TIME **0** minutes

Quick summary
Teams must relay while transporting Maltesers using straws.

Equipment / resources needed
One bag of Maltesers (very light chocolate-covered malt sweets).
One straw per person.

How it works
Divide the group into teams and give each person a straw. On your word, one by one, each member of the team must take a Malteser to the other end of the room using only a straw – no hands allowed! The idea is that by sucking the straw, they should be able to carry the Malteser using suction pressure.

> #### Suggested tip
> *Vary this game by telling the group that to transport their Malteser, they must tilt their head back, blow out of the straw and balance the Malteser using the stream of their breath.*

INTRODUCTION

- I hope you're enjoying the weekend/course so far

- Yesterday/earlier we looked at the Holy Spirit and had a chance to pray for each other

- Today/now we're going to look at what happens next – what we do with the rest of our lives (a small topic, I know)?

Choose one of the following 4 options:

GROUNDHOG DAY

PREPARATION TIME **5** minutes

Quick summary
In this clip, we see Bill Murray replaying the same day over and over again. This is an example of someone getting a second chance at life.

Equipment / resources needed
A copy of the film Groundhog Day, Columbia Pictures, 1993. Certificate PG.

▷ *Chapter 18: 0:55:10* ☐ *Chapter 18: 0:58:01*

Projector and screen (or a TV), and a DVD player.

How to link to talk

- Contrary to that clip, we only get one shot at life, no matter who we are. As the saying goes, 'Life is not a dress rehearsal'

- So how do we make the most of it?

8 MILE MOVIE TRAILER

PREPARATION TIME **5** minutes

Quick summary

This clip shows the movie trailer for the film 8 Mile. The lyrics to the Eminem song 'Lose Yourself' go like this: 'If you had one shot, one opportunity to seize everything you ever wanted, would you capture it or just let it slip ... you only get one shot ... do not miss your chance ...'

Equipment / resources needed

To find the link for this clip, please visit youthalpha.org/lgmedia
You may want to use a projector and a screen in order to show the trailer to the whole group.

How to link to talk

- Like Eminem says in that song, we only get one shot at life

- As the saying goes, 'Life is not a dress rehearsal'

- So how do we make the most of it?

THE FACTORY VIRAL

PREPARATION TIME **5** minutes

Quick summary

In this film, we see two people being born, growing up, and dying on a 'conveyor belt' of life, demonstrating that life is meaningless without God. This viral was used in UK cinemas to promote the Alpha Course in 2007.

Equipment / resources needed

The link for this video can be found online at youthalpha.org/lgmedia
You may want to use a projector and a screen in order to show the film to the whole group.

How to link to talk

- Is there more to life than just living each day and eventually dying? Is life about existing or is it about living? How do we make the most of life?

^{OPTION 4}

THE IMPOSSIBLE NUMBER GAME

PREPARATION TIME **0** minutes

Quick summary
This game is about repetition – is this what life should be like?

Equipment / resources needed
None.

How it works
Tell everyone in the room to close their eyes. Explain that the aim of the game is to count from one to a hundred, but people can only call out one number at a time, and must do so randomly (ie: there is no system for who goes when). As soon as two people say the same number at the same time, the game must tediously start again. Stop when you have had enough.

How to link to talk
- What is the point of life? Sometimes it can seem very repetitive

- Contrary to that game, we only get one shot at life, no matter who we are. As the saying goes, 'Life is not a dress rehearsal'

- So how do we make the most of it?

POINT 1 – WHAT SHOULD WE DO?

- The amazing yet strange thing about the kingdom of God is that it seems upside-down in comparison to the world. Some would say it makes no sense! Following Jesus involves living counter-culturally – living differently to the culture around us

Read Romans 12:1–2 (or to end of chapter):

- 'Therefore, I urge you, brothers, in view of God's mercy, to offer your bodies as living sacrifices, holy and pleasing to God – this is your spiritual act of worship. Do not conform any longer to the pattern of this world, but be transformed by the renewing of your mind. Then you will be able to test and approve what God's will is – his good, pleasing and perfect will' (Romans 12:1–2)

- The way to make the most of our lives is to offer them to God

- Make a break with the past and your 'old' life

- It is tough living for God in today's world, especially at school. It can be easy to let pressure from the world squeeze and force us to 'fit the mould' of everyone else

- First of all, Romans 12:2 says, 'Don't conform.' Let's look at that

OPTION 1

THE ASCH EXPERIMENT

PREPARATION TIME **0** minutes

Quick summary

This true story of an experiment done by Solomon Asch shows how easily people will conform to certain standards, even if they are wrong, in a bid to go unnoticed. Christians must not blend in – they must live differently.

Equipment / resources needed
None.

How it works

In the 1950s, a very famous experiment was done by a guy called Solomon Asch. It was designed to test how easily people would go along with the rest of a group. Asch put people into groups of five (four actors and one non-actor), showed them four lines on a page and asked them which two lines were same length. The actors all gave the same answer, which was obviously wrong. Seventy-five per cent of the non-actors went with the group and gave the wrong answer, even though it was blatantly incorrect!

How to link to talk

- Often, it is much easier to blend in and go along with what everyone else is doing, even when it is obviously wrong

- But the verse we just read tells us that, as Christians, we shouldn't aim to blend in – we should live differently

OPTION 2

ASCH EXPERIMENT CLIP

PREPARATION TIME **5** minutes

Quick summary

This clip shows the experiment done by Solomon Asch, demonstrating how easily people will conform to certain standards, even if they are wrong, in a bid to go unnoticed. Christians must not blend in – they must live differently.

Equipment / resources needed
To find the link for this clip, please visit youthalpha.org/lgmedia
You may want to use a projector and a screen in order to show the clip to the whole group.

How to link to talk

- Often, it is much easier to blend in and go along with what everyone else is doing, even when it is obviously wrong

- But the verse we just read tells us that, as Christians, we shouldn't aim to blend in – we should live differently

POLICEMAN

PREPARATION TIME **0**
minutes

Quick summary
This story shows how much easier we find it to blend in, even when doing the right thing is at stake. Christians must not blend in – they must live differently.

Equipment / resources needed
None.

How it works
I heard about a young police officer who was taking his final exam at Hendon Police College in North London. The first three questions in the exam were relatively easy, but question four went like this:

'You're on patrol in outer London when an explosion occurs in a gas main in a nearby street. On investigation, you find that a large hole has been blown in the footpath and that there is an overturned van lying nearby. Inside the van there's a strong smell of alcohol. Both occupants, a man and a woman, are injured. You recognise the woman as the wife of your Divisional Inspector, who is currently away in the United States. A passing motorist stops to offer you assistance, but you realise that he is a man who's wanted for armed robbery. Suddenly another man runs out of a nearby house shouting that his wife is expecting a baby and the shock of the explosion has made the birth imminent. Another man is crying for help, having been blown into an adjacent canal by the explosion, and he cannot swim. Bearing in mind the provisions of the Mental Health Act, describe in a few words what action you would take.'

The police officer thought for a moment, picked up his pen and wrote: 'I would take off my uniform and mingle with the crowd.'

How to link to talk
- Often, it is much easier to blend in and go along with what everyone else is doing, even when it is obviously wrong

- But the verse we just read tells us that, as Christians, we shouldn't aim to blend in – we should live differently

WILL IT BLEND?

PREPARATION TIME **5**
minutes

Quick summary
This clip is part of a YouTube series called 'Will it Blend?' In this episode, Tom Dickson blends an iPhone. Christians must not blend in – they must live differently.

Equipment / resources needed
To find the link for this clip, please visit youthalpha.org/lgmedia
You may want to use a projector and a screen in order to show the film to the whole group.

How to link to talk
- Okay, so there wasn't much point in showing you that, other than it was about blending!

- The point I wanted to make is that it can often be much easier to 'blend in' with everyone else, to conform to what they are doing and saying

- But the verse we just read tells us that, as Christians, we shouldn't aim to blend in – we should live differently

POINT 2 – HOW DO WE DO IT?

- So how do we live differently to the world around us? How do we offer our lives to God?

- The second part of Romans 12:2 says, 'Be transformed.' The secret is to let God transform us from the inside out

- We can pray to God and offer all areas of our life to him. Let me run through the different areas that we should offer

You may like to include this optional extra, but it is not essential

OPTIONAL EXTRA – GOING DEEPER   PREPARATION TIME 30
                                                        minutes

HUMAN BODY

Quick summary
As you make each of the following points, mark down which body part you are referring to on a life-size human cut-out.

Equipment / resources needed
One large sheet of paper.
Scissors.
Sticky notes.

How it works
Before the session starts, make a life-size cut-out of a human body. Have some sticky notes ready to stick on the appropriate body part as you speak.

How to link to talk
As follows.

1. **Our time**. Time is our most valuable possession. How do we use our time? How would God want us to use it? You could pray, 'God, please help me give all of my time to you', and see how your priorities change. There are two things I would encourage you to do to start: first, try to spend time with God each day by praying and reading the Bible, and secondly, spend time with other Christians each week in a church or youth group.

2. **Our ambitions/dreams**. Are our personal goals the same as God's goals for us? Jesus said, 'Seek first the kingdom of God, and all these [other] things will be given to you too' (Matthew 6:33). What are your ambitions? Do they fit in with the kingdom of God?

3. **Our money/wallets**. How do we use what we have? Selfishly, or by giving? Jesus says, 'Do not store up for yourselves treasures on earth, where moth and rust destroy, and where thieves break in and steal. But store up for yourselves treasures in heaven, where moth and rust do not destroy, and where thieves do not break in and steal. For where your treasure is, there your heart will be also' (Matthew 6:19–21). Where are we storing up our treasure? In piles of cash or in the kingdom of God?

4. **Our ears**. Do we choose to listen to gossip, or do we believe the best about others?

5. **Our eyes**. What do we chose to look at and watch – particularly on TV or in magazines?

6. **Our mouth/tongue**. The tongue is very powerful. What do we say?

7. **Our hands**. Do we use our hands to give and to serve others, or to take?

8. **Our sexuality**. God has made us sexual beings, and he knows the best way for us to enjoy it. Let's chat a bit about God's view of sex, as it's a relevant issue for a lot of young people.

Choose one of the following 3 options:

OPTION 1

VANILLA SKY

PREPARATION TIME **5** minutes

Quick summary
In this clip, Julie crashes the car as she tells David what the consequences of their relationship are – 'your body made a promise to me'. This shows the power that sex has over people.

Equipment / resources needed
A copy of Vanilla Sky, *Paramount Pictures, 2002. Certificate 15.*

▷ *Chapter 9: 0:40:39*　　☐ *Chapter 9: 0:41:47*

NB: there is use of profanity shortly before this scene begins

Projector and screen (or a TV), and a DVD player.

How to link to talk

- Sex is an amazing and powerful thing. It is not just a physical act, it is also a spiritual act. There is much more to it than just the union of two bodies

- God's plan is not to stop us having sex – not at all. God is love, he designed sex! But he wants us to enjoy sex, not be hurt by it. That's why he created marriage as the context for sex. Sex is for a man and a woman who have committed to each other for life

- That clip shows how painful it can be when people who have had sex break up. Sex can hurt us if used in the wrong context. The amazing thing is that God forgives, and it is possible for him to make us clean and whole again if we have been hurt in this way

CARDBOARD PEOPLE

PREPARATION TIME **1–2** hours

Quick summary
Show that two people who are glued together can't be pulled apart without lasting damage being done to both of them. Sex should only be used in the context of marriage.

Equipment / resources needed
Two sheets of cardboard or paper, each a different colour (pink and blue, ideally).
Scissors.
Glue.

How it works
The night before this session, cut a simple outline of a man (blue) and a woman (pink) out of coloured paper. Glue them together and leave them to dry. Put heavy books on top of them to ensure they are firmly stuck. At the right moment, hold up the paper people and explain that they represent a couple who have had sex. Tell the group that the Bible says once a couple have had sex, they become spiritually attached (1 Corinthians 6:16). As you speak, try to pull the two people apart – you should find that they do separate, but each is left with bits of the other coloured paper still attached.

How to link to talk

- Sex is an amazing and powerful thing. It is not just a physical act, it is also a spiritual act. There is much more to it than just the union of two bodies

- God's plan is not to stop us having sex – not at all. God is love, he designed sex! But he wants us to enjoy sex, not be hurt by it. That's why he created marriage as the context for sex. Sex is for a man and a woman who have committed to each other for life

(Show your cardboard figures and explain that they have had sex!)

- Sex is like glue – it joins us together with the other person

- When we try to separate these two *[pull them apart at this point]*, we see that it is hard to do. We can't make a clean break – each of them leaves pieces of themselves on the other. Sex is much more than just the union of two bodies

- It can be really painful when people who have had sex break up. Sex can hurt us if used in the wrong context. The amazing thing is that God forgives, and it is possible for him to make us clean and whole again if we have been hurt in this way

- Christians are not anti-sex at all! We believe that God invented sex, but designed it to be part of a committed, loving relationship

OPTION 3

GOD INVENTED SEX

PREPARATION TIME **0** minutes

Quick summary
This analogy explains that God created sex, but it should only be used in the context of marriage.

Equipment / resources needed
None.

How it works
Sex was God's idea! When he made us, he could have decided that babies should be made by shaking hands, by kissing or by giving someone a 'high-five'! But God designed sex to be pleasurable for both the guy and the girl. God isn't sitting 'up there' in heaven thinking, 'Oh my goodness, what the heck are those two doing? I never knew you could do that', of course not. Sex was God's idea – his invention – as a gift to us. But, with this gift comes rules on how best to use it so it won't hurt us. God is our creator, and he gives us an instruction manual – the Bible – to help us live our lives.

How to link to talk
- Jesus said that God's intended context for sex is in marriage – he said: 'For this reason a man will leave his father and mother and be united to his wife, and the two will become one flesh' (Matthew 19:5)

- Sex is a very powerful thing – it is not just a physical act, it is also a spiritual act. There is much more to it than just the union of two bodies

- It can be really painful when people who have had sex break up. Sex can hurt us if used in the wrong context. The amazing thing is that God forgives, and it is possible for him to make us clean and whole again if we have been hurt in this way

- All of those areas are things that we should offer to God. If we do this, we will maximise life, not lose it

- Of course, this is not the easiest way to live and it may well involve sacrifice but Jesus promises to be with us and give us life (John 10:10)

POINT 3 – WHY SHOULD WE OFFER OUR LIVES TO GOD?

- Why should we offer our lives to God? Because God has a great plan for our future and this is the way to follow it (Romans 12:2), and because of all that God has done for us – we owe it to him ('in view of God's mercy', Romans 12:1). The sacrifices we may have to make are small in comparison to the sacrifices he has made for us

Choose one of the following 2 options:

'WHOEVER BUYS MY SON GETS EVERYTHING'

PREPARATION TIME **0** minutes

Quick summary
This analogy shows us that God will give us everything if we only live for him.

Equipment / resources needed
None.

How it works
I once heard about a wealthy English baron called Fitzgerald. This man had one son. His son left home and, while he was away from home, died. Fitzgerald never got over this loss, but as his wealth increased, he invested in very valuable paintings by the 'old masters'.
When he died, his will called for all the paintings to be sold. He had such a great collection, collectors and museum representatives came from all over the world to attend the auction. Before it began, the lawyer read from Fitzgerald's will, and it said this: 'The first painting to be sold in this auction is a portrait of my beloved son.' The portrait was by an unknown painter, it was poor quality. Only one person even bothered to bid for it – somebody who'd worked for the family and who'd known and loved the boy. He bought it for sentimental value and for the memories it held. Then the lawyer said, 'I must now read the second clause of the will. It says this: "Whoever buys *My Son* gets everything." The auction is over.' The man who bought the painting of the son was given everything.

How to link to talk
- Jesus said, 'Seek first the kingdom of God … and all these things will be given to you' (Matthew 6:33)

- The simple truth is that if we live for Jesus, then we will not miss out on life – in fact, our lives will be as full as they could possibly be

OPTION 2

'WHOEVER BUYS MY SON GETS EVERYTHING' ANIMATION

PREPARATION TIME 5 minutes

Quick summary
This animated version of the story from the previous option shows us that God will give us everything if we live for him.

Equipment / resources needed
This video can be found online at youthalpha.org/lgmedia
You may want to use a projector and a screen in order to show the animation to the whole group.

How to link to talk
- Jesus said, 'Seek first the kingdom of God … and all these things will be given to you' (Matthew 6:33)

- The simple truth is that if we live for Jesus, then we will not miss out on life – in fact, our lives will be as full as they could possibly be

CONCLUSION

- So, in summary, how do we make the most of the rest of our lives?

  - the Bible says, 'Don't conform, but be transformed'

  - we must offer our lives to Jesus and live life with him. Yes, the way we live may well look a little different to the rest of the world, but it will be worth it

- Let's pray

QUICK PRAYER TO CLOSE

PREPARATION TIME 0 minutes

Quick summary
Pray to end your talk.

Equipment/resources needed
None.

How it works
- I am just going to say a short prayer to close

- Lord, thank you for this time together. I pray that you would show us more of what it means to not conform to the patterns of the world around us. Please come and transform us by your Holy Spirit. In Jesus' name, Amen

We would strongly encourage you to have another time of prayer ministry at this point instead of small group discussion. Simply invite the Holy Spirit to come, and wait on him like you did in the previous session. Make sure your team are ready to pray for people.

SESSION 7

HOW CAN I RESIST EVIL?

SESSION 7
HOW CAN I RESIST EVIL?

SUMMARY

AIMS OF THIS SESSION

- To encourage the group to know that we have God on our side, and he has defeated the devil

- To explain the reality of evil in our world

- To explore how we can resist evil

NOTES

- If you have had your Weekend/Day, ask people to feed back from it

- Let group leaders know that this session can sometimes raise some tricky pastoral questions and subjects, such as the occult. These are issues they should be aware of before the small groups begin. You might like to pray in to this before the session

SESSION OVERVIEW

- Food
- Welcome
- Ice breaker game
- Worship *(if applicable)*
- Talk
  - Introduction
  - Point 1 – Why should we believe in the devil?
  - Point 2 – What's the devil got to do with me?
  - Point 3 – Should I be worried?
  - Point 4 – How do we defend ourselves?
  - Point 5 – How do we attack?
  - Conclusion
- Small groups

WELCOME

- Welcome back to Youth Alpha!

- It's great to have you here with us

- Before we get going, let's start with an ice breaker game

ICE BREAKER GAME

Choose one of the following 3 options:

OPTION 1

STICKY NOSE RELAY

PREPARATION TIME **5** minutes

Quick summary
A relay that requires 'sticky noses' for transporting cotton balls.

Equipment / resources needed
Lots of cotton wool balls.
Tub of Vaseline.
Two shallow baskets.

How it works
This is a simple relay race in which team members must crawl on their hands and knees to a basket at the other end of the room. From this basket, they must retrieve a cotton wool ball. The catch is that the cotton wool ball must be picked up using only players' noses, which will be sticky after being coated with Vaseline.
Arrange the players into two (or more) teams behind a starting line. Place the basket filled with cotton wool balls at the other end of the room. Once players' noses have been coated in Vaseline, say, 'Go!' to start the relay. Contestants must crawl down the room and plunge their noses into the basket until a cotton wool ball sticks. With the cotton wool balls on their noses, they must crawl back down the course to their team.
When they return to their team, they are not allowed to use their hands to remove the cotton wool ball. They can only do this by shaking their heads vigorously. Only when the cotton wool ball is dislodged can the next team member start their turn. The team with the most cotton wool balls at the end of the game wins.
We suggest you spend no longer than three minutes on this game.

GOOD OR EVIL?

PREPARATION TIME **0** minutes

Quick summary
A game in which the group decides what, from the list below, is good and evil.

Equipment / resources needed
None.

How it works
Explain to the group that you are going to read out a list, and it is up to them to decide whether they think the things on the list are good, evil, or inbetween. Designate one side of the room as 'good' and the other as 'evil' – and let them know that it is okay to stand somewhere inbetween. They each have to move around and stand wherever they think that item best fits on the good/evil scale.

- Starbucks coffee
- Reading horoscopes
- Plastic surgery
- Pornography
- Gossip
- Ouija boards
- Child slavery
- Palm reading
- Agony aunts (in magazines)
- Global warming

Once you have finished 'voting', discuss these questions:

- How can we judge when something is evil?

- Isn't it interesting that we have such different opinions of what is evil?

FIRE DRILL

PREPARATION TIME **0** minutes

Quick summary
Present this question to your small groups and allow it to initiate discussion.

Equipment / resources needed
None.

How it works
Ask the group to imagine that their home is on fire. Make clear that the right thing to do in this situation is to run for your life, but explain that in this case, they have a few minutes of safety to grab a few precious items from the flames. Assuming that all people and animals are already safe, what would they take with them? Ask each person to make a list

of the three items that they would save. When they have finished, they should read their list to the rest of the group. Ask some of the following questions to get a discussion going:

- What is the most expensive thing that has been saved by the group?

- Has anyone saved anything that belongs to someone else?

- If you had to let one item on your list burn, which item would it be?

- If you could only save one of the items on your list which one would you save?

- Is there anything on your list that has only sentimental value?

INTRODUCTION

- Welcome to week seven of Youth Alpha

- Last time we looked at the question, 'How does God guide us?' and we talked about five different ways that God leads us. Can anyone remember what they were? *[Prize for anyone who can!]*

- This week we'll be looking at the subject of evil. That may seem like a strange thing to do on a course like this, but I'll explain why

- In Romans 12:21, the Bible says, 'Do not be overcome by evil, but overcome evil with good'

- Have you ever noticed that if you add one letter to the word 'God' you get 'good'? If you add one letter to the word 'evil' you get 'devil'. The claim of the New Testament is that, just as behind goodness lies God himself, behind the evil in the world lies the devil

POINT 1 – WHY SHOULD WE BELIEVE IN THE DEVIL?

Choose one of the following 3 options:

OPTION 1

THE SIMPSONS

PREPARATION TIME **5** minutes

Quick summary
In this clip, Homer Simpson sells his soul to the devil for a doughnut. This demonstrates how often popular culture portrays the devil in a caricatured and unbelievable way.

Equipment / resources needed

A copy of The Simpsons: *'Treehouse of Horror IV' (season 5, episode 5), Twentieth Century Fox Home Entertainment LLC, 2005, Certificate 12.*

▷ *Chapter 2: 0:02:36* ☐ *Chapter 2: 0:04:46*

Projector and screen (or a TV), and a DVD player.

How to link to talk

- The way the devil is portrayed on TV and in movies is usually over exaggerated and silly – a complete caricature

- Just because he's regularly portrayed in this way, doesn't mean he isn't real

CARICATURES

PREPARATION TIME **30** minutes

Quick summary

Show caricatures of famous people, followed by a caricature of the devil.

Equipment / resources needed

Caricatures/cartoons.
You may want to use a projector and a screen in order to show this to the whole group.

How it works

Find some caricatures/cartoons of well-known people and one of the devil. Ask the group to identify the people shown – maybe have prizes for each correct answer. Try to find pictures that are very exaggerated, but not too offensive.
Finish with the caricature of the devil.

How to link to talk

- Sometimes it's easy to get the wrong impression of someone based on how they are portrayed in cartoons or in the media

- This last picture is also a kind of a caricature: the devil doesn't really look like this, but that doesn't mean that he is not real

- Many people have a picture of the devil that is based on a caricature – they think that he walks around with a big fork saying, 'Boo!' to people

NEWSPAPER STORIES

PREPARATION TIME **5** minutes

Quick summary

Group activity to find real-life stories of suffering; this should prompt a discussion of the reasons for this kind of adversity.

Equipment / resources needed
Newspapers.
Scissors.
Glue.

How it works
Hand out newspapers to the group. Have them cut out photos from the negative stories that they find. Stick these photos onto a sheet of paper. Choose a few of the photos that appear interesting and ask these questions:

- Who is it that is suffering in this story?

- Who is to blame?
    - the people who are suffering
    - people that are causing the suffering
    - God
    - devil
    - other

- What is the cause of this situation?
    - the evil (sin) done by humanity in general
    - the evil (sin) done by those involved in this particular situation
    - evil generally

How to link to talk
- These are just a few examples of things that show the reality of evil in our world

---

- Some people find it easy to believe in the devil, perhaps because of the evil they have experienced or seen

- Others find it almost impossible, perhaps because they are thinking of a red devil with horns, a pointed tail and a big fork, or because they are thinking of the devil as portrayed in comedies

- Why should we believe in the devil's existence? There are good reasons to believe:

    - because it is clear from the horror and evil in our world that he is at work

    - because Christians have believed in his existence down the ages

    - because the Bible speaks of him in the Old Testament
      (Job 1; 1 Chronicles 21:1; Isaiah 14) and in the New Testament
      (Ephesians 6:11–12; Luke 10:17–20)

- But – taking too much of an interest in the devil is just as dangerous as doubting that he even exists (Deuteronomy 18:10)

You may choose to use one or both of these quotes to help illustrate your point:

OPTIONAL QUOTES

William Peter Blatty (writer and producer of *The Exorcist*)

'As far as God goes, I'm a non-believer. But when it comes to the devil – well, that's something else. The devil keeps advertising; the devil does lots of commercials.'

(Alan Macdonald, Films in Close Up*, Frameworks, 1991.)*

C. S. Lewis (author of the 'Narnia' books)

'There are two equal and opposite errors into which we can fall about the devils. One is to disbelieve in their existence; the other is to believe and to feel an excessive and unhealthy interest in them. They themselves are equally pleased by both errors.'

(C. S. Lewis, The Screwtape Letters, *Macmillan, 1951.)*

POINT 2 – WHAT'S THE DEVIL GOT TO DO WITH ME?

- What does the Bible say? 'Put on the full armour of God so that you can take your stand against the devil's schemes. For our struggle is not against flesh and blood, but against the rulers, against the authorities, against the powers of this dark world and against the spiritual forces of evil in the heavenly realms' (Ephesians 6:11–12)

- In other words, there is a kind of spiritual war going on that we can't see. We must resist the unseen forces in the world

- In John's Gospel, the Bible tells us that the devil's aim is to steal from us, kill our life, our fun and our freedom and destroy us (John 10:10). He wants to prevent us from having a proper relationship with God, and will do anything he can to stop this

- What are the devil's tactics?

    - he creates doubt in our minds

    - he causes us to take our eyes off Jesus

    - he tempts us to sin

You may like to include this option extra, but it is not essential.

OPTIONAL EXTRA – GOING DEEPER

PREPARATION TIME 5
minutes

GENESIS 3:1b–7

Quick summary
Read Genesis 3:1b–7 aloud to your group.

Equipment / resources needed
If you want the group to follow the text on screen, you may need a projector and a computer.

How it works
- We can see some of this in Genesis, chapter 3: the story of Adam and Eve being tempted by the snake and eating the apple

Genesis 3:1b–7

'He said to the woman, "Did God *really* say, 'You must not eat from any tree in the garden'?"

The woman said to the serpent, "We may eat from the trees in the garden, but God did say, 'You must not eat fruit from the tree that is in the middle of the garden, and you must not touch it, or you will die.'"

"You will not surely die," the serpent said to the woman.

"For God knows that when you eat of it your eyes will be opened, and you'll be like God, knowing good and evil. When the woman saw the fruit of the tree was good for food and pleasing to the eye, and also desirable for gaining wisdom, she took some of it and ate it.

She also gave some to her husband, who was with her, and he ate it.

Then the eyes of both of them were opened, and they realised they were naked; so they sewed fig leaves together and made coverings for themselves.'

How to link to talk
- Check out the devil's tactics in this passage. He:

    - creates doubt: he tries to feed doubts into our minds – 'did God really say that?'

    - creates distractions: the devil tries to turn our eyes away from God, he focuses on the negative and tells us that following Jesus will be boring and no fun at all. He made Eve forget that God said they could eat *anything else* and focused on the forbidden fruit – 'you will be like God'

    - creates lies: he tells them that if they eat the forbidden fruit they will be like God, and that there will be no consequences to sin – 'you will not surely die'

POINT 3 – SHOULD I BE WORRIED?

- No! Jesus is all powerful and he has set us free. We have all the forces of heaven on our side

Choose one of the following 3 options:

BRIDGE TO TERABITHIA

PREPARATION TIME 5 minutes

Quick summary
In this clip, Jesse and Leslie are about to be overwhelmed by wild beasts until hundreds of Terabithian warriors come to their aid. This is an example of a hero being protected by a strong force of hidden friends, making attackers turn and run.

Equipment/resources needed
A copy of the film Bridge to Terabithia, *Walden Media LLC, 2006. Certificate PG.*

▷ *Chapter 10: 0:59:00* ☐ *Chapter 10: 1:02:19*

Projector and screen (or a TV), and a DVD player.

How to link to talk
- It's quite natural to be freaked out by the thought that the devil is out to get you, but we have nothing to fear

- As Christians, we have transferred from the devil's team to Jesus' team. Jesus is in charge of us now, not the devil (Colossians 1:13)

- Jesus won the war and has completely defeated Satan (Colossians 2:15), but there are still battles going on, and, as soldiers in God's army we are involved in these (Luke 10:17–20)

- Like in this video clip, we have the full resources of heaven supporting us

FOOTBALL TRANSFER SKIT

PREPARATION TIME 30 minutes

Quick summary
The point we want to communicate is that, as Christians, we have been transferred from the devil's kingdom of darkness to Jesus' kingdom of light and life. We are now under Jesus' authority, not the devil's. This option uses a skit, based on the football (soccer) world's practice of transferring players from one club to another, to illustrate this.

Equipment / resources needed
None.

How it works

If you like, you can rehearse this in advance with a few members of the team, but if you pick confident volunteers it is also possible to do it ad-lib in front of the group. Keeping your guests in mind, make a decision based on what will work best and be the most amusing.

SKIT SCRIPT

Scene 1 – The newsroom

Sports anchorman: 'Good evening and welcome to Channel Five's sports report. The big news tonight is of a rumoured transfer. Rotundo, Brazil's leading striker, and scorer of the winning goal in the last world cup, could be leaving Inferno FC to play for the Saints. While we're here, why don't we look at that goal one more time and remind ourselves what all of the fuss is about?' *[Points to his left.]*

Commentator: 'And Rotundo is off, barrelling down the wing ... beats one defender with some silky skills, plays it past the second, and sprints onto the ball. Now he's in lots of space. Fakes the long cross and instead takes it into the box himself – oh this is too much, fantastic skills, amazing footwork, such confidence! And now it's only the goalkeeper to beat. Rotundo draws back his powerful right foot, shoots ... scorcher ... the goalkeeper's not even moved ... goal!'

[As the commentator is commentating, Rotundo is acting out everything he/she says.]

Sports anchorman: 'Well, I think that says it all, and I never tire of watching that clip. I think that we can safely say there are going to be some very excited Saints fans tonight as they contemplate the difference Rotundo could make to their club's chances of winning the championship.'

Scene 2 – A press conference

Reporter: 'Rotundo how does it feel to be one of the Saints now?'

Rotundo: 'Amazing. I can't tell you how glad I am to be free of Inferno. It feels like a new life to me. I can't tell you how badly our old manager, Lucius, treated us. Anyone would have thought he hated us. He always made us play with injuries, trained us too hard, punished us when we lost and dropped us when we won. It was hell.'

Second reporter: 'How does it feel to be the most expensive transfer ever?'

Rotundo: 'I'm just thrilled that the manager here at the Saints felt I was worth it.'

Scene 3 – Rotundo's mansion in the middle of the night

[A phone rings beside the bed. Rotundo picks it up.]

Rotundo: Huh?! Who's calling?

Lucius: 'Rotundo? Rotundo? This is your manager speaking, you useless lump of lard. Why haven't you been at training?'

Rotundo: 'Lucius? Is that you? It's the middle of the night ...'

Lucius: '... not here in Brazil it's not. I don't know what you're doing on the other side of the world anyway. Get back here!'

Rotundo: 'But I'm not your player anymore! You can't order me around. The Saints bought me and now I play for them. Now get off the phone!'

How to link to talk

- As Christians, we have transferred from the devil's team to Jesus' team. Jesus is in charge of us now, not the devil (Colossians 1:13)

- Jesus won the war and has completely defeated Satan (Colossians 2:15), but there are still battles going on, and, as soldiers in God's army we are involved in these (Luke 10:17–20)

- We have the full resources of heaven supporting us

D-DAY AND VE-DAY

PREPARATION TIME **0** minutes

Quick summary
Use the analogy of D-day and VE-day to show that although the devil has been defeated (D-day), his battle for our individual lives will continue until Jesus returns (VE-day).

Equipment / resources needed
None.

How it works

- There were two key days in the Second World War: 'D-day' and 'VE-day' (Victory in Europe Day). D-day (6 June 1944) was the decisive moment of World War Two; it was the day that determined its outcome. There was no real doubt about the future of the Second World War at that point, but it still wasn't over – there were lots of smaller battles raging that took nearly a year to finish, despite the fact the conclusion had already been made. VE-day (8 May 1945) was the day that all that fighting finally finished

How to link to talk

- In a sense, we live between D-day and VE-day now. Jesus' death has decided the war, but there are still battles raging over our individual lives. The devil is keen to destroy as many people as possible before that final day

- We don't need to worry, but the battle is not over yet. On the cross, the devil was defeated and demoralised. The cross and the resurrection are the decisive moments in history. But the devil is not yet destroyed. There will come a moment when he is destroyed: when Jesus returns

POINT 4 – HOW DO WE DEFEND OURSELVES?

You may like to include this optional extra, but it is not essential:

OPTIONAL EXTRA – GOING DEEPER   PREPARATION TIME 1
hour

ARMOUR OF GOD ILLUSTRATION

Quick summary
Use this illustration to show the group how Christians can defend themselves against the devil using 'God's armour'.

Equipment / resources needed
A whiteboard/flip chart to draw the outline of a person on to.
Equipment needed to make the 'armour'.
Blu-Tack to stick armour to person's outline

How it works
Draw the outline of a person on a flip chart or whiteboard. Have the elements of the armour ready to stick on the outline, ie: belt, breastplate, boots, shield, helmet, sword. In order to make the idea of 'putting on' God's armour less abstract, write the relevant name of the armour on each of the elements. For example, write 'peace' on the boots, 'righteousness' on the breastplate and so on.

How to link to talk
As you mention each of the following, stick the appropriate part of armour on the figure.

- Given that there's still a battle going on, and knowing that we're all vulnerable, how do we defend ourselves? Let's have a look at the Bible. In Ephesians 6 in the New Testament it gives us six practical tips on how to defend ourselves:

    1. Focus on Jesus – 'the belt of truth'. We can know Jesus' truth to counter the devil's lies (Ephesians 6:14)

    2. Keep your relationships right – 'the breastplate of righteousness'. Keep short accounts with God and with other people. We can support each other (Ephesians 6:14)

3. Get involved in serving God – 'the boots of the gospel of peace'. Tell others about Jesus when we are ready to do so – more on that in another session (Ephesians 6:15)

4. Keep trusting God – 'the shield of faith'. Being sure of God's promises (Ephesians 6:16)

5. Protect your mind – 'the helmet of salvation'. Watch what we fill our minds with (Ephesians 6:17)

6. Know your Bible – 'the sword of the Spirit'. Get to know the Bible and attack the devil with its truth (Ephesians 6:17)

POINT 5 – HOW DO WE ATTACK?

- We are not limited to just defending ourselves. We can also attack!

Choose one of the following 2 options:

DRIVING THE WRONG WAY

PREPARATION TIME **0** minutes

Quick summary
This story about a man driving down the motorway in the wrong direction demonstrates how following Jesus goes against the grain of society.

Equipment / resources needed
None.

How it works
There was a man called Herman who was driving down the motorway when his mobile phone rang. He answered it (using his hands free kit, of course) and heard his wife's voice urgently warning him, 'Herman, I've just heard the news —there's a car going the wrong way down Highway 280. I know that's the way that you're going, so please be careful!' Herman replied, 'It's not just *one* car, there are *hundreds* of them!'

How to link to talk
- It may seem like following Jesus is like driving against the traffic, and that in resisting the devil's schemes we face a lot of opposition

LIGHT IN THE DARKNESS

PREPARATION TIME **0** minutes

Quick summary
This illustration shows the power that light has over darkness.

Equipment / resources needed
One candle.

How it works
Darken the room as much as possible. Have a candle ready to light. As you light the candle, say:

- Darkness may seem powerful but light is always stronger

How to link to talk

- Light always triumphs over darkness; darkness can never overpower light. Just one small light in a dark room makes a big impression

- So how do we attack?

- By praying – the Bible tells us to 'be alert and always keep on praying' (Ephesians 6:18). Our prayers can attack the devil!

- By action – we attack the devil by doing the things that Jesus told us to do (Luke 7:22)

CONCLUSION

- The devil is real, as is his influence in the world, but he is no match for God.

- There is no reason to have a great interest in the devil. Why worry about a loser?

- We have no cause to fear the devil because we are now in Jesus' kingdom

- We can put on the armour of God and resist the devil

QUICK PRAYER TO CLOSE

PREPARATION TIME 0 minutes

Quick summary
Pray to end your session.

Equipment / resources needed
None.

How it works

- I am just going to say a short prayer to close

- Lord, thank you that you have defeated the power of the devil. Thank you that we can live with you and with your authority. Please help us to always resist evil, and not to fear. In Jesus' name, Amen

How to link to talk

- Now we're going to have a quick break and then go into our small groups

- Thanks so much for coming to Youth Alpha today – see you next time!

SESSION 7
HOW CAN I RESIST EVIL?
SMALL GROUP DISCUSSION QUESTIONS

[These can be combined at the end of the talk or interspersed after each teaching point. You can find an additional copy of this sheet online at youthalpha.org/lgmedia]

POINTS 1 & 2 – WHY SHOULD WE BELIEVE IN THE DEVIL / WHAT'S THE DEVIL GOT TO DO WITH ME?

- If somebody had mentioned the devil to you yesterday, what would have sprung immediately into your mind?

- Why do you think there are bad things in the world?

- Do you believe in the devil?

- Is it right to blame the devil for everything that goes wrong in the world?

- Is it right to blame the devil for everything that goes wrong in our lives?

POINT 3 – SHOULD I BE WORRIED?**

- Do you think the idea of the devil wanting to destroy our lives is scary?

- What do you think it means to say that Jesus 'defeated' the devil by dying on the cross and then rising again?

- Is it reassuring to you to hear that Jesus has won this victory?

- Do you believe there is power in magic/witchcraft/the occult?

- Do you think being involved in these areas has a positive or negative effect on someone's life? Do you know anyone who is active in these areas? How does it affect them?

- How do you feel about the idea of having all the resources of heaven on your side?

*** BE AWARE: this discussion could throw up some pastoral issues. Before you begin this session, it would be helpful to decide how you will deal with anyone who may be concerned about past experiences with the occult. In the group context, it is important to make sure that everyone feels safe and affirmed, confident in the knowledge that God is far greater than any power of evil. It is often a good idea to end this session with some fun and humour and/or a powerful Bible verse about our loving, heavenly Father.*

POINTS 4 & 5 – HOW DO WE DEFEND OURSELVES / HOW DO WE ATTACK?

- How do you feel about the idea of putting on the 'armour of God'?

- Which bits of the armour of God (Ephesians 6) do you like the idea of the most?

- Are you up for praying and living in such a way as to attack the devil?

- Has your view of the devil changed because of this session?

You may like to include this optional extra, but it is not essential:

OPTIONAL EXTRA – GOING DEEPER

SESSION 7 BIBLE STUDY

Quick summary
This is an advanced option for small groups who may be ready for Bible study.

Equipment / resources needed
A Bible.

How it works
Read: Ephesians 6:10–20 – The armour of God

Then, in your small group, discuss the following questions:

- What do verses 11 and 12 tell us about the kind of spiritual fight that Christians face?

- What do you think each piece of armour represents? What do you think we need to do to be sure that we have each piece protecting us?

SESSION 7A

HOW CAN I LIVE FREE?

SESSION 7a
HOW CAN I LIVE FREE?

SUMMARY

AIMS OF THIS SESSION

- To encourage the group to know that we have God on our side, and he has defeated the Devil

- To explain the kingdom of God, and the reality of evil and suffering in our world

- To explore how we can resist evil and how we can pray for healing

NOTES

- This session is the combination of two talks: 'How Can I Resist Evil?' and 'Does God Heal Today?' so there is a lot to get through!

- This talk is to be used in eight and nine week courses only – not in the ten week version. See course overview for clarity

- Take some time as a team to ask God for 'words of knowledge' about healing that you can share at the end of the talk

- In small groups, give people a chance to respond to these words, and pray (by the laying on of hands) as a group for anyone who wants it

- If you have had your Weekend/Day, ask people to feed back from it

- As you are drawing near the end of the course, begin to talk about church and what will happen at the end of the course (perhaps invite the group along to a service)

SESSION OVERVIEW

- Food
- Welcome
- Ice breaker game
- Worship *(if applicable)*
- Talk
    - Introduction
    - Point 1 – The kingdom of God
    - Point 2 – Freedom from evil
    - Point 3 – Freedom from pain and disease
    - Conclusion
- Small groups

WELCOME

- Welcome back to Youth Alpha!

- It's great to have you here with us

- Before we get going, let's start with an ice breaker game

ICE BREAKER GAME

Choose one of the following 3 options:

STICKY NOSE RELAY

PREPARATION TIME **5** minutes

Quick summary
A relay that requires 'sticky noses' for transporting cotton balls.

Equipment / resources needed
Lots of cotton wool balls.
Tub of vaseline.
Two shallow baskets.

How it works
This is a simple relay race in which team members must crawl on their hands and knees to a basket at the other end of the room. From this basket, they must retrieve a cotton wool ball. The catch is that the cotton wool ball must be picked up using only players' noses, which will be sticky after being coated with Vaseline.
Arrange the players into two (or more) teams behind a starting line. Place the basket filled with cotton wool balls at the other end of the room. Once players' noses have been coated in Vaseline, say, 'Go!' to start the relay. Contestants must crawl down the room and plunge their noses into the basket until a cotton wool ball sticks. With the cotton wool balls on their noses, they must crawl back down the course to their team.
When they return to their team, they are not allowed to use their hands to remove the cotton wool ball. They can only do this by shaking their heads vigorously. Only when the cotton wool ball is dislodged can the next team member start their turn. The team with the most cotton wool balls at the end of the game wins. We suggest you spend no longer than three minutes on this game.

GOOD OR EVIL?

PREPARATION TIME **0** minutes

Quick summary
A game in which the group decides what, from the list below, is good and evil.

Equipment / resources needed
None.

How it works
Explain to the group that you are going to read out a list, and it is up to them to decide whether they think the things on the list are good, evil, or inbetween. Designate one side of the room as 'good' and the other as 'evil' – and let them know that it is okay to stand somewhere inbetween. They each have to move around and stand wherever they think that item best fits on the good/evil scale.

- Starbucks coffee
- Reading horoscopes
- Plastic surgery
- Pornography
- Gossip
- Ouija boards
- Child slavery
- Palm reading
- Agony aunts (in magazines)
- Global warming

Once you have finished 'voting', discuss these questions:

- How can we judge when something is evil?

- Isn't it interesting that we have such different opinions of what is evil?

SHAVING FOAM GAME

PREPARATION TIME **5** minutes

Quick summary
Teams must attempt to throw popcorn onto someone's shaving foam-covered face!

Equipment / resources needed
One can of shaving foam.
Two bags of popcorn/cheese puffs/crisps.
Baby wipes/towels to clean up.

How it works
Split the group into two teams and ask for two volunteers from each. In the teams, one volunteer should cover the other's face in shaving foam (we suggest you use non-perfumed foam). Once this is done, the rest of the team must stand behind a line (about two metres away from the foam-covered volunteer), and try to throw popcorn or cheese puffs at the volunteer's face. Give them one minute to see how many pieces they can stick to the foam. The team with the most wins!

INTRODUCTION

- Welcome to week seven of Youth Alpha

- Last week we looked at the question, 'How does God guide us?' and we talked about five different ways that God leads us. Can anyone remember what they were? *[Prize for anyone who can!]*

- This week we're looking at the subject of how we can live free: how we can be free from evil, and free from pain and sickness?

POINT 1 – THE KINGDOM OF GOD

- One of the biggest questions a lot of us have is, 'Why is there so much suffering in the world?' This is a huge and very valid question

- The kingdom of God is the key to understanding our experience of healing in the world today

- There are many things we could and should say here, but there is no concrete answer. The one thing I keep coming back to time and again is this: the Bible promises us that God is especially close to those who are in pain and suffering and in pain

- You only have to look to Jesus on the cross to know that God understands what it is to suffer

- Another incredible promise from God is that freedom is possible: freedom from the evil and disease in the world

- These promises all centre around what the Bible calls 'the kingdom of God'. This can be a pretty complicated thing to get our heads around

- Mark 1:15: Jesus says this, 'The time has come, the kingdom of God is near. Repent and believe the good news!'

- In that verse Jesus says, 'The time has come' – meaning that the reign of God is here today

- But it's also about the future – 'the kingdom is near'. The promise of the coming kingdom will be fulfilled in the future when Jesus returns

- The kingdom of God is both 'now' and 'not yet'. That means that when Jesus came to earth, he brought the kingdom of God. The healings that he did were a sign that the kingdom of God had arrived, but it hasn't arrived in its completeness yet

- In the meantime, now, we live in the inbetween times – the kingdom is here in part, but not completely. *(See Sheet 7a at the end of this session, or download the 'Now and not yet' diagram from* youthalpha.org/lgmedia *and, using this, explain that healing today is made possible through God's kingdom on earth)*

- It's a bit like this:

THE LION, THE WITCH AND THE WARDROBE

PREPARATION TIME 5 minutes

Quick summary
In this clip, Aslan is bringing in the start of summer and the snow melts away. Use this to demonstrate to the group the concept of God's kingdom: it is both 'now' (summer) and 'not yet' (winter). In terms of heaven on earth, we live in the season of spring today.

Equipment / resources needed
A copy of the film The Chronicles of Narnia: The Lion, the Witch and the Wardrobe *(episode 4), BBC, 1988. Certificate U.*

▶ *Chapter 13: 1:13:21*   ☐ *Chapter 13: 1:16:17*

Projector and screen (or a TV), and a DVD player.

How to link to talk
- Aslan represents Jesus. In this clip, it is Aslan's power that's melting the snow and turning winter to summer. The kingdom of heaven is represented by the warmth of summer, and the earth is represented by the cold of winter. In the Old Testament, it was like the earth was covered in snow

- Occasionally, the sun would shine and the earth would warm up (when God performed healings), but the snow never melted

- When Jesus came (like Aslan), he brought sunshine with him and it began to melt the snow

- Today, we live in the 'spring' – it isn't quite summer, so there are warm days and cold days. Not every person we pray for will get healed, but some will. Warm days give us a foretaste of what heaven will be like

- One day, Jesus will return again and bring heaven in its fullness on earth

WINTER/SUMMER

PREPARATION TIME 0 minutes

Quick summary
Use this seasonal analogy to demonstrate to the group the concept of God's kingdom: it is both 'now' (summer) and 'not yet' (winter). In terms of heaven on earth, today we live in the season of spring.

Equipment / resources needed
None.

How it works

In some ways it's a bit like the seasons. The kingdom of heaven is represented by the warmth of summer, and the earth is represented by the cold of winter. In the Old Testament, the earth was covered in snow. Occasionally, the sun would shine and the earth would warm up (when God performed healings), but the snow never melted. When Jesus came, he brought sunshine with him and it began to melt the snow. Today, we live in the 'spring' – it isn't quite summer, so there are warm days *and* cold days. Not every person we pray for will get healed, but some will. Warm days give us a foretaste of what heaven will be like. One day, Jesus will return again and bring heaven in its fullness on earth

How to link to talk

- This shows the importance of knowledge about the kingdom of God in our understanding of healing

- The first time Jesus came, he came in weakness. When he returns again (what is known as the Second Coming), Jesus says he'll come with power and great glory. All of history is moving towards that climax. There are over 300 references in the New Testament to the Second Coming of Jesus

- That will be a day of universal resurrection, a day of judgment, a new heaven and a new earth … perfection! And the Bible says there will be no more suffering or pain (Revelation 21:4)

- On that day in the future, all who put their trust in him will know total freedom, on all levels

- But until then, we don't – and evil seems to be all around us

POINT 2 – FREEDOM FROM EVIL

- The Bible says, in Romans 12:21, 'Do not be overcome by evil, but overcome evil with good'

- Where do you think evil comes from?

- Have you ever noticed that if you add one letter to the word 'God' you get 'good'? If you add one letter to the word 'evil' you get 'devil'. The claim of the New Testament is that, just as behind goodness lies God himself, behind the evil in the world lies the devil

- A lot of people find it almost impossible to believe there is a devil, perhaps because they are thinking of a caricature: horns, a pointed tail, a big fork. They may be thinking of the devil as portrayed in comedies

- Many have a false image of God – you know: old man, big white beard, white dress, sitting on the clouds …

- Many people also have a false image of the devil

THE SIMPSONS

PREPARATION TIME **5** minutes

Quick summary
In this clip, Homer Simpson sells his soul to the Devil for a doughnut. This demonstrates how often popular culture portrays the Devil in a caricatured and unbelievable way.

Equipment / resources needed
A copy of The Simpsons: *'Treehouse of Horror IV' (season 5, episode 5), Twentieth Century Fox Home Entertainment LLC, 2005, Certificate 12.*

▷ *Chapter 2: 0:02:36*   ☐ *Chapter 2: 0:04:46*
Projector and screen (or a TV), and a DVD player.

How to link to talk
- The way the devil is portrayed on TV and in movies is usually over exaggerated and silly – a complete caricature

- Just because he's regularly portrayed in this way, doesn't mean he isn't real

CARICATURES

PREPARATION TIME **30** minutes

Quick summary
Show caricatures of famous people, followed by a caricature of the devil.

Equipment / resources needed
Caricatures/cartoons.
You may want to use a projector and a screen in order to show this to the whole group.

How it works
Find some caricatures/cartoons of well-known people and one of the devil. Ask the group to identify the people shown – maybe have prizes for each correct answer. Try to find pictures that are very exaggerated, but not too offensive.
Finish with a caricature of the devil.

How to link to talk
- Sometimes it's easy to get the wrong impression of someone based on how they are portrayed in cartoons or in the media

- This last picture is also a kind of a caricature: the devil doesn't really look like this, but that doesn't mean that he is not real

- Many people have a picture of the devil that is based on a caricature – they think that he walks around with a big fork saying, 'Boo!' to people

OPTION 3

NEWSPAPER STORIES

PREPARATION TIME **5** minutes

Quick summary
Group activity to find real-life stories of suffering; this should prompt a discussion of the reasons for this kind of adversity.

Equipment / resources needed
Newspapers.
Scissors.
Glue.

How it works
Hand out newspapers to the group. Have them cut out photos from the negative stories that they find. Stick these photos onto a sheet of paper. Choose a few of the photos that appear interesting and ask these questions:

- Who is it that is suffering in this story?

- Who is to blame?
  - the people who are suffering
  - people that are causing the suffering
  - God
  - devil
  - other

- What is the cause of this situation?
  - the evil (sin) done by humanity in general
  - the evil (sin) done by those involved in this particular situation
  - evil generally

How to link to talk
- These are just a few examples of things that are evil in our world

---

- Why should we believe in the devil's existence? There are good reasons to believe:

  - because it is clear from the horror and evil in our world that he is at work

  - because Christians have believed in him down the ages

  - because the Bible speaks of him in the Old Testament (Job 1; 1 Chronicles 21:1; Isaiah 14) and in the New Testament (Ephesians 6:11–12; Luke 10:17–20)

- But – taking too much of an interest in the devil is just as dangerous as doubting that he even exists (Deuteronomy 18:10)

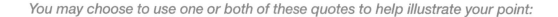

You may choose to use one or both of these quotes to help illustrate your point:

> ## OPTIONAL QUOTES
>
> William Peter Blatty (writer and producer of *The Exorcist*)
>
> 'As far as God goes, I'm a non-believer. But when it comes to the devil – well, that's something else. The devil keeps advertising; the devil does lots of commercials.'
>
> *(Alan Macdonald, Films in Close Up, Frameworks, 1991.)*
>
> C. S. Lewis (author of the 'Narnia' books)
>
> 'There are two equal and opposite errors into which we can fall about the devils. One is to disbelieve in their existence; the other is to believe and to feel an excessive and unhealthy interest in them. They themselves are equally pleased by both errors.'
>
> *(C. S. Lewis, The Screwtape Letters, Macmillan, 1951.)*

- What does the Bible say? 'Put on the full armour of God so that you can take your stand against the devil's schemes. For our struggle is not against flesh and blood, but against the rulers, against the authorities, against the powers of this dark world and against the spiritual forces of evil in the heavenly realms' (Ephesians 6:11–12)

- In other words, there is a kind of spiritual war going on that we can't see. We must resist the unseen forces in the world

- In John's Gospel, the Bible tells us that the devil's aim is to steal from us, kill our life, our fun and our freedom and destroy us (John 10:10). He wants to prevent us from having a proper relationship with God, and will do anything he can to stop this

- What are the devil's tactics?

  - he creates doubt in our minds

  - he causes us to take our eyes off Jesus

  - he tempts us to sin

- But Jesus said that his desire is exactly the opposite: 'I have come that they may have life, and have it to the full' (John 10:10)

- And it's only in Jesus, as we concentrate on him, rather than the powers of evil, that we discover the life and freedom that he offers

POINT 3 – FREEDOM FROM PAIN AND DISEASE

- As well as being free from the power of evil, Jesus also offers us freedom from pain and disease

- People today believe all sorts of things about healing. Some believe that illnesses can only be healed through doctors, hospitals and medicine. Others believe in 'faith healing' through things like crystals, Chinese medicines or other spiritual paths. Some, of course, believe that there is no such thing as supernatural healing. And others, such as myself, believe that God can heal us through prayer

Choose one of the following 4 options:

OPTION 1

VOX POPS: 'DOES GOD HEAL TODAY?'

PREPARATION TIME **5** minutes

Quick summary
Show the group a video in which members of the public share their views on the question, 'Does God heal today?' The purpose of this is to show the many different views and opinions that people have on the subject of healing.

> **Suggested tip**
> *If you have time, you could even make your own video showing the public's views on this topic.*

Equipment / resources needed
The vox pops video can be found online at youthalpha.org/lgmedia
You may want to use a projector and screen in order to show the clip to the whole group.

How to link to talk
- So different people have lots of different views on healing

OPTION 2

'HEALING' TESTIMONY

Share a story (your own, or perhaps the story of someone else who is also running the course) about a time in your life when God healed you.

HEALING IN THE GROCERY STORE

PREPARATION TIME 5 minutes

Quick summary
This is an amazing story about God's healing power, as told by Chad Dedmon from Jesus Culture in California. In this video, Chad tells of how he felt God telling him to pray for people as he was shopping, and how God healed people as he prayed over the shop's loud speaker!

Equipment / resources needed
To find the link for this clip, please visit youthalpha.org/lgmedia
You may want to use a projector and a screen in order to show the clip to the whole group.

How to link to talk
- So do you believe that God can heal people today?

AJAY GOHILL

PREPARATION TIME 0 minutes

Quick summary
This true story tells of a man who was healed after crying out to God.

Equipment / resources needed
None.

How it works
Ajay Gohill was born in Kenya but moved to England in 1971. He was brought up as a Hindu and worked in the family business as a newsagent in Neasden. At the age of twenty-one he contracted Erythrodermic Psoriasis, a chronic skin disease. His weight dropped from 11.5 [73 kg] to 7.5 stone [47.5 kg]. He was treated all over the world – in the United States, Germany, Switzerland and Israel, as well as all over England. He said that he spent eighty per cent of his earnings on trying to find a cure and he took strong drugs which affected his liver. Eventually, he had to give up his job. The disease covered his body from head to toe; he was so horrible to look at, he couldn't even wear a t-shirt. He lost all his friends, and his wife and son left him. He wanted to die. One October, Ajay was lying in his hospital bed. He cried out, 'God if you are watching, let me die – I am sorry if I have done something wrong.' From his locker he pulled out a Good News Bible. He opened it at random and read Psalm 38:

'O Lord, don't punish me in your anger! You have wounded me with your arrows; you have struck me down. Because of your anger, I am in great pain; my whole body is diseased because of my sins. I am drowning in the flood of my sins; they are a burden too heavy to bear. Because I have been foolish, my sores stink and rot. I am bowed down, I am crushed; I mourn all day long. I am burning with fever and I am near to death. I am worn out and utterly crushed; my heart is troubled and I groan with pain. O Lord, you know what I long for; you hear all my groans. My heart is pounding, my strength is gone, and my eyes have lost their brightness. My friends and neighbours will not come near me, because of my sores; even my family keeps away from me … Do not abandon me, O God; do not stay away from me, my God! Help me now, O Lord my saviour!' (Psalm 38:1–11, 21–22 Good News Bible).

Each and every verse seemed relevant to him. He prayed for God to heal him, and then he fell into a deep sleep. When he awoke the next morning 'everything looked new'. He went to relax in the bath and when he looked at the water, he saw his skin had lifted off and his body was floating. He called in the nurses and told them that God was healing him: all of his skin was new, like a baby's. He was totally healed and has since been reunited with his son. Ajay says that the inner healing that has taken place in his life is even greater than the physical healing. He says, 'Every day I live for Jesus. I am his servant today.'

How to link to talk
- So do you believe that God can heal people today?

- As I read the Bible, especially the Gospels, I see a God who heals. Actually it's quite hard to read about Jesus' ministry without talking about healing. In fact, twenty-five percent of the gospels are about healing!

- God promised to heal his people in the Old Testament. He says, 'I am the God who heals you' (Exodus 15:26). It is his nature to heal

- Occasionally we see God healing people in the Old Testament, but it wasn't a regular thing. In the book of 2 Kings, for example, Naaman, the military commander, is healed of leprosy. However, in the Old Testament we only get glimpses of God's kingdom breaking through onto earth

- Jesus sent his disciples out to pray for healing. He gave them authority to heal the sick in his name (the twelve disciples – Matthew 9:35–10:8; the seventy-two disciples – Luke 10:1–20). He also said that we would see greater things than he had (John 14:12). Jesus saw the sick healed and the dead raised – just imagine what we will see!

- As Jesus went up to heaven, he commissioned his disciples – and that includes all of us – to go and do as he did (Matthew 28:16–20)

- That's exactly what the disciples did. The early church went out and preached the gospel and healed the sick. They believed that the two went side by side. We should believe the same today

- So Jesus taught about healing and he went out and healed people. As a result, even the earliest churches in the Bible believed healing was possible and they acted on it. But it didn't stop there – the church has been praying for the sick and seeing God perform miracles ever since

- Throughout the history of the Christian church there have been examples of healing and miracles. It didn't just stop with the disciples in the early church

- Here's an example:

THE STORY OF INNOCENTIUS   PREPARATION TIME 0
minutes

Quick summary
This true story of a man named Innocentius demonstrates the power of prayer in healing.

Equipment / resources needed
None.

How it works
[Read this story with as much drama and horror as possible.]

St Augustine of Hippo (a place, not the animal), one of the greatest theologians of the first five centuries of the church, showed that he wasn't squeamish by writing this story down for us.

St Augustine was staying with a man called Innocentius, who was being treated by doctors for 'fistulae' of which he had 'a large number intricately seated in his rectum'! He had undergone one very painful operation. It was not thought that he would survive another.

St Augustine and some others prayed for him, and as they did so, Innocentius was thrown to the floor as if someone had hurled him violently to earth. He groaned and sobbed and his whole body shook so much that he couldn't talk.

The dreaded day of the operation came. 'The surgeons arrived ... the frightful instruments [were] produced ... the part [was] bared; the surgeon ... with knife in hand, eagerly look[ed] for the sinus that [had] to be cut. He searche[d] for it with his eyes; he [felt] for it with his finger' but he found a perfectly healed wound.

God had healed Innocentius, much to his relief!

How to link to talk
- As time went on, the Church set up hospitals and other institutions to help the sick get better, but God was, and is, still in the business of intervening miraculously too. And we can ask him to do so!

- So how do we pray for healing?

- Well, our job is simply to pray – it is God who does the healing

- We need to check our motive – Jesus healed people because he loved them. It is important that we care and want the best for anyone we pray for

- Prayers for healing should be simple, not long and complicated. There are no special prayers to pray – remember, it is God's power, not our words, that heal

- There is no set way in which to pray for healing – Jesus did it in different ways. But I'll give you a helpful model to follow

- We usually recommend that you pray with someone of the same gender as you, and in groups of either two or three

- When we pray for healing we should:

    - ask where it hurts, how long it has hurt, and why it hurts

    - pray that God would heal in the name of Jesus – we normally place our hands on the person's shoulder when we pray

    - ask that the Holy Spirit would heal the person

    - continue to be open to more guidance from the Holy Spirit

- Afterwards we should:

    - ask the person how they feel

    - make sure that they are happy and that they understand all that has happened

- We should not give up if nothing seems to happen or if the person is only partially healed. Jesus once prayed for a blind man and asked him, 'Do you see anything?' The man said, 'I see people, but they look like trees walking around.' So Jesus prayed a second time, and this time the man's eyes were opened and his sight was restored completely (Mark 8:24). If Jesus sometimes had to pray twice, we shouldn't feel discouraged at having to do so!

CONCLUSION

- In a moment, we're going to go into our small groups and I want to encourage you to have a go at praying for healing for anyone in your group who might want it. Don't be embarrassed to ask for prayer

- So, to conclude: we believe that God is the creator of all things good, but there is also a power of evil that causes suffering and pain. But God wants to set us free

- We have no cause to fear the devil because we are now in Jesus' kingdom

- We can put on the armour of God and resist the devil

- As Christians, we should pray for the sick. A guy called John Wimber, someone whom God used a lot in the area of healing, used to say, 'When we pray for no one, no one gets healed. But when we pray for lots of people, some of them are healed.' So it is important to pray

- One day, we will live in heaven with Jesus and there will be no sickness. Until then, he calls us to pray and ask him to heal the sick

- Sometimes, the kingdom of heaven will break through and we will see amazing things before our very eyes

QUICK PRAYER TO CLOSE

PREPARATION TIME 0 minutes

Quick summary
Pray to end your talk.

Equipment / resources needed
None.

How it works
- I am just going to say a short prayer to close

- Lord, thank you that you have defeated the power of the devil. Thank you that we can live with you and with your authority. Thank you so much that you are a God who heals today, and Lord, we pray tonight that once again you will come by your Spirit among us and heal people here. In Jesus' name, Amen

How to link to talk
- Now we're going to have a quick break and then go into our small groups

- Thanks so much for coming to Youth Alpha today – see you next time!

[If you prayed as a team before the session began and felt you received some words of knowledge for the group, share them before you break into small groups.]

SESSION 7a
HOW CAN I LIVE FREE?
SMALL GROUP DISCUSSION QUESTIONS

If you are doing your small groups after the talk, the best thing to do would be to begin by immediately offering to pray for anyone who wants it. Ask if anyone identified with any of the words of knowledge that were read out. If so, ask them if they are happy to sit/stand in the middle of the group and let everyone place their hands on them and pray.
If there were no words of knowledge, or if no one responds, ask if anyone would like prayer for healing and then pray for them.

After that, feel free to use any of the questions below.

[These can be combined at the end of the talk or interspersed after each teaching point. You can find an additional copy of this sheet online at youthalpha.org/lgmedia]

POINT 1 – THE KINGDOM OF GOD

- Does the idea that we live in the time between Jesus's death and heaven on earth make any sense to you? Explain …

- Is it reassuring to you to hear that Jesus has won this victory?

- What do you feel about the idea of one day living in heaven with Jesus?

POINT 2 – FREEDOM FROM EVIL**

- If somebody had mentioned the devil to you yesterday, what would have immediately sprung in to your mind?

- Why do you think there are bad things in the world?

- Do you believe in the devil?

- Is it right to blame the devil for everything that goes wrong in the world?

- Do you think the idea of the devil wanting to destroy our lives is scary?

- Are you up for praying and living in such a way as to attack the devil?

** BE AWARE: this discussion could throw up some pastoral issues. Before you begin this session, it would be helpful to decide how you will deal with anyone who may be concerned about past experiences with the occult. In the group context, it is important to make sure that everyone feels safe and affirmed, confident in the knowledge that God is far greater than any power of evil. It is often a good idea to end this session with some fun and humour and/or a powerful Bible verse about our loving, heavenly Father.

POINT 3 – FREEDOM FROM PAIN AND DISEASE

- Has anyone here ever experienced anything miraculous?

- Do you believe that God can heal people today? Why/why not?

- How does the fact that the early church, and the church ever since, have prayed for healing and seen miracles make you feel?

- How did you find praying for healing for each other?

You may like to include this optional extra, but it is not essential:

OPTIONAL EXTRA – GOING DEEPER

SESSION 7a BIBLE STUDY

Quick summary
This is an advanced option for small groups who may be ready for Bible study.

Equipment / resources needed
A Bible.

How it works
Read: Ephesians 6:10–20 – The armour of God

Then, in your small group, discuss the following questions:

- How do you feel about the idea of putting on the 'armour of God'?

- Which bits of the armour of God (Ephesians 6) do you like the idea of the most?

- What do verses 11 and 12 tell us about the kind of spiritual fight that Christians face?

- What do you think each piece of armour represents? What do you think we need to do to be sure that we have each piece protecting us?

SHEET 7a
NOW AND NOT YET
HAND OUT

CHART 1

THIS AGE | AGE TO COME

CHART 2

The age to come realised in principle

AGE TO COME

First coming of Jesus

The period in which we now live

Second coming of Jesus

THIS AGE

SESSION 8

WHY AND HOW SHOULD I TELL OTHERS?

SESSION 8
WHY AND HOW SHOULD I TELL OTHERS?

SUMMARY

AIMS OF THIS SESSION

- To encourage the group that sharing our faith should be natural and non-pressurised

- To explain that Jesus wants us all to share our faith

- To explore the idea that sharing our faith is about more than just words

NOTES

- If you have had your Weekend/Day recently, get people to feed back from it

- As you are drawing near to the end of the course, begin to talk about church and what will happen at the end of the course (perhaps invite the group along to a service)

- Mention details about the next Youth Alpha course, and ask the group to think about who they could invite

SESSION OVERVIEW

- Food
- Welcome
- Ice breaker game
- Worship *(if applicable)*
- Talk
    - Introduction
    - Point 1 – Live the message
    - Point 2 – Talk the message
    - Point 3 – Present the message
    - Point 4 – Empower the message
    - Point 5 – Pray the message
    - Conclusion
- Small groups

WELCOME

- Welcome back to Youth Alpha!

- It's great to have you here with us

- Before we get going, let's start with an ice breaker game

ICE BREAKER GAME

Choose one of the following 3 options:

OPTION 1

WATER BALLOON THROW

PREPARATION TIME 30 minutes

Quick summary
In pairs, guests play a game of catch with water balloons.

Equipment / resources needed
Lots of filled water balloons (enough for one balloon per pair, plus spares).

How it works
Take your group outside, or to a place where it is okay to spill water. Split everyone who would like to play into pairs, and ask each pair to choose one person to be 'number one' and the other to be 'number two'. All the 'ones' stand shoulder to shoulder facing the same direction. All the 'twos' stand opposite their partners, facing them toe-to-toe.
Give a water balloon to every 'number one'.
On your word, the 'ones' must pass the balloon to the 'twos'. Assuming all the pairs accomplish this successfully, both the ones and the twos take a step backwards. On 'go', the twos must now toss the balloon back to the ones. If anybody drops the balloon, or if the balloon bursts as it is caught, that pair is eliminated.
Every time a pair successfully completes a throw and a catch, they must both take a step backwards. The winning pair is the one that lasts the longest, or that manages a successful throw and catch at the greatest distance. We suggest you spend no longer than ten minutes on this game.

OPTION 2

PULSE RELAY

PREPARATION TIME 2 minutes

Quick summary
A game in which teams must pass a 'pulse' along a line as fast as possible.

NB: this game can be used as an icebreaker, or for Point 1 of the teaching.

Equipment / resources needed
Two chairs.
One ball/object to grab.
One coin.

How it works

Split the group into two equal teams, and ask them to form two parallel lines. Instruct everyone to hold hands with the team members next to them, thus creating two human chains. At one end, between the teams, place a chair with a small object (eg: a tennis ball, a handkerchief, etc) on it. The referee should stand at the opposite end.

Ask the two players nearest to the referee to keep their eyes on him/her at all times. Everyone else should watch the object on the chair only.

For each round, the referee must flip a coin and quietly show it only to the two players nearest to him/her. Whenever the coin shows 'heads', the first two players must squeeze the hand of the next person in line as quickly as possible.

Whenever a player's hand gets squeezed, he or she must quickly continue to 'pass the pulse', by squeezing the next person's hand, and so on, down the line.

The aim of the game is to be the first team to grab the object from the chair, once the 'pulse' reaches the 'object' end of the line. If 'heads' is flipped and a team successfully grabs the ball, that team wins. After each coin flip, wait several seconds and then flip again.

This can be done as best of five, seven or nine, and you could give out prizes (or respect points!) to the winning team. We suggest you spend no longer than five minutes on this game.

NB: keep an eye out for cheating!

ADVERTISING CHRISTIANITY

PREPARATION TIME **0** minutes

Quick summary
Get groups to create an advertising campaign for Christianity.

Equipment / resources needed
Paper and pens for each group to write down their ideas.

How it works

Ask everyone to get into their small groups. Tell them to imagine that they are a highly paid, highly skilled creative team at a top advertising agency. The day's challenge is to provide a top-drawer campaign for one of their agency's biggest clients: they need to sell Christianity.

Ask them:

- What are the chief selling points you can base your campaign on?
- What might your logo be?
- What slogans can you use to catch people's attention?
- What might your posters look like?
- What could you do for radio and television slots?

You will want to set an appropriate time limit for this activity (eg: ten minutes).

INTRODUCTION

- Welcome to week eight of Youth Alpha

- Last time we looked at the question, 'How can I resist evil?' We talked about the fact that there is a spiritual battle going on between the forces of good and evil, but Jesus has won the war, so there's no need to fear

- This week, we're looking at the subject of why and how we should tell others about what we believe

- Looking at the history of the church, it is quite clear that there is something highly infectious and contagious about the Christian faith. After all, it started with just a handful of believers huddled together in an insignificant city in the Middle East. Yet today, there are not just millions, but billions of believers across the whole world

- But sometimes, those of us who are Christians can be a bit insensitive in sharing our faith with others …

Choose one of the following 3 options:

HORTON HEARS A WHO!

PREPARATION TIME **5** minutes

Quick summary
In this clip, we see Horton trying to explain to the Mayor of Whoville that he is external to their world, and that Whoville is just a small speck. This demonstrates how difficult it can be to explain what we believe, or how we feel, to others.

Equipment / resources needed
A copy of the film Horton Hears a Who!, *Twentieth Century Fox Film Corporation, 2008. Certificate U*

▷ *Chapter 17: 0:35:09* ☐ *Chapter 17: 0:36:08*

Projector and screen (or a TV), and a DVD player.

How to link to talk
- In this clip we see Horton trying to explain to the Mayor of Whoville that Whoville is just a speck in his world, and that he is actually an elephant!

- In a similar way, it can sometimes be tricky to find the right words to explain what we believe to others, as the idea of God being real can be as hard to grasp as the situation we see in this clip

EVANGELISM LINEBACKER

PREPARATION TIME **5** minutes

Quick summary
In this clip we meet the 'Evangelism Linebacker' – a man who goes around tackling those who won't share their faith! This is an example of how not to do evangelism.

Equipment / resources needed
To find the link for this clip, please visit youthalpha.org/lgmedia
You may want to use a projector and a screen in order to show the clip to the whole group.

How to link to talk
- There are good ways and bad ways to share our faith – I'll focus on the good ways! (And don't worry: no one is going to come and 'get you' if you don't share your faith!)

SHARING THE GOOD NEWS

PREPARATION TIME **0** minutes

Quick summary
This story shows how some people can respond negatively to Christians sharing their message.

Equipment / resources needed
None.

How it works
Two church members were going door to door, telling people about Jesus. They knocked on the door of a woman who was not happy to see them. She told them in no uncertain terms that she did not want to hear their message, and slammed the door in their faces.
To her surprise, the door did not close and, in fact, bounced back open. She tried again; she really put her pack into it, and slammed the door with the same result – it bounced back open.
Convinced these rude young people were sticking their feet in the door, she reared back to give it a slam that would teach them a lesson, when one of them said, 'Ma'am, before you do that again you need to move your cat.'

How to link to talk
- In this session we are looking at how we can share our faith

---

- Why should we tell other people about our faith in Jesus?

Reason 1 Because Jesus told us to. Jesus died for us, he rose again from the dead, and then he said, 'Now go and tell people about this amazing news: you can be forgiven, you can be set free. You can have eternal life.' Jesus wants to use us to tell other people.

- The word 'go' appears 1,514 times in the Bible – I didn't count them all, but somebody did! In the New Testament it appears 233 times, in Matthew's Gospel it's 54 times. Jesus says, 'Go and tell ... Go and invite ... Go and make disciples'

Reason 2 Because we love our friends and family. Love must be what motivates us, because we want people to discover what we have found in Jesus.

Reason 3 Because it is good news! And usually, good news travels fast. People are very good at passing on good news. We can't just keep it to ourselves – we want to tell people.

- Right from the start it is good to recognise two possible mistakes:

    - some go the religious fanatic route, trying to force their views down other people's throats
    - some go silent and never let anyone know about their faith

- The key to avoiding these two mistakes is to really care about the person you are telling, and to trust God

- We're quickly going to look at five ways we can share our faith

POINT 1 – LIVE THE MESSAGE

Choose one of the following 4 options:

OPTION 1 AMAZING GRACE

PREPARATION TIME **5** minutes

Quick summary
In this clip, we see William and his followers put their faith into action. They are living the message, and living out their faith.

Equipment / resources needed
A copy of the film Amazing Grace, *Bristol Bay Productions LLC, 2006. Certificate PG.*

▷ *Chapter 6: 0:54:16*   ☐ *Chapter 6: 0:55:13*

Projector and screen (or a TV), and a DVD player.

How to link to talk
- We are called by God to love those around us, and to love the poor. We must stand up against injustice in our world

OPTION 2 STARFISH

PREPARATION TIME **0** minutes

Quick summary
This analogy about a boy saving the lives of starfish – one at a time – shows that our even our tiny acts of kindness can make a huge difference. Telling just one person about Jesus could change their life forever.

Equipment / resources needed
None.

How it works
A man was walking along a beach in Mexico when he saw a remarkable sight – the beach was covered in tens of thousands of starfish! The tide had gone out and left them stranded on the beach, dying in the heat of the sun. The man saw a young boy standing among the starfish. The boy was picking them up one at a time, running down to the sea and throwing them into the water, before going back to get another starfish and repeating the process again.

The man went up to him and said, 'Look, can't you see — there are tens of thousands of starfish out here! I don't really think what you're doing is going to make any difference.'

The young boy picked up another starfish, went down to the water's edge, threw it in the sea and said, 'I bet it made a difference for that one!'

How to link to talk
- We may not be able to change the world on our own, but we can change the lives of those around us, one by one

- We are called by God to love those around us, and to love the poor. We must stand up against injustice in our world

OPTION 3

STARFISH ANIMATION
PREPARATION TIME **5** minutes

Quick summary
This cartoon animation about a boy saving the lives of starfish – one at a time – shows that even our tiny acts of kindness can make a huge difference. Telling just one person about Jesus could change their life forever.

Equipment / resources needed
The animation can be found online at youthalpha.org/lgmedia
You may want to use a projector and a screen in order to show the animation to the whole group.

How to link to talk
- We may not be able to change the world on our own, but we can change the lives of those around us, one by one

- We are called by God to love those around us, and to love the poor. We must stand up against injustice in our world

OPTION 4

BONO'S QUOTE
PREPARATION TIME **0** minutes

Quick summary
Bono's quote shows how he puts his faith into action. He is living the message, and living out his faith.

Equipment / resources needed
None.

How it works
Bono, the lead singer of the band U2, is a big campaigner for the poor.
He is a Christian, and his faith inspires him to make a difference.
He was once invited to speak at a big political gathering in Brighton, UK,
and this is some of what he said:

'My name is Bono. I'm a rock-star. Excuse me if I appear a little nervous
– I'm not used to appearing before crowds of less than 80,000 people. I
heard the word "party" – obviously got the wrong idea!'

He went on to speak of his time working in an Ethiopian orphanage. He
said:

'We lived for a month working at the orphanage. The locals knew me as
"Dr Good Morning". The children called me "the girl with a beard". Don't
ask! [It was because of his long hair!]
It just blew my mind; it opened my mind. On our last day at the
orphanage, a man handed me his baby and said, "Take him with you."
He knew in Ireland his son would live; in Ethiopia his son would die. I
turned him down. In that moment, I started this journey. In that moment I
became the worst thing of all: a rock-star with a cause. Except this isn't
a cause – 6,500 Africans dying a day of treatable, preventable disease,
dying for want of medicines you and I can get at our local chemist: that's
not a cause; that's an emergency.'

(Bono, speaking at the Labour Party Conference*, 29 September 2004.)*

How to link to talk
- As Christians, God calls us to live the message of Christianity. This
  means loving those around us, and loving the poor. We must stand up
  against injustice in our world

- When people know that we are Christians, they will watch how we live. Our actions
  should match our words

- The way that we live is sometimes more important than the words we speak
  (Matthew 5:13–16)

- In particular, we should be careful to always treat other people well. To be a Christian
  – a follower of Jesus – is to live by his example and put others first (Philippians 2:3)

- Jesus spoke a lot about loving the poor. One of the ways our faith should be
  noticeable to our others is through how we treat the poor and needy in our
  communities. Jesus didn't say this was an optional extra – it's an essential part of
  living the Christian life

POINT 2 – TALK THE MESSAGE

Choose one of the following 4 options:

YES MAN

PREPARATION TIME **5** minutes

Quick summary
In this clip, we see Carl attending a seminar in which he is pressured into saying 'yes'. This is an example of how not to share our faith and how not to do evangelism.

NB: there is a brief reference to sexual behaviour in this clip.

Equipment / resources needed
A copy of the film Yes Man, Village Roadshow Films (BVI) Limited, 2008. Certificate 15.

▶ *Chapter 4: 0:15:09* ⬜ *Chapter 4: 0:18:37*

Projector and screen (or a TV), and a DVD player.

How to link to talk
- We believe that evangelism should never involve pressuring people like we saw in that clip. There are good ways and bad ways to share our faith – I'll focus on the good ways!

EXPLANATION GAME

PREPARATION TIME **5** minutes

Quick summary
Without using the actual words that they are trying to describe, players must try and explain a list of words for the rest of the group to guess. Just like trying to tell people about our faith, this game can be tricky.

Equipment / resources needed
Lists of words, written/printed on paper (enough for one per player).

How it works
Ask for two (or more) volunteers to come forward. They will each have between thirty and sixty seconds to try and describe as many words as they can from a list that you will give them (you can either use the following list or make one up yourself).The rest of the group must try to guess the word that they are describing. As soon as the group calls out the correct word, they may do the next one.
The person who successfully explains the most objects in the allotted time is the winner (you may like to give them a prize).

Possible words:

- *Football*
- *Church*

- *The person giving the talk now*
- *The Pope*
- *Tom Cruise*
- *David Beckham*
- *Star Wars*
- *Father Christmas*

How to link to talk

- Just like *[names of players]* demonstrated in this game, Jesus wants us to be able to explain to others what we believe. For some people, this comes naturally and is quite easy, but for others it is much harder to do

'LEADING PEOPLE TO FAITH' TESTIMONY

Share a story, either about someone who came to faith because a friend told them about their belief, or about someone who has led a friend to faith.

- Jesus wants us all to be able to explain to others what we believe. We all have a story or a testimony, and it is great to be able to share it. For some, this comes naturally and is quite easy, but for others it is much harder to do

NOT TELLING OTHERS!

PREPARATION TIME **0** minutes

Quick summary
This short story shows the group how simple it can be to share your faith with people, even if you feel uncomfortable about it.

Equipment / resources needed
None.

How it works
A young man was going to church, but was hesitant about becoming a Christian because he was absolutely petrified at the thought of having to speak to his friends and family about Jesus. In fact, it sounded like such a horrendous idea, he didn't think he could ever become a Christian. The young man went to see an older, wiser Christian and explained how he was feeling. The older man said, 'Look, in your case God has made an exception. You don't have to tell anybody. It can just be a private thing between you and God.' The young man was very pleased about this, and when he went home, he went straight up to his bedroom, knelt down by his bed and he gave his life to Jesus. At that very moment, the Holy Spirit came upon him and filled him. It flooded his whole being and he was filled with an overflowing joy. He rushed downstairs to the kitchen, where he found his family and five of his friends. Breathless with excitement, he exclaimed, 'It's amazing! You can become a Christian and you don't have to tell anybody!'

How to link to talk

- Jesus wants us all to be able to explain to others what we believe. We all have a story or a testimony, and it is great to be able to share it. For some, this comes naturally and is quite easy, but for others it is much harder to do

---

- If we live like Christians it is quite likely that people will notice and want us to talk about it

- There is no formula for how to speak about your faith – the important thing is to tell your story and be natural. Never use force – very few people have ever come to faith through a heated argument!

- When we talk about what we believe, people may well have some very good questions to ask us. 'What about science – doesn't that disprove Christianity?' 'What about suffering?' 'What about other religions?'

- We should take these questions seriously (if the person is asking seriously) and try to answer, either right then, or later, when we've had a chance to talk to another Christian about it or look it up somewhere (2 Corinthians 5:11)

- If you don't know the answer, don't worry, and don't pretend you do! Just be willing to go away and find out

POINT 3 – PRESENT THE MESSAGE

Choose one of the following 4 options:

A KNIGHT'S TALE

PREPARATION TIME 5 minutes

Quick summary
In this clip, the herald 'preaches' Sir Ulrich's praise. This is an example of a great preacher.

Equipment / resources needed
A copy of the film A Knight's Tale, Columbia Pictures Industries, Inc, 2001. Certificate PG.

▷ *Chapter 12: 0:37:00* ☐ *Chapter 12: 0:39:45*

Projector and screen (or a TV), and a DVD player.

How to link to talk
- The good news is that we do not all have to be great preachers!

- We are all called to be witnesses. A witness is someone who tells of what they have seen or experienced. Just tell people about your experience of God

- It can also be effective to take friends to hear the truth as presented by someone (or a group) who are especially good at explaining the faith (John 1:39–42)

FAMOUS SPEECH

PREPARATION TIME **5** minutes

Quick summary

Find a clip of a famous speech, given by a gifted speaker, such as Martin Luther King Junior's 'I have a dream' or Barack Obama's 'Yes we can'.

Equipment / resources needed

You can find an appropriate video online at youtube.com or other video sites. You may want to use a projector and a screen in order to show the film to the whole group.

How to link to talk

- The good news is that we do not all have to be great preachers!

- We are all called to be witnesses. A witness is someone who tells of what they have seen or experienced. Just tell people about your experience of God

- It can also be effective to take friends to hear the truth as presented by someone (or a group) who are especially good at explaining the faith (John 1:39–42)

MONEY QUESTION

PREPARATION TIME **0** minutes

Quick summary

Use this analogy about money to show the group that by telling just one person at a time about Jesus, we could see many people coming to faith over the years.

Equipment / resources needed

None.

How it works

- Which would you rather have: £10,000 every day for twenty days or £1 that doubles its cumulative value every day for twenty days?

It isn't obvious, but the £1 option will earn them £524,288 not just £200,000.

- It is easy to think, 'I could never be a great preacher, so there's no point in making any effort to talk about Jesus to my friends. What difference could I make?'

- That's wrong. Just as the £1 that kept doubling grew bigger than the £10,000 every day, if we all brought just one friend to Jesus each year, and then helped *them* to bring one of their friends to

Jesus the next year, we would see huge numbers of young people coming to Christ. It is better for us to aim to share our faith one-by-one than thinking we must reach thousands at a time

How to link to talk

- Could you try doing one of these in the next week?

  - pray for a friend

  - ask a friend to a youth event

  - make an effort to talk to a lonely person at school

  - tell somebody the story of how you came to be a Christian

BILLY GRAHAM

PREPARATION TIME **0** minutes

Quick summary

This is the true story of how Billy Graham came to faith. Use it to show the group how even bringing just one person to Jesus can have an impact on millions of people's lives.

Equipment / resources needed

None.

How it works

There was a man called Albert McMakin. He was twenty-four years of age and he was a farmer. He had just become a Christian, and was really excited about his faith. He knew that people were going to be speaking about Jesus at a series of events nearby, so he got hold of a van in order to bring all his friends to hear the speakers.

There was one friend in particular that he wanted to bring. This guy was a farmer's son and he really wasn't interested in Christianity. He was very good-looking and popular with the ladies, but Albert didn't think he'd want to hear about Jesus. He wondered how he could get this guy to come. Eventually, Albert decided to ask him to drive the van. The guy said, 'Okay, I'll drive the van. I don't want to come in to the meetings but I'll drive the van for you.'

So he did. Once he was there, he was curious to see what was going on, so he decided to sit at the back and listen. He was completely enthralled by what he heard, and he went back night after night. On the last night of the meetings, the speaker said, 'If you want to become a Christian and give your life to Jesus Christ, then come to the front.' The farmer's son got up and went to the front.

Since that day, that man has spoken in person to 210 million people about the Christian faith, he's been the friend and confidant of nine American Presidents and he's spoken, not live, but through the media, to half of the world's population.

His name is Billy Graham and he is probably the most famous evangelist of recent times.

How to link to talk
- We can't all be Billy Grahams, but we can all be Albert McMakins!
- We can all be the one who says, 'Come and see' to our friends

POINT 4 – EMPOWER THE MESSAGE

- Before we run out of time, I'll quickly race through the last two points
- Point four is 'empower the message': in the New Testament God used miracles to back up the message (Acts 3)
- God still does miracles today, and we shouldn't be afraid to ask him to show his power to people

You may like to include this optional extra, but it is not essential:

OPTIONAL EXTRA – GOING DEEPER

'EXPERIENCING GOD'S POWER' TESTIMONY

If you have anyone on your team who came to faith through experiencing the power of God, you could ask them to share their story now.

POINT 5 – PRAY THE MESSAGE

- Last, but definitely not least (it's actually the most important point) – pray the message
- Prayer is the power behind any attempt to tell people the good about Jesus
- If we haven't been praying, then we shouldn't expect to see anything happen
- We can pray that people's eyes would be opened to the truth about God. It says in 2 Corinthians 4:4 that the 'god of this age' (the devil) has blinded people so that they cannot see God. We need to pray that they can be set free from that blindness
- We can pray that God would give us boldness to talk about our faith (Acts 4:29–31)

CONCLUSION

Choose one of the following 4 options:

PAY IT FORWARD

PREPARATION TIME **5** minutes

Quick summary
In this clip, Trevor explains his strategy and shows how acts of kindness can have a huge impact on the world.

Equipment / resources needed
A copy of the film Pay It Forward, *Warner Bros. and Bel Air Pictures LLC, 2000. Certificate 12.*

▷ *Chapter 10: 0:32:04* ☐ *Chapter 10: 0:33:32*

Projector and screen (or a TV), and a DVD player.

How to link to talk
- Jesus calls us to pass on our faith: it is good news for everyone!

- If all of us 'pass it on' to others then the message will quickly spread to lots of people

- We should remember to never give up (Romans 1:16)

CANDLE ILLUSTRATION

PREPARATION TIME **0** minutes

Quick summary
Lighting a candle in a dark room shows the impact of just one light. If we light many candles in a dark room, we see how big the difference is.

Equipment / resources needed
One candle per person.
Lighter/matches.

How it works
In as quiet and reflective an atmosphere as possible, give one candle to each person and darken the room. Light one candle and use this to light the candles of the people on either side of you. They in turn light their neighbour's candle and so on, until the whole group has their candles alight.

NB: HEALTH AND SAFETY WARNING – be careful with fire, especially with younger groups!

How to link to talk

- Jesus calls us to pass on our faith: it is good news for everyone!

- If all of us 'pass it on' to others then the message will quickly spread to lots of people

- We should remember to never give up (Romans 1:16)

SUNDAY SCHOOL TEACHER
PREPARATION TIME **0** minutes

Quick summary
This story demonstrates the importance of continuing to spread the good news about Jesus, even when we feel it is going unheard.

Equipment / resources needed
None.

How it works
A man, injured in war, lay dying in the trenches. His friend, who was beside him, turned to him and asked, 'Is there anything I can do for you?' The dying man replied, 'No, I'm dying. There's nothing you can do.' 'Well,' said his friend, 'is there anything I could do when I get home, any message I could take?' The dying man responded, 'Yes. I'd like you to take a message to someone', and he gave him the name and address of a man at home. 'Tell him that what he taught me as a child is helping me to die now.' The soldier died.
When the soldier's friend went home, he went to visit the person the soldier had asked him to see, and told him the story. The man said, 'God forgive me. I taught that man in Sunday school [children's church] many years ago. Soon after I taught him I gave up teaching on Sundays because I thought that what I was doing was having no effect.'

How to link to talk
- We should never give up sharing our faith (Romans 1:16)

- We might never know the effect of something that we have said or done, but God will use our lives and our words if we trust him

ST FRANCIS OF ASSISI'S QUOTE
PREPARATION TIME **0** minutes

Quick summary
This quote, said by St Francis of Assisi, shows that more often than not, it is our actions, not our words, that have the greatest effect when spreading the gospel.

Equipment / resources needed
None.

How it works
- Saint Francis of Assisi said this: 'Preach the gospel at all times; if necessary, use words'

How to link to talk
- Our lives should always speak of what God has done for us. Sometimes we will need to say the words, but often it is how we live and how we love others that says more

- So to conclude: we should share our faith with others because Jesus told us to, because we love our friends and family and because it is good news!

- We should remember that evangelism isn't only about what we say it is about who we are and how we live

- We must always remember that God calls us to love the poor, broken people of this world

- Let's pray now

QUICK PRAYER TO CLOSE

PREPARATION TIME 0
minutes

Quick summary
Pray to end your session.

Equipment / resources needed
None.

How it works
- I am just going to say a short prayer to close

- Father, thank you so much that your message is such good news. Please help us this week to share the love of Jesus with our friends and family, and also with the poor and broken people of this world. Help us to live our lives as a witness to everything you have given us. In Jesus' name, Amen

How to link to talk
- Now we're going to have a quick break and then go into our small groups

- Thanks so much for coming to Youth Alpha today – see you next time!

SESSION 8
WHY AND HOW SHOULD I TELL OTHERS?

SMALL GROUP DISCUSSION QUESTIONS

[These can be combined at the end of the talk or interspersed after each teaching point. You can find an additional copy of this sheet online at youthalpha.org/lgmedia]

POINT 1 – LIVE THE MESSAGE

- How do you feel about the idea that we should all share our faith because it is good news?

- How do you feel about Jesus' message that tells us we should love the poor and needy among us?

- What do you think should be the main thing that marks those who are Christians apart from those who aren't?

- How can we show our faith to others without getting in their faces?

POINTS 2 & 3 – TALK THE MESSAGE / PRESENT THE MESSAGE

- If you did not know anything at all about Christianity how would you like to find out about it?

- If somebody was going to tell you about Christianity what would be the best thing they could say?

- How do you feel about the idea of speaking about your faith to others?

- Has anyone told a friend about Youth Alpha?

- Has anyone told a friend about what we talk about on the course?

POINTS 4 & 5 – EMPOWER THE MESSAGE / PRAY THE MESSAGE

- How do you feel about the idea of praying for your friends/family to become Christians?

- Do your family or your school friends know you come here/to church? What do they think about it?

- How do you feel about the idea of telling others?

You may like to include this optional extra, but it is not essential:

OPTIONAL EXTRA – GOING DEEPER

SESSION 8 BIBLE STUDY

Quick summary
This is an advanced option for small groups who may be ready for Bible study.

Equipment / resources needed
A Bible.

How it works
Read: John 4:1–26 – Jesus talks with a Samaritan woman

Then, in your small group, discuss the following questions:

- What does this story tell us about the woman?

- How did Jesus make contact with her?

- What illustration did Jesus use? Why did he choose this image at this time? (vv.10, 13–14)

- How can we try to be relevant to our friends' interests and needs when we talk to them about Christianity?

SESSION 8A

WHAT ABOUT THE CHURCH AND TELLING OTHERS?

SESSION 8a
WHAT ABOUT THE CHURCH AND TELLING OTHERS?

SUMMARY

AIMS OF THIS SESSION

- To encourage the group that we can all be part of the Church, and that sharing our faith should be natural and non-pressurised

- To explain that Jesus is passionate about the church; it is his only plan to share his message with the world

- To explore the idea that sharing our faith is about more than just words

NOTES

- This session is two talks combined: 'What about the Church?' and 'Why and How Should I Tell Others?' so there is a lot to get through!

- This talk should only be used on the eight week course, after 'How can I live free?'

- As this is the last session of the course, talk about your church and/or youth group and invite everyone along

- Group leaders should talk about what their small group can do next if they want to keep meeting together

- Mention details about the next Youth Alpha course, and ask the group to think about who they could invite

SESSION OVERVIEW

- Food
- Welcome
- Ice breaker game
- Worship *(if applicable)*
- Talk
    - Introduction
    - Point 1 – How do we tell others?
    - Point 2 – What about the church?
    - Conclusion
- Small groups

WELCOME

- Welcome back to Youth Alpha!

- It's great to have you here with us for the last session of the course

- Before we get going, let's start with an ice breaker game

ICE BREAKER GAME

Choose one of the following 3 options:

WATER BALLOON THROW

PREPARATION TIME 30 minutes

Quick summary
In pairs, guests play a game of catch with water balloons.

Equipment / resources needed
Lots of filled water balloons (enough for one balloon per pair, plus spares).

How it works
Take your group outside, or to a place where it is okay to spill water. Split everyone who would like to play into pairs, and ask each pair to choose one person to be 'number one' and the other to be 'number two'. All the 'ones' stand shoulder to shoulder facing the same direction. All the 'twos' stand opposite their partners, facing them toe-to-toe.
Give a water balloon to every 'number one'.
On your word, the 'ones' must pass the balloon to the 'twos'. Assuming all the pairs accomplish this successfully, both the ones and the twos take a step backwards. On 'go', the twos must now toss the balloon back to the ones. If anybody drops the balloon, or if the balloon bursts as it is caught, that pair is eliminated.
Every time a pair successfully completes a throw and a catch, they must both take a step backwards. The winning pair is the one that lasts the longest, or that manages a successful throw and catch at the greatest distance. We suggest you spend no longer than ten minutes on this game.

BODY PARTS GAME

PREPARATION TIME 0 minutes

Quick summary
People must get into pairs as quickly as possible and connect the specified body parts.

Equipment / resources needed
None.

How it works

Ask everyone to find a partner – they will remain in these pairs throughout the game. Explain that when you play the music, everyone must move around the room, away from their partner. When the music stops and you call out two body parts (eg: 'forehead … elbow'), the pairs must find each other and make those two body parts touch. The last pair to do so are out, and you should keep going until you have a winning pair. Suggestions for body parts to call out: knee/foot; nose/cheek; forehead/ shoulder; bottom/knee; shoulder/foot, etc. We suggest you spend no longer than five minutes on this game.

ABSOLUTELY POSITIVELY BINGO PREPARATION TIME **10**
minutes

Quick summary

Give each person a copy of the 'Absolutely positively bingo' worksheet: this game provides a great opportunity for the group to encourage each other.

Equipment / resources needed

You can find the 'Absolutely positively bingo' worksheet on Sheet 8a at the end of this session, or online at youthalpha.org/lgmedia
One pen per person.

How it works

Give everyone a worksheet and a pen. The aim of this exercise is to encourage each other.
Each player must try to fill their grid with the signatures of other members of the group. In order to achieve this, players must match the descriptions on the grid with one of their fellow group members, and then ask that person to sign their name in the corresponding box. All of the descriptions are positive, and each player must decide which attribute most accurately describes other group members. Each person can only sign someone's sheet once. The first person to complete their grid wins. We suggest you spend no longer than ten minutes on this game.

INTRODUCTION

- Welcome to the final session of Youth Alpha – well done, you have made it!

- Last week we looked at how we can resist evil and whether God still heals people today

- This week, we're looking at the subject of why and how we should tell others about what we believe, and all about the church

- Looking at the history of the church, it is quite clear that there is something highly infectious and contagious about the Christian faith. After all, it started with just a handful of believers huddled together in an insignificant city in the Middle East. Yet today, there are not just millions, but billions of believers across the whole world

- But sometimes, those of us who are Christians can be a bit insensitive in sharing our faith with others …

Choose one of the following 3 options:

HORTON HEARS A WHO!

PREPARATION TIME **5** minutes

Quick summary
In this clip, we see Horton trying to explain to the Mayor of Whoville that he is external to their world, and that Whoville is just a small speck. This demonstrates how difficult it can be to explain what we believe, or how we feel, to others.

Equipment / resources needed
A copy of the film Horton Hears a Who!, *Twentieth Century Fox Film Corporation, 2008. Certificate U*

▷ *Chapter 17: 0:35:09*   ☐ *Chapter 17: 0:36:08*

Projector and screen (or a TV), and a DVD player.

How to link to talk
- In this clip we see Horton trying to explain to the Mayor of Whoville that Whoville is just a speck in his world, and that he is actually an elephant!

- In a similar way, it can sometimes be tricky to find the right words to explain what we believe to others, as the idea of God being real can be as hard to grasp as the situation we see in this clip

EVANGELISM LINEBACKER

PREPARATION TIME **5** minutes

Quick summary
In this clip we meet the 'Evangelism Linebacker' – a man who goes around tackling those who won't share their faith! This is an example of how not to do evangelism.

Equipment / resources needed
To find the link for this clip, please visit youthalpha.org/lgmedia
You may want to use a projector and a screen in order to show the clip to the whole group.

How to link to talk
- There are good ways and bad ways to share our faith - I'll focus on the good ways! (And don't worry: no one is going to come and 'get you' if you don't share your faith!)

OPTION 3

SHARING THE GOOD NEWS

PREPARATION TIME **0**

minutes

Quick summary
This story shows how some people can respond negatively to Christians sharing their message.

Equipment / resources needed
None.

How it works
Two church members were going door to door, telling people about Jesus. They knocked on the door of a woman who was not happy to see them. She told them in no uncertain terms that she did not want to hear their message, and slammed the door in their faces.

To her surprise, the door did not close and, in fact, bounced back open. She tried again; she really put her pack into it, and slammed the door with the same result – it bounced back open.

Convinced these rude young people were sticking their feet in the door, she reared back to give it a slam that would teach them a lesson, when one of them said, 'Ma'am, before you do that again you need to move your cat.'

How to link to talk
- In this session we are looking at the church, and how we can share our faith

- Why should we tell other people about our faith in Jesus?

Reason 1   Because Jesus told us to. Jesus died for us, he rose again from the dead, and then he said, 'Now go and tell people about this amazing news: you can be forgiven, you can be set free. You can have eternal life.' Jesus wants to use us to tell other people.

- The word 'go' appears 1,514 times in the Bible – I didn't count them all, but somebody did! In the New Testament it appears 233 times, in Matthew's Gospel it's 54 times. Jesus says, 'Go and tell … Go and invite … Go and make disciples'

Reason 2   Because we love our friends and family. Love must be what motivates us, because we want people to discover what we have found in Jesus.

Reason 3   Because it is good news! And usually, good news travels fast. People are very good at passing on good news. We can't just keep it to ourselves – we want to tell people.

- Right from the start it is good to recognise two possible mistakes:

  - some go the religious fanatic route, trying to force their views down other people's throats
  - some go silent and never let anyone know about their faith

- The key to avoiding these two mistakes is to really care about the person you are telling, and to trust God

POINT 1 – HOW DO WE TELL OTHERS?

- We're quickly going to look at five ways we can share our faith

1. LIVE THE MESSAGE

Choose one of the following 4 options:

OPTION 1

AMAZING GRACE

PREPARATION TIME **5** minutes

Quick summary
In this clip, we see William and his followers put their faith into action. They are living the message, and living out their faith.

Equipment / resources needed
A copy of the film Amazing Grace, *Bristol Bay Productions LLC, 2006. Certificate PG.*

▷ *Chapter 6: 0:54:16*   ☐ *Chapter 6: 0:55:13*

Projector and screen (or a TV), and a DVD player.

How to link to talk
- We are called by God to love those around us, and to love the poor. We must stand up against injustice in our world

OPTION 2

STARFISH

PREPARATION TIME **0** minutes

Quick summary
This analogy about a boy saving the lives of starfish – one at a time – shows that our even our tiny acts of kindness can make a huge difference. Telling just one person about Jesus could change their life forever.

Equipment / resources needed
None.

How it works
A man was walking along a beach in Mexico when he saw a remarkable sight – the beach was covered in tens of thousands of starfish! The tide had gone out and left them stranded on the beach, dying in the heat of the sun. The man saw a young boy standing among the starfish. The boy was picking them up one at a time, running down to the sea and throwing them into the water, before going back to get another starfish and repeating the process again.
The man went up to him and said, 'Look, can't you see – there are tens of thousands of starfish out here! I don't really think what you're doing is going to make any difference.'
The young boy picked up another starfish, went down to the water's edge, threw it in the sea and said, 'I bet it made a difference for that one!'

How to link to talk

- We may not be able to change the world on our own, but we can change the lives of those around us, one by one

- We are called by God to love those around us, and to love the poor. We must stand up against injustice in our world

OPTION 3

STARFISH ANIMATION

PREPARATION TIME **5** minutes

Quick summary

This cartoon animation about a boy saving the lives of starfish – one at a time – shows that even our tiny acts of kindness can make a huge difference. Telling just one person about Jesus could change their life forever.

Equipment / resources needed

The animation can be found online at youthalpha.org/lgmedia
You may want to use a projector and a screen in order to show the animation to the whole group.

How to link to talk

- We may not be able to change the world on our own, but we can change the lives of those around us, one by one

- We are called by God to love those around us, and to love the poor. We must stand up against injustice in our world

OPTION 4

BONO'S QUOTE

PREPARATION TIME **0** minutes

Quick summary

Bono's quote shows how he puts his faith into action. He is living the message, and living out his faith.

Equipment / resources needed

None.

How it works

Bono, the lead singer of the band U2, is a big campaigner for the poor. He is a Christian, and his faith inspires him to make a difference.
He was once invited to speak at a big political gathering in Brighton, UK, and this is some of what he said:

'My name is Bono. I'm a rock-star. Excuse me if I appear a little nervous – I'm not used to appearing before crowds of less than 80,000 people. I heard the word "party" – obviously got the wrong idea!'

He went on to speak of his time working in an Ethiopian orphanage. He said:

'We lived for a month working at the orphanage. The locals knew me as "Dr Good Morning". The children called me "the girl with a beard". Don't ask! [It was because of his long hair!]

It just blew my mind; it opened my mind. On our last day at the orphanage, a man handed me his baby and said, "Take him with you." He knew in Ireland his son would live; in Ethiopia his son would die. I turned him down. In that moment, I started this journey. In that moment I became the worst thing of all: a rock-star with a cause. Except this isn't a cause – 6,500 Africans dying a day of treatable, preventable disease, dying for want of medicines you and I can get at our local chemist: that's not a cause; that's an emergency.'

(Bono, speaking at the Labour Party Conference, *29 September 2004.)*

How to link to talk

- As Christians, God calls us to live the message of Christianity. This means loving those around us, and loving the poor. We must stand up against injustice in our world

- When people know that we are Christians, they will watch how we live. Our actions should match our words

- The way that we live is sometimes more important than the words we speak (Matthew 5:13–16)

- In particular, we should be careful to always treat other people well. To be a Christian – a follower of Jesus – is to live by his example and put others first (Philippians 2:3)

- Jesus spoke a lot about loving the poor. One of the ways our faith should be noticeable to our others is through how we treat the poor and needy in our communities. Jesus didn't say this was an optional extra – it's an essential part of living the Christian life

2. TALK THE MESSAGE

- If we live like Christians it is quite likely that people will notice and want us to talk about it

- There is no formula for how to speak about your faith – the important thing is to tell your story and be natural. Never use force – very few people have ever come to faith through a heated argument!

- When we talk about what we believe, people may well have some very good questions to ask us. What about science – doesn't that disprove Christianity? What about suffering? What about other religions?

- We should take these questions seriously (if the person is asking seriously) and try to answer, either right then, or later, when we've had a chance to talk to another Christian about it or look it up somewhere (2 Corinthians 5:11)

- If you don't know the answer, don't worry, and don't pretend you do! Just be willing to go away and find out

3. PRESENT THE MESSAGE

- One of the best ways of sharing your faith is to simply say, 'Come and see!'

- The good news is that we do not all have to be great preachers!

- We are all called to be witnesses. A witness is someone who tells of what they have seen or experienced. Just tell people about your experience of God

- It can also be effective to take friends to hear the truth as presented by someone (or a group) who are especially good at explaining the faith (John 1:39–42)

4. EMPOWER THE MESSAGE

- Point four is 'empower the message': in the New Testament God used miracles to back up the message (Acts 3)

- God still does miracles today, and we shouldn't be afraid to ask him to show his power to people

You may like to include this optional extra, but it is not essential:

OPTIONAL EXTRA – GOING DEEPER

'EXPERIENCING GOD'S POWER' TESTIMONY

If you have anyone on your team who came to faith through experiencing the power of God, you could ask them to share their story now

---

5. PRAY THE MESSAGE

- Last, but definitely not least (it's actually the most important point) – pray the message

- Prayer is the power behind any attempt to tell people the good about Jesus

- If we haven't been praying, then we shouldn't expect to see anything happen

- We can pray that people's eyes would be opened to the truth about God. It says in 2 Corinthians 4:4 that the 'god of this age' (the devil) has blinded people so that they cannot see God. We need to pray that they can be set free from that blindness

- We can pray that God would give us boldness to talk about our faith (Acts 4:29–31)

You may like to include this optional extra, but it is not essential:

- And if we are sharing our faith, then lives will be changed, and the church will grow

POINT 2 – WHAT ABOUT THE CHURCH?

- So what is church all about?

Choose one of the following 3 options:

OPTION 1

VOX POPS: 'WHAT IS CHURCH?' PREPARATION TIME 5
minutes

Quick summary
Show the group a video in which members of the public share their views on the church. The purpose of this is to give the group an idea of what others think about this topic. The question being asked is, 'What is the first thing you think of when I say the word "church"?'

Equipment / resources needed
*The vox pops video can be found online at youthalpha.org/lgmedia
You may want to use a projector and a screen in order to show the video to the whole group.*

Suggested tip
If you have time, you could even make your own video showing the public's views on this topic.

How to link to talk
- Many people think of church as being mind-numbingly boring and totally pointless

MR BEAN

PREPARATION TIME 5

minutes

Quick summary
In this clip, we see Mr Bean going to church. This clip perpetuates common misconceptions about the church.

Equipment / resources needed
A copy of the film Mr Bean Volume 1, *Tiger Television Ltd, 1990. Certificate U.*

▷ *Chapter 3: 0:21:22*   ☐ *Chapter 3: 0:23:28*

Projector and screen (or a TV), and a DVD player.

How to link to talk
- Many people think of church as being mind-numbingly boring and totally pointless

ALL TIED TOGETHER

PREPARATION TIME 0

minutes

Quick summary
Each person in the group holds on to the same piece of string, demonstrating that if everyone is connected, they are able to support each other.

Equipment / resources needed
A very big ball of string.
Scissors.

How it works
Ask everyone to stand in a circle (do not join in yourself; you should remain outside the circle). If there are more than ten or fifteen people, it may be better to divide into two groups. Give one person a big ball of string, and ask them to pass the ball to someone across the circle while still holding on to the end of the string. This person should also hold on to the string (so it is pulled taut) and then pass the ball on to someone else. The idea is that in the end everyone should be holding on to part of the string, creating a sort of spider web in the middle. Get everyone to hold on tightly and then lean back so that everyone is relying on and is supported by all the others in the group.
Now use a pair of scissors to cut one strand of the web. Someone will fall away starting a chain reaction.

How to link to talk
- The church is an interconnected group of people, united by their relationship with God and with one another

- It can often seem that what is important to the church is totally different to what is important to us

- The question is, what is the church? Is it just another club? Just a type of building? Just somewhere to waste a couple of hours on a Sunday morning? Or is it much, much more?

- The New Testament is packed full of images of what the church is like. Just as we had five ways to share our faith, I'm now going to quickly look at five images that I think can really help us to understand what the church is

1. THE PEOPLE OF GOD

- When we hear the word church, we often think of a building, don't we? The Bible tells us that the actual 'church' is the people of God. It is people that make the church of Jesus Christ, not buildings. The buildings that we refer to as 'churches' are just special places where the 'church' (the people of God) meet together

- Being a Christian is about having a relationship with God, but it is also about having relationships with other people

- Today the church is huge – it consists of over 2 billion people, which is a third of the world's population

- We become part of the church by new birth through our relationship with Jesus – just like we talked about earlier in the course. The Bible says we have been 'baptised into Christ Jesus' (Romans 6:1–4). We become part of Jesus – so as he died, we have now also died, and as he rose into new life, we do too. We are now living new lives with Jesus! Pretty cool!

- So the church is the people of God – it's a great idea to join a church, to be part of a Christian youth group and to build our relationships with each other as the people of God

2. THE FAMILY OF GOD

- 1 John 5:1 says: 'Everyone who believes that Jesus is the Christ is born of God, and everyone who loves the father loves his child as well'

- Have you heard the saying, 'You can choose your friends but you can't choose your family'? Have a look around the room – these are your new brothers and sisters! That's possibly a strange thought!

- Sometimes family members argue, but they are still family. It's the same in the church. Over the years, different parts of the church (denominations) have argued sometimes about what the Bible really says about certain things, or about how we live out our faith. It's a real shame, as it can often put people off Jesus, but we are still family

- Jesus' prayer before he died was that we would all be one – that we would all be united, unified (John 17:11)

- That's actually one of the cool things about this course – just as we are running it here, so there are thousands of other groups all over the world doing the same thing: Roman Catholic, Baptist, Anglican, Pentecostal and Russian Orthodox churches as well as schools, youth clubs and many others. We are all united together. We are family.

Choose one of the following 2 options:

THE NUTTY PROFESSOR

PREPARATION TIME **5** minutes

Quick summary
This clip shows the Klumps farting while they're having dinner together.

Equipment / resources needed
A copy of the film The Nutty Professor, *Universal Studios, 1996. Certificate 12.*

▶ *Chapter 2: 0:11:04*   ☐ *Chapter 2: 0:15:31*

Projector and screen (or a TV), and a DVD player.

How to link to talk
- The church is meant to be a family. Not necessarily a family like this one, but a family nonetheless

COALS IN A FIRE

PREPARATION TIME **0** minutes

Quick summary
This analogy shows the importance of getting involved with church in order to keep our faith burning all the time.

Equipment / resources needed
None.

How it works
A young man was really struggling with his Christianity. He had come to faith in Christ, but found himself drifting away from the church and from God. He had lots of doubts and lots of difficulties and was starting to lose his faith. He went to see an older man to get some advice. They sat down by a big fireplace and started to chat about life.

The young man explained how he was feeling. The older man didn't say anything; instead, he stood up, went over to the fire and picked up the tongs. He took a red-hot coal out of the fire, and he put it on the ground in front of the fireplace. As the young man talked, he watched the coal to go from red-hot to black, dark, and cold.

The old man took the tongs again and put the coal back in the fire. Within a few minutes the coal was red-hot again. He didn't need to say anything. The young man left knowing exactly why his faith had gone a bit cold.

How to link to talk

- It's the same with our Christian lives. If we get involved with church, our faith can stay 'hot' for Jesus. However, if we don't connect to other Christians we can get discouraged and our faith can get cold

- So we need each other

3. THE BODY OF CHRIST

- 1 Corinthians 12: 27 says: 'Now you are the body of Christ, and each one of you is a part of it'

- That's the next image of the church – the body of Christ

Choose one of the following 4 options:

OPTION 1

GLADIATOR

PREPARATION TIME **5** minutes

Quick summary
In this clip we see the gladiators working as a team as they face their attackers in the arena.

NB: WARNING – contains strong bloody violence.

Equipment / resources needed
A copy of the film Gladiator, *DreamWorks LLC and Universal Studios, 2000. Certificate 15.*

▷ *Chapter 15: 1:19:10*   ☐ *Chapter 15: 1:25:07*

Projector and screen (or a TV), and a DVD player.

How to link to talk
- In that clip Maximus says, 'Whatever comes out of there, we're better off facing it together.' They work together as a team

- The church is the body of Christ – Jesus' physical body on earth – and we must all work together too

HONDA ADVERT

Quick summary
Just like the church body must work together, so this Honda advert shows how all the different parts of a car need to work in unison in order to achieve anything.

Equipment / resources needed
To find the link for this clip, please visit youthalpha.org/lgmedia
You may want to use a projector and a screen in order to show the clip to the whole group.

How to link to talk
- The church is the body of Christ – Jesus' physical body on earth – and we must all work together

'I WANNA BE YOUR HANDS!'

Quick summary
A messy game where one person becomes another person's 'arms' while helping them to do all kinds of activities! This demonstrates the importance of team work in the church.

Equipment / resources needed
Two or three bin bags/bin liners (to wear over clothes for protection).
Food to eat.
Two or three toothbrushes.
Toothpaste.
Two or three cups of water.
Two or three cloths.
Two or three blindfolds.
Baby wipes/towels to clean up with.

How it works
Ask for some volunteers, enough to make between one and three pairs of people. Ask one person from each pair to stand with their hands behind their back, wearing some sort of covering to protect their clothes (eg, a bin bag). The second person, who must wear a blindfold, should stand behind the first volunteer, and put their arms through the arms of their partner. It should look as though the second volunteer's arms belong to the person standing in front of them. The blindfolded volunteer is now the 'hands' of their partner, and will be instructed to carry out various tasks such as:

- *Feeding them (messy food is the best!)*
- *Brushing their teeth*
- *Giving them a drink*
- *Washing their face*

We suggest you spend no longer than five minutes on this game.

How to link to talk

- The church is the body of Christ – Jesus' physical body on earth – and we must all work together

TEAM WORK ACTIVITY

PREPARATION TIME **10** minutes

Quick summary

The group must work together to perform a simple task, demonstrating the importance of team work in the church.

Equipment / resources needed

One can of mandarin oranges (or another type of canned fruit).
One can opener.
One spoon.
One copy of the 'Roles and instructions' worksheet (can be found on Sheet 9a at the end of this session, or online at youthalpha.org/lgmedia).

How it works

Before the session begin you should:

- *Hide a can of fruit somewhere near a window*
- *Hide a can opener near the door*
- *Hide a spoon near a light switch*

Cut out the role descriptions from the 'Roles and instructions' worksheet, which you can find on Sheet 9a at the end of this session, or online at youthalpha.org/lgmedia

The items should be out of sight but not difficult to find. If other locations are more convenient then adapt the following instructions to fit.

Ask for eight volunteers to take part in this game. (If there are less than eight, the roles of B and G; C and H; D and E may be combined with only slight adaptation.) The key player is the speaker. It is essential that you choose someone who is an imaginative thinker and good leader. He or she needs to try and identify which tasks everyone else in the team can and cannot do and give directions accordingly.

Explain that the object of the game is to give the leader (choose someone to play this role) a spoonful of their favourite snack. The leader will need help achieving this, as their hands should be held behind their back throughout the game.

Each player needs to be given a file card with their instructions, which they should read and then put away without showing anyone else.

Tell the group not to bend the rules by gesturing or muttering. Set the game in motion and do not interrupt it again unless the participants are struggling so badly that they are giving up hope.

How to link to talk

- The church is the body of Christ – Jesus' physical body on earth – and we must all work together

- Just like different parts of the body have different roles, we all have different gifts from God, therefore we all have a different part to play. Together we form the body of Christ, united by the Holy Spirit

- The Bible uses this example: 'The eye cannot say to the hand, "I don't need you!" And the head cannot say to the feet, "I don't need you!" ' (1 Corinthians 12:21) – we all need each other. We can't do it alone. Similarly, we shouldn't feel envious of other people's gifts, because we all have a different role to do

- We can ask God to show us our gifts so we can play our part in the body of Christ

4. A HOLY TEMPLE

- Ephesians 2:19–22 says: 'Consequently, you are no longer foreigners and aliens, but fellow-citizens with God's people and members of God's household, built on the foundation of the apostles and prophets, with Christ Jesus himself as the chief cornerstone. In him the whole building is joined together and rises to become a holy temple in the Lord. And in him you too are being built together to become a dwelling in which God lives by his Spirit'

- God lives in us! That is his dwelling place now, today. Just as in the Old Testament God lived in a physical temple, a building; so he now lives in his church, his people. The church building is just where we happen to meet up

- The Bible says that our bodies are the temple of the Holy Spirit, and Jesus is the cornerstone of that temple

5. THE BRIDE OF CHRIST

- The last image we'll look at is that of the bride of Christ

- Ephesians 5:25 and 32 says: 'Husbands, love your wives, just as Christ loved the church and gave himself up for her to make her holy, cleansing her by the washing with water through the word, and to present her to himself as a radiant church, without stain or wrinkle or any other blemish, but holy and blameless … This is a profound mystery – but I'm talking about Christ and the church'

- The church is the bride of Christ! That's you and me. Jesus gave his life for his bride, for us, so that he can be united with us forever

- Our response should be to love him, to worship him, and to want to live holy lives for him

CONCLUSION

- Our lives should always speak of what God has done for us. Sometimes we will need to say the words, but often it is how we live and how we love others that says more

- We must always remember that God calls us to love the poor, broken people of this world

- The church is about people: people in relationship with Jesus, people working together, people looking after one another, people serving and sharing good news with others

- Let's pray

QUICK PRAYER TO CLOSE

PREPARATION TIME **0** minutes

Quick summary
Pray to end your session.

Equipment / resources needed
None.

How it works
- I am just going to say a short prayer to close

- Lord, we thank you that we can all be part of your church. Thank you so much that you make us part of your family. Please help us to share this good news with those around us. In Jesus' name, Amen

How to link to talk
- Now we're going to have a quick break and then go into our small groups

- Thanks so much for coming to Youth Alpha! It's been great having you as part of this course. We'd love to keep seeing you, so stay in touch

- Do feel free to bring your friends along to our next course, which starts *[insert dates]*

You may want to take a moment to invite the group to a future youth meeting or to a church service with you.

SESSION 8a
WHAT ABOUT THE CHURCH AND TELLING OTHERS?

SMALL GROUP DISCUSSION QUESTIONS

[These can be combined at the end of the talk or interspersed after each teaching point. You can find an additional copy of this sheet online at youthalpha.org/lgmedia]

POINT 1 – HOW DO WE TELL OTHERS?

- How do you feel about the idea that we should all share our faith because it is good news?

- How do you feel about Jesus' message that we should love the poor and needy among us?

- What do you think should be the main thing that marks those who are Christians apart from those who aren't?

- How can we show our faith to others without getting in their faces?

- Has anyone told a friend about Youth Alpha?

- How do you feel about the idea of praying for your friends/family to become Christians?

POINT 2 – WHAT ABOUT THE CHURCH?

- How do you feel about being part of:

    - the people of God?

    - the family of God?

    - Jesus' body on earth?

    - a holy temple (your body is a temple of the Holy Spirit!)

    - Jesus' bride?

- Does any of this change your view of what church is?

GENERAL DISCUSSION POINTS

- Can you summarise your experience on Youth Alpha?

- Has your view of the church changed over the last few weeks?

- Do you want to continue meeting up as a group, and/or going to church?

- Is there anything that you would like prayer for?

You may like to close by praying together as a group.

SHEET 8a
ABSOLUTELY POSITIVELY
BINGO WORKSHEET

Get a different person to sign their name in each square of your grid. Choose someone who has the quality described in that square – and tell them that they have it! The first person to fill every square is the winner.

Welcoming person	Natural leader	Amazing footballer	Inspiring person
Kind person	Thoughtful	Good at praying	Great actor
Great singer	Dresses with style	Incredible eyes	Incredible hair
Always encouraging	Amazing dancer	Generous person	Humble person
Very friendly	Great cook	Good at sports	Best smile

SHEET 9a
TEAM WORK ACTIVITY

ROLES AND INSTRUCTIONS WORKSHEET

Cut out these roles and ensure that each member of every group is given one before the game starts.

✂ –

A. You are the speaker. You may talk as much as you like, but you may not move.

✂ –

B. The only words you may use are, 'Yes', 'No', 'I know' and 'I don't know'. You may not move. The can of fruit is hidden near the window.

✂ –

C. The only words you may use are, 'Yes', 'No', 'I know' and 'I don't know'. You may not move. The can opener is hidden near the door.

✂ –

D. The only words you may use are, 'Yes', 'No', 'I know' and 'I don't know'. You may not move. The spoon is hidden near the light switch.

✂ –

E. The only words you may use are, 'Yes', 'No', 'I know' and 'I don't know'. You may move, but only when you are absolutely sure where the can of fruit, the can opener and the spoon are. You are allowed to touch and carry them, but you must not take them near the leader.

✂ –

F. The only words you may use are, 'Yes', 'No', 'I know' and 'I don't know'. You may only move if you have the can of fruit in your hand. You are not allowed to touch anything else that contains metal.

✂ –

G. The only words you may use are, 'Yes', 'No', 'I know' and 'I don't know'. You may only move if you have the can opener in your hand. You are not allowed to touch anything else that contains metal.

✂ –

H. The only words you may use are, 'Yes', 'No', 'I know' and 'I don't know'. You may only move if you have the spoon in your hand. You are not allowed to touch anything else that contains metal.

SESSION 9

DOES GOD HEAL TODAY?

SESSION 9
DOES GOD HEAL TODAY?

SUMMARY

AIMS OF THIS SESSION

- To encourage the group to realise that God does perform miracles today

- To explain the idea of the kingdom of God and the reasons why we don't always see answers to prayer

- To explore how we can pray for healing

NOTES

- Before the session begins, take some time as a team to ask God for 'words of knowledge' about healing that you can share at the end of the talk

- In your small groups, give people a chance to respond to these words, and pray (by the laying on of hands) as a group for anyone who wants it

- As you are drawing near the end of the course, begin to talk about church and what will happen at the end of the course (perhaps invite the group along to a specific service)

SESSION OVERVIEW

- Food
- Welcome
- Ice breaker game
- Worship *(if applicable)*
- Talk
  - Introduction
  - Point 1 – Healing in the Bible
  - Point 2 – Healing in history
  - Point 3 – How do we pray for healing?
  - Conclusion
- Small groups including prayer ministry time

WELCOME

- Welcome back to Youth Alpha!

- It's great to have you here with us

- Before we get going, let's start with an ice breaker game

ICE BREAKER GAME

Choose one of the following 2 options:

TAIL GRAB GAME

PREPARATION TIME **0** minutes

Quick summary
Teams of 'snakes' try to catch each other's 'tails'.

Equipment / resources needed
One handkerchief or cloth per team (minimum of two teams).

How it works
Get everyone into groups of between six and ten people. Each group forms a 'snake' by having each team member put their hands on the hips of the person in front. The person at the end of the snake should have a handkerchief or a strip of cloth tucked into their belt/pocket, the end of which should be visible and grab-able. This is the snake's tail. The object of the game is to grab the tails of the other snakes without losing your own. The person at the front of the snake (the 'head') is the only person allowed to grab other snakes' tails, and the snakes must remain complete and unbroken at all times. Give the command, 'Go!' and watch the mayhem! We suggest you spend no longer than five minutes on this game.

SHAVING FOAM GAME

PREPARATION TIME **5** minutes

Quick summary
Teams must attempt to throw popcorn onto someone's shaving foam-covered face!

Equipment / resources needed
One can of shaving foam.
Two bags of popcorn/cheese puffs/crisps.
Baby wipes/towels to clean up.

How it works
Split the group into two teams and ask for two volunteers from each. In the teams, one volunteer should cover the other's face in shaving foam (we suggest you use non-perfumed foam). Once this is done, the rest of the team must stand behind a line (about two metres away from the

foam-covered volunteer), and try to throw popcorn or cheese puffs at the volunteer's face. Give them one minute to see how many pieces they can stick to the foam. The team with the most wins!

You may like to include this optional extra, but it is not essential:

OPTIONAL EXTRA   PREPARATION TIME (5)
                                                                        minutes

SPORTS BLOOPERS

Quick summary
Show a 'bloopers' clip of gymnastic accidents or spectacular skiing wipeouts (nothing too serious, though). You may want to follow the link below in order to show the suggested clip.

Equipment / resources needed
To find the link for this clip, please visit youthalpha.org/lgmedia
Alternatively, you may prefer to search online for a different clip of amusing sporting accidents to show. You may want to use a projector and a screen in order to show the clip to the whole group.

How to link to talk
• I'll tell you why I showed you these in a minute – it ties in with today's topic!

INTRODUCTION

- Welcome to week nine of Youth Alpha

- Last time we looked at why and how we should share our faith with others

- This week we're looking at the subject of healing – does God still perform miracles today?

Choose one of the following 4 options:

OPTION 1

VOX POPS: PREPARATION TIME (5)
'DOES GOD HEAL TODAY?'   minutes

Quick summary
Show the group a video in which members of the public share their views on the question 'Does God heal today?' The purpose of this is to show the many different views and opinions that people have on the subject of healing.

Equipment / resources needed
The vox pops video can be found online at youthalpha.org/lgmedia
You may want to use a projector and a screen in order to show the film to the whole group.

How to link to talk
- So in this session, we're looking at the question 'Does God heal today?'

'HEALING' TESTIMONY

Share a story (your own, or perhaps the story of someone else who is also running the course) about a time in your life when God healed you.

HEALING IN THE GROCERY STORE

PREPARATION TIME **5** minutes

Quick summary
This is an amazing story about God's healing power, as told by Chad Dedmon from Jesus Culture in California. In this video, Chad tells of how he felt God telling him to pray for people as he was shopping, and how God healed people as he prayed over the shop's loud speaker!

Equipment / resources needed
To find the link for this clip, please visit youthalpha.org/lgmedia
You may want to use a projector and a screen in order to show the film to the whole group.

How to link to talk
- So in this session, we're looking at the question 'Does God heal today?'

AJAY GOHILL

PREPARATION TIME **0** minutes

Quick summary
This true story tells of a man who was healed after crying out to God.

Equipment / resources needed
None.

How it works
Ajay Gohill was born in Kenya but moved to England in 1971. He was brought up as a Hindu and worked in the family business as a newsagent in Neasden. At the age of twenty-one he contracted

Erythrodermic Psoriasis, a chronic skin disease. His weight dropped from 11.5 [73 kg] to 7.5 stone [47.5 kg]. He was treated all over the world – in the United States, Germany, Switzerland and Israel, as well as all over England. He said that he spent eighty per cent of his earnings on trying to find a cure and he took strong drugs which affected his liver. Eventually, he had to give up his job. The disease covered his body from head to toe; he was so horrible to look at, he couldn't even wear a t-shirt. He lost all his friends, and his wife and son left him. He wanted to die. One October, Ajay was lying in his hospital bed. He cried out, 'God if you are watching, let me die – I am sorry if I have done something wrong.' From his locker he pulled out a Good News Bible. He opened it at random and read Psalm 38:

'O Lord, don't punish me in your anger! You have wounded me with your arrows; you have struck me down. Because of your anger, I am in great pain; my whole body is diseased because of my sins. I am drowning in the flood of my sins; they are a burden too heavy to bear. Because I have been foolish, my sores stink and rot. I am bowed down, I am crushed; I mourn all day long. I am burning with fever and I am near to death. I am worn out and utterly crushed; my heart is troubled and I groan with pain. O Lord, you know what I long for; you hear all my groans. My heart is pounding, my strength is gone, and my eyes have lost their brightness. My friends and neighbours will not come near me, because of my sores; even my family keeps away from me … Do not abandon me, O God; do not stay away from me, my God! Help me now, O Lord my saviour!' (Psalm 38:1–11, 21–22 Good News Bible).

Each and every verse seemed relevant to him. He prayed for God to heal him, and then he fell into a deep sleep. When he awoke the next morning 'everything looked new'. He went to relax in the bath and when he looked at the water, he saw his skin had lifted off his body and was floating. He called in the nurses and told them that God was healing him: all of his skin was new, like a baby's. He was totally healed and has since been reunited with his son. Ajay says that the inner healing that has taken place in his life is even greater than the physical healing. He says, 'Every day I live for Jesus. I am his servant today.'

How to link to talk
- So do you believe that God can heal people today?

- People today believe all sorts of things about healing. Some believe that illnesses can only be healed through doctors, hospitals and medicine. Others believe in 'faith healing' through things like crystals, Chinese medicines or other spiritual paths. Some, of course, believe that there is no such thing as supernatural healing. And others, such as myself, believe that God can heal us through prayer

- Let's look at what the Bible says

POINT 1 – HEALING IN THE BIBLE

- As I read the Bible, especially the Gospels, I see a God who heals. Actually it's quite hard to read about Jesus' ministry without talking about healing. In fact, twenty-five percent of the Gospels are about healing!

- God promised to heal his people in the Old Testament. He says, 'I am the God who heals you' (Exodus 15:26). It is his nature to heal

- Occasionally we see God healing people in the Old Testament, but it wasn't a regular thing. In the book of 2 Kings, for example, Naaman, the military commander, is healed of leprosy. However, in the Old Testament we only get glimpses of God's kingdom breaking through onto earth

- In the New Testament, we read about Jesus' teaching. He said that 'the kingdom of God is near'. He showed the closeness of God's kingdom by performing miracles such as healing. Healing is possible because there is no sickness in heaven

You may like to include this optional extra, but it is not essential:

OPTIONAL EXTRA – GOING DEEPER   PREPARATION TIME
minutes

THE KINGDOM OF GOD

Quick summary
Using the 'Now and not yet' diagram, explain that healing today is made possible through God's kingdom on earth.

Equipment / resources needed
You can find the 'Now and not yet' diagram on Sheet 7 at the end of this session, or online at youthalpha.org/lgmedia
You may want to use a projector and screen to show the diagram to the whole group.

How it works
- The kingdom of God is the key to understanding our experience of healing in the world today

- The kingdom of God is both 'now' and 'not yet'. That means that when Jesus came to earth, he brought the kingdom of God. The healings that he did were a sign that the kingdom of God had arrived, but it hasn't yet arrived in its completeness

- That will only happen when Jesus comes again. Today, we live in the in-between time. The kingdom is here, but not yet completely

- When healing occurs, we see signs that the kingdom of God is here

- Where healing doesn't happen we are reminded that we still have to wait to see the kingdom come fully

How to link to talk
- This shows the importance of knowledge about the kingdom of God in our understanding of healing

Choose one of the following 2 options:

THE LION, THE WITCH AND THE WARDROBE

PREPARATION TIME **5** minutes

Quick summary
In this clip, Aslan is bringing in the start of summer and the snow melts away. Use this to demonstrate to the group the concept of God's kingdom: it is both 'now' (summer) and 'not yet' (winter). In terms of heaven on earth, we live in the season of spring today.

Equipment / resources needed
A copy of the film The Chronicles of Narnia: The Lion, the Witch and the Wardrobe *(episode 4), BBC, 1988. Certificate U.*

▷ *Chapter 13: 1:13:21*   ☐ *Chapter 13: 1:16:17*

Projector and screen (or a TV), and a DVD player.

How to link to talk
- Aslan represents Jesus. In this clip, it is Aslan's power that's melting the snow and turning winter to summer. The kingdom of heaven is represented by the warmth of summer, and the earth is represented by the cold of winter. In the Old Testament, it was like the earth was covered in snow

- Occasionally, the sun would shine and the earth would warm up (when God performed healings), but the snow never melted

- When Jesus came (like Aslan), he brought sunshine with him and it began to melt the snow

- Today, we live in the 'spring' – it isn't quite summer, so there are warm days and cold days. Not every person we pray for will get healed, but some will. Warm days give us a foretaste of what heaven will be like

- One day, Jesus will return again and bring heaven in its fullness on earth

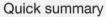

OPTION 2

WINTER/SUMMER

PREPARATION TIME **0** minutes

Quick summary

Use this seasonal analogy to demonstrate to the group the concept of God's kingdom: it is both 'now' (summer) and 'not yet' (winter). In terms of heaven on earth, today we live in the season of spring.

Equipment / resources needed
None.

How it works

In some ways it's a bit like the seasons. The kingdom of heaven is represented by the warmth of summer, and the earth is represented by the cold of winter. In the Old Testament, the earth was covered in snow. Occasionally, the sun would shine and the earth would warm up (when God performed healings), but the snow never melted. When Jesus came, he brought sunshine with him and it began to melt the snow. Today, we live in the 'spring' – it isn't quite summer, so there are warm days *and* cold days. Not every person we pray for will get healed, but some will. Warm days give us a foretaste of what heaven will be like. One day, Jesus will return again and bring heaven in its fullness on earth.

How to link to talk
- This shows the importance of knowledge about the kingdom of God in our understanding of healing

- Jesus sent his disciples out to pray for healing. He gave them authority to heal the sick in his name (the twelve disciples – Matthew 9:35–10:8; the seventy-two disciples – Luke 10:1–20). He also said that we would see greater things than he had (John 14:12). Jesus saw the sick healed and the dead raised – just imagine what we will see!

- As Jesus went up to heaven, he commissioned his disciples – and that includes all of us – to go and do as he did (Matthew 28:16–20)

- That's exactly what the disciples did. The early church went out and preached the gospel and healed the sick. They believed that the two went side by side. We should believe the same today

- That's why the book of Acts, which is the story of the first church, is called 'Acts' rather than 'Theories' – because the disciples went out and acted upon Jesus' instructions

POINT 2 – HEALING IN HISTORY

- So Jesus taught about healing and he went out and healed people. As a result, even the earliest churches in the Bible believed healing was possible and they acted on it. But it didn't stop there – the church has been praying for the sick and seeing God perform miracles ever since

- Throughout the history of the Christian church there have been examples of healing and miracles. It didn't just stop with the disciples in the early church

- Here's an example:

THE STORY OF INNOCENTIUS   PREPARATION TIME   **0**
minutes

Quick summary
This true story of a man named Innocentius demonstrates the power of prayer in healing.

Equipment / resources needed
None.

How it works
[Read this story with as much drama and horror as possible.]

St Augustine of Hippo (a place, not the animal), one of the greatest theologians of the first five centuries of the church, showed that he wasn't squeamish by writing this story down for us.
St Augustine was staying with a man called Innocentius, who was being treated by doctors for 'fistulae' of which he had 'a large number intricately seated in his rectum'! He had undergone one very painful operation. It was not thought that he would survive another.
St Augustine and some others prayed for him, and as they did so, Innocentius was thrown to the floor as if someone had hurled him violently to earth. He groaned and sobbed and his whole body shook so much that he couldn't talk.
The dreaded day of the operation came. 'The surgeons arrived ... the frightful instruments [were] produced ... the part [was] bared; the surgeon ... with knife in hand, eagerly look[ed] for the sinus that [had] to be cut. He searche[d] for it with his eyes; he [felt] for it with his finger' but he found a perfectly healed wound.
God had healed Innocentius, much to his relief!

How to link to talk
- As time went on, the Church set up hospitals and other institutions to help the sick get better, but God was, and is, still in the business of intervening miraculously too. And we can ask him to do so!

POINT 3 – HOW DO WE PRAY FOR HEALING?

- How do we do it? Well, our job is to pray – it is God who does the healing

- We need to check our motive – Jesus healed people because he loved them. It is important that we care and want the best for anyone we pray for

- Prayers for healing should be simple, not long and complicated. There are no special prayers to pray – remember, it is God's power, not our words, that heals

- We can ask God for 'words of knowledge' to help us pray for healing. This is when the Holy Spirit guides us in how to pray by giving us a 'word' about a medical condition we wouldn't have known about otherwise. This could be:

    - a picture in our minds

    - a sympathy pain (we feel pain in our bodies that isn't normal for us)

    - a strong feeling

    - words in our minds

    - words that we speak

- There is no set way in which to pray for healing – Jesus did it in different ways. But I'll give you a helpful model to follow

- We usually recommend that you pray with someone of the same gender as you, and in groups of either two or three

- When we pray we should:

    - ask where it hurts, how long it has hurt, and why it hurts

    - pray that God would heal in the name of Jesus – we normally place our hands on the person's shoulder when we pray

    - ask that the Holy Spirit would heal the person

    - continue to be open to more guidance from the Holy Spirit

- Afterwards we should:

    - ask the person how they feel

    - make sure that they are happy and that they understand all that has happened

- We should not give up if nothing seems to happen or if the person is only partially healed. Jesus once prayed for a blind man and asked him, 'Do you see anything?' The man said, 'I see people, but they look like trees walking around.' So Jesus prayed a second time, and this time the man's eyes were opened and his sight was restored completely (Mark 8:24). If Jesus sometimes had to pray twice, we shouldn't feel discouraged at having to do so!

CONCLUSION

- In a moment, we're going to go into our small groups and I want to encourage you to have a go at praying for healing for anyone in your group who might want it. Don't be embarrassed to ask for prayer

- In conclusion: as Christians, we should pray for the sick. A guy called John Wimber, someone whom God used a lot in the area of healing, used to say, 'When we pray for no one, no one gets healed. But when we pray for lots of people, some of them are healed.' So it is important to pray

- We should remember that doctors don't have a 100 per cent success rate, but they don't stop being doctors and they don't stop trying. It's the same for us

- All of us can pray for healing. Some people seem to have specialist gifts in healing, like others do in evangelism, but we are all still called to pray

- God can heal our bodies, and he can also heal other types of hurts too, whether it's emotional pain or any other kind of pain. Nothing is impossible for God

- One day, we will live in heaven with Jesus and there will be no sickness. Until then, he calls us to pray and ask him to heal the sick

- Sometimes, the kingdom of heaven will break through and we will see amazing things before our very eyes

QUICK PRAYER TO CLOSE

PREPARATION TIME **0** minutes

Quick summary
Pray to end your talk.

Equipment / resources needed
None.

How it works
- I am just going to say a short prayer to close

- Father, we thank you so much that you are a God who heals today, and Lord, we pray tonight that once again you will come by your Spirit among us and heal people here. In Jesus' name, Amen

How to link to talk
[If you prayed as a team before the session began and felt you received some words of knowledge for the group, share them before you break into small groups.]

- Now we're going to have a quick break then go into our small groups

- Thanks so much for coming to Youth Alpha today – see you next time!

SESSION 9
DOES GOD HEAL TODAY?
SMALL GROUP DISCUSSION QUESTIONS

If you are doing your small groups after the talk, the best thing to do would be to begin by immediately offering to pray for anyone who wants it. Ask if anyone identified with any of the words of knowledge that were read out. If so, ask them if they are happy to sit/stand in the middle of the group and let everyone place their hands on them and pray.
If there were no words of knowledge, or if no one responds, ask if anyone would like prayer for healing and then pray for them.

After that, feel free to use any of the questions below.

[These can be combined at the end of the talk or interspersed after each teaching point. You can find an additional copy of this sheet online at youthalpha.org/lgmedia]

POINT 1 – HEALING IN THE BIBLE

- What did you think about the testimony at the beginning?

- Has anyone here ever experienced anything miraculous?

- Do you believe that God can heal people today? Why/why not?

- Did you know that twenty-five per cent of the Gospels are about people getting healed by Jesus?

- Does the idea that we live in the time between Jesus's death and heaven on earth make any sense to you? Explain …

POINT 2 – HEALING IN HISTORY

- How does it make you feel to know that the early church, and the church ever since, have prayed for healing and seen miracles?

- Did you know that it was the church that set up hospitals?

POINT 3 – HOW DO WE PRAY FOR HEALING?

Before these questions, try praying for each other.

- How did you find praying for healing for each other?

- How do you feel about the idea that God sometimes gives us words of knowledge?

SHEET 7
NOW AND NOT YET
HAND OUT

CHART 1

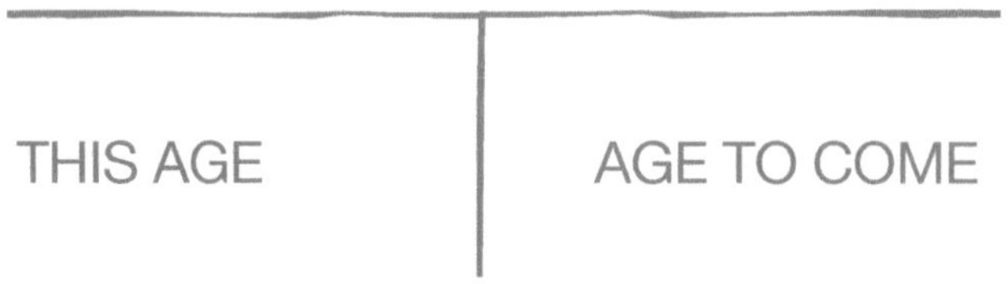

THIS AGE | AGE TO COME

CHART 2

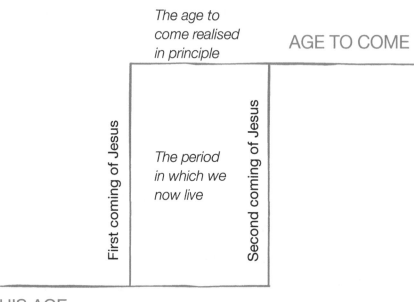

The age to come realised in principle

AGE TO COME

First coming of Jesus

The period in which we now live

Second coming of Jesus

THIS AGE

SESSION 10

WHAT ABOUT THE CHURCH?

SESSION 10
WHAT ABOUT THE CHURCH?

SUMMARY

AIMS OF THIS SESSION

- To encourage the group that we can all be part of the church

- To explain that Jesus is passionate about the church

- To explore the idea of being part of the church – what happens next?

NOTES

- As this is the last session of the course, talk about your church and/or youth group and invite everyone along

- Group leaders should talk about what their small group can do next if they want to keep meeting together

- Mention details about the next Youth Alpha course, and ask the group to think about who they could invite

SESSION OVERVIEW

- Food
- Welcome
- Ice breaker game
- Worship *(if applicable)*
- Talk
  - Introduction
  - Point 1 – The people of God
  - Point 2 – The family of God
  - Point 3 – The body of Christ
  - Point 4 – A holy temple
  - Point 5 – The bride of Christ
  - Conclusion
- Small groups

WELCOME

- Welcome back to Youth Alpha!

- It's great to have you here with us for the last session of the course

- Before we get going, let's start with an ice breaker game

ICE BREAKER GAME

Choose one of the following 3 options:

OPTION 1

WATER RELAY

PREPARATION TIME **5** minutes

Quick summary
A relay in which teams must fill an empty jug with water, using only their mouths to transport cups with water in them.

Equipment / resources needed
Two jugs per team.
Lots of water to hand for refills.
One small plastic/paper cup per person.

How it works
Split the group into two or more teams of about eight people. You will need two jugs per team, one of which should be empty, and the other filled with water (make sure you have enough water on hand to refill it if you need to).
The object of the game is to get as much water as possible out of the full jug and into the empty one. The fun part is this: the only way the teams are allowed to transfer water is in a chain: from person to person and from cup to cup. The twist is that the cups must be held in the players' mouths at all times.
Line teams up shoulder to shoulder in order to form 'chains'. The player nearest the full jug (at the start of the line-up) is the only person allowed to use their hands. They must pick up the jug and pour some water into the cup that is being held in their mouth. Then, they must tilt their head so that the water is poured out of their cup into the cup of the person next to them, who will need to crouch slightly to make sure that their cup is lower than their teammate's. This continues down the line until the last team member tips what remains of the water into the empty jug.
The team with the most water in their jug at the end of play wins.
We suggest you spend no longer than ten minutes on this game.

NB: teams may get wet!

BODY PARTS GAME

PREPARATION TIME **0** minutes

Quick summary
People must get into pairs as quickly as possible and connect the specified body parts.

Equipment / resources needed
None.

How it works
Ask everyone to find a partner – they will remain in these pairs throughout the game. Explain that when you play the music, everyone must move around the room, away from their partner. When the music stops and you call out two body parts (eg: 'forehead … elbow'), the pairs must find each other and make those two body parts touch. The last pair to do so are out, and you should keep going until you have a winning pair. Suggestions for body parts to call out: knee/foot; nose/cheek; forehead/shoulder; bottom/knee; shoulder/foot, etc. We suggest you spend no longer than five minutes on this game.

ABSOLUTELY POSITIVELY BINGO PREPARATION TIME **10** minutes

Quick summary
Give each person a copy of the 'Absolutely positively bingo' worksheet: this game provides a great opportunity for the group to encourage each other.

Equipment / resources needed
You can find the 'Absolutely positively bingo' worksheet on Sheet 8 at the end of this session, or online at youthalpha.org/lgmedia
One pen per person.

How it works
Give everyone a worksheet and a pen. The aim of this exercise is to encourage each other.
Each player must try to fill their grid with the signatures of other members of the group. In order to achieve this, players must match the descriptions on the grid with one of their fellow group members, and then ask that person to sign their name in the corresponding box. All of the descriptions are positive, and each player must decide which attribute most accurately describes other group members. Each person can only sign someone's sheet once. The first person to complete their grid wins. We suggest you spend no longer than ten minutes on this game.

INTRODUCTION

- Welcome to the final session of Youth Alpha – well done, you have made it!

- Over the last few weeks we have looked at who Jesus was and why he died for us, prayer and the Bible, the Holy Spirit, healing, evil, and guidance. For our final session we are going to look at the church

Choose one of the following 3 options:

VOX POPS: 'WHAT IS CHURCH?'   PREPARATION TIME 5 minutes

Quick summary
Show the group a video in which members of the public share their views on the church. The purpose of this is to give the group an idea of what others think about this topic. The question being asked is, 'What is the first thing you think of when I say the word "church"?'

Equipment / resources needed
The vox pops video can be found online at youthalpha.org/lgmedia
You may want to use a projector and a screen in order to show the video to the whole group.

> Suggested tip
> If you have time, you could even make your own video showing the public's views on this topic.

How to link to talk
- Many people think of church as being mind-numbingly boring and totally pointless

MR BEAN   PREPARATION TIME 5 minutes

Quick summary
In this clip, we see Mr Bean going to church. This clip perpetuates common misconceptions about the church.

Equipment / resources needed
A copy of Mr Bean Volume 1, *Tiger Television Ltd, 1990. Certificate U.*

▷ *Chapter 3: 0:21:22*   ☐ *Chapter 3: 0:23:28*

Projector and screen (or a TV), and a DVD player.

How to link to talk
- Many people think of church as being mind-numbingly boring and totally pointless

OPTION 3

ALL TIED TOGETHER

Quick summary

Each person in the group holds on to the same piece of string, demonstrating that if everyone is connected, they are able to support each other.

Equipment / resources needed

A very big ball of string.
Scissors.

How it works

Ask everyone to stand in a circle (do not join in yourself; you should remain outside the circle). If there are more than ten or fifteen people, it may be better to divide into two groups. Give one person a big ball of string, and ask them to pass the ball to someone across the circle while still holding on to the end of the string. This person should also hold on to the string (so it is pulled taut) and then pass the ball on to someone else. The idea is that in the end everyone should be holding on to part of the string, creating a sort of spider web in the middle. Get everyone to hold on tightly and then lean back so that everyone is relying on and is supported by all the others in the group. Now use a pair of scissors to cut one strand of the web. Someone will fall away starting a chain reaction.

How to link to talk

- The church is an interconnected group of people, united by their relationship with God and with one another

You may choose to use this quote to further illustrate your point:

OPTIONAL QUOTE

Abraham Lincoln (former president of the USA)

'If all the people who fell asleep in church on Sunday morning were laid out end to end … they would be a great deal more comfortable.'

(Abraham Lincoln, president of the USA 1861–1865.)

- It can often seem that what is important to the church is totally different to what is important to us

- The question is, what is the church? Is it just another club? Just a type of building? Just somewhere to waste a couple of hours on a Sunday morning? Or is it much, much more?

- The New Testament is packed full of images of what the church is like. I'm going to look at five that I think can really help us to understand what the church is

POINT 1 – THE PEOPLE OF GOD

- 1 Peter 2:9 says, 'But you are a chosen people, a royal priesthood, a holy nation, a people belonging to God, that you may declare the praises of him who called you out of darkness into his wonderful light. Once you were not a people, but now you are the people of God'

- When we think of the word 'church', we often think of a building, don't we? The Bible tells us that the actual 'church' is the people of God. It is people that make the church of Jesus Christ, not buildings. The buildings that we refer to as 'churches' are just special places where the 'church' (the people of God) meet together

- Being a Christian is about having a relationship with God, but it is also about having relationships with other people

- Today the church is huge – it consists of over 2 billion people, which is a third of the world's population

- We become part of the church by new birth through our relationship with Jesus – just like we talked about earlier in the course. The Bible says we have been 'baptised into Christ Jesus' (Romans 6:1–4). We become part of Jesus – so as he died, we have now also died, and as he rose into new life, we do too. We are now living new lives with Jesus! Pretty cool!

- So the church is the people of God – it's a great idea to join a church, to be part of a Christian youth group and to build our relationships with each other as the people of God

POINT 2 – THE FAMILY OF GOD

- 1 John 5:1 says: 'Everyone who believes that Jesus is the Christ is born of God, and everyone who loves the father loves his child as well'

- Have you heard the saying, 'You can choose your friends but you can't choose your family'? Have a look around the room – these are your new brothers and sisters! That's possibly a strange thought!

- Sometimes family members argue, but they are still family. It's the same in the church. Over the years, different parts of the church (denominations) have argued sometimes about what the Bible really says about certain things, or about how we live out our faith. It's a real shame, as it can often put people off Jesus, but we are still family

- Jesus' prayer before he died was that we would all be one – that we would all be united, unified (John 17:11)

- That's actually one of the cool things about this course – just as we are running it here, so there are thousands of other groups all over the world doing the same thing: Roman Catholic, Baptist, Anglican, Pentecostal and Russian Orthodox churches as well as schools, youth clubs and many others. We are all united together. We are family

THE NUTTY PROFESSOR

PREPARATION TIME **5** minutes

Quick summary
This clip shows the Klumps farting while they're having dinner together.

Equipment / resources needed
A copy of the film The Nutty Professor, *Universal Studios, 1996. Certificate 12.*

▷ *Chapter 2: 0:11:04* ☐ *Chapter 2: 0:15:31*

Projector and screen (or a TV), and a DVD player.

How to link to talk
- The church is meant to be a family. Not necessarily a family like this one, but a family nonetheless

COALS IN A FIRE

PREPARATION TIME **0** minutes

Quick summary
This analogy shows the importance of getting involved with church in order to keep our faith burning all the time.

Equipment / resources needed
None.

How it works
A young man was really struggling with his Christianity. He had come to faith in Christ, but found himself drifting away from the church and from God. He had lots of doubts and lots of difficulties and was starting to lose his faith. He went to see an older man to get some advice. They sat down by a big fireplace and started to chat about life.

The young man explained how he was feeling. The older man didn't say anything; instead, he stood up, went over to the fire and picked up the tongs. He took a red-hot coal out of the fire, and he put it on the ground in front of the fireplace. As the young man talked, he watched the coal go from red-hot to black, dark and cold.

The old man took the tongs again and put the coal back in the fire. Within a few minutes the coal was red-hot again. He didn't need to say anything. The young man left knowing exactly why his faith had gone a bit cold.

How to link to talk
- It's the same with our Christian lives. If we get involved with church, our faith can stay 'hot' for Jesus. If we don't connect to other Christians, however, we can get discouraged and our faith can get cold

- So we need each other

POINT 3 – THE BODY OF CHRIST

- 1 Corinthians 12: 27 says: 'Now you are the body of Christ, and each one of you is a part of it'

- That's the next image of the church – the body of Christ

Choose one of the following 4 options:

GLADIATOR

PREPARATION TIME **5** minutes

Quick summary
In this clip we see the gladiators working as a team as they face their attackers in the arena.

NB: WARNING – contains strong bloody violence.

Equipment / resources needed
A copy of the film Gladiator, *DreamWorks LLC and Universal Studios, 2000. Certificate 15.*

▷ *Chapter 15: 1:19:10*   ☐ *Chapter 15: 1:25:07*

Projector and screen (or a TV), and a DVD player.

How to link to talk
- In that clip Maximus says, 'Whatever comes out of there, we're better off facing it together.' They work as a team

  - The church is the body of Christ – Jesus' physical body on earth – and we must all work together too

HONDA ADVERT

PREPARATION TIME **5** minutes

Quick summary
Just like the church body must work together, so this Honda advert shows how all the different parts of a car need to work in unison in order to achieve anything.

Equipment / resources needed
To find the link for this clip, please visit youthalpha.org/lgmedia
You may want to use a projector and a screen in order to show the clip to the whole group.

How to link to talk
- The church is the body of Christ – Jesus' physical body on earth – and we must all work together

OPTION 3

'I WANNA BE YOUR HANDS!'

PREPARATION TIME **5** minutes

Quick summary
A messy game where one person becomes another person's 'arms' while helping them to do all kinds of activities! This demonstrates the importance of team work in the church.

Equipment / resources needed
Two or three bin bags/bin liners (to wear over clothes for protection).
Food to eat.
Two or three toothbrushes.
Toothpaste.
Two or three cups of water.
Two or three cloths.
Two or three blindfolds.
Baby wipes/towels to clean up with.

How it works
Ask for some volunteers, enough to make between one and three pairs of people. Ask one person from each pair to stand with their hands behind their back, wearing some sort of covering to protect their clothes (eg, a bin bag). The second person, who must wear a blindfold, should stand behind the first volunteer, and put their arms through the arms of their partner. It should look as though the second volunteer's arms belong to the person standing in front of them. The blindfolded volunteer is now the 'hands' of their partner, and will be instructed to carry out various tasks such as:

- *Feeding them (messy food is the best!)*
- *Brushing their teeth*
- *Giving them a drink*
- *Washing their face*

We suggest you spend no longer than five minutes on this game.

How to link to talk
- The church is the body of Christ – Jesus' physical body on earth – and we must all work together

OPTION 4

TEAM WORK ACTIVITY

PREPARATION TIME **10** minutes

Quick summary
The group must work together to perform a simple task, demonstrating the importance of team work in the church.

Equipment / resources needed
One can of mandarin oranges (or another type of canned fruit).
One can opener.
One spoon.

One copy of the 'Roles and instructions' worksheet (can be found on Sheet 9 at the end of this session, or online at youthalpha.org/lgmedia).

How it works
Before the session begin you should:

- *Hide a can of fruit somewhere near a window*
- *Hide a can opener near the door*
- *Hide a spoon near a light switch*

Cut out the role descriptions from the 'Roles and instructions' worksheet, which you can find on Sheet 9 at the end of this session, or online at youthalpha.org/lgmedia
The items should be out of sight but not difficult to find. If other locations are more convenient then adapt the following instructions to fit.
Ask for eight volunteers to take part in this game. (If there are less than eight, the roles of B and G; C and H; D and E may be combined with only slight adaptation.) The key player is the speaker. It is essential that you choose someone who is an imaginative thinker and good leader. He or she needs to try and identify which tasks everyone else in the team can and cannot do and give directions accordingly.
Explain that the object of the game is to give the leader (choose someone to play this role) a spoonful of their favourite snack. The leader will need help achieving this, as their hands should be held behind their back throughout the game.
Each player needs to be given a file card with their instructions, which they should read and then put away without showing anyone else. Tell the group not to bend the rules by gesturing or muttering. Set the game in motion and do not interrupt it again unless the participants are struggling so badly that they are giving up hope.

How to link to talk
- The church is the body of Christ – Jesus' physical body on earth – and we must all work together

- Just like different parts of the body have different roles, we all have different gifts from God, therefore we all have a different part to play. Together we form the body of Christ, united by the Holy Spirit

- The Bible uses this example: 'The eye cannot say to the hand, "I don't need you!" And the head cannot say to the feet, "I don't need you!" ' (1 Corinthians 12:21) – we all need each other. We can't do it alone. Similarly, we shouldn't feel envious of other people's gifts, because we all have a different role to do

- We can ask God to show us our gifts so we can play our part in the body of Christ

POINT 4 – A HOLY TEMPLE

You may choose to use this joke to help illustrate your point:

OPTIONAL JOKE   PREPARATION TIME 0
                                                              minutes

Quick summary
This joke raises the question about where God 'lives' in a light-hearted way.

Equipment / resources needed
None.

How it works
There was a little boy called Tommy who was very naughty. His mother despaired of him, and after trying everything she eventually thought, 'I know! I'll take him down to see the vicar – that will sort him out!' So she took young Tommy down to see the vicar. The vicar was quite a serious man. He had a great big leather desk, and he sat down Tommy opposite himself and decided to find out how much the little boy knew about God. So he asked, 'Tommy, where is God?' The little boy began to look nervous, so again the vicar said: 'Tommy, where is God?' The boy looked even more nervous. So in an even bigger voice, the vicar asked, 'Tommy, where is God?' By this time the boy was so terrified he got up and ran out of the vicar's study, out of the house and all the way home. His mother thought this was amazing, 'This has done it! This has really sorted him out!' The little boy ran in through his front door, and saw his father sitting watching TV. His father said, 'Tommy, what's the matter?' Tommy said, 'Dad, Dad, they've lost God down at the church and now they're trying to blame me for it!'

How to link to talk
- Well, I know it's a bad joke, but it's a good question – where is God? Where does God live? What is the answer?

- Ephesians 2:19-22 says: 'Consequently, you are no longer foreigners and aliens, but fellow-citizens with God's people and members of God's household, built on the foundation of the apostles and prophets, with Christ Jesus himself as the chief cornerstone. In him the whole building is joined together and rises to become a holy temple in the Lord. And in him you too are being built together to become a dwelling in which God lives by his Spirit'

- God lives in us! That is his dwelling place now, today. Just as in the Old Testament God lived in a physical temple, a building; so he now lives in his church, his people. The church building is just where we happen to meet up

- The Bible says that our bodies are the temple of the Holy Spirit (1 Corinthians 6:19), and Jesus is the cornerstone of that temple

POINT 5 – THE BRIDE OF CHRIST

- The last image we'll look at is that of the bride of Christ

Choose one of the following 4 options:

LOVE ACTUALLY

PREPARATION TIME **5** minutes

Quick summary
In this clip, we see a couple get married while their friends celebrate. Just like Keira Knightley is the bride in this film, so the church is the bride of Christ.

Equipment / resources needed
A copy of the film Love Actually, *Universal Pictures/Working Title, 2003. Certificate 15.*

▷ *Chapter 2: 0:09:21*   ☐ *Chapter 2: 0:10:55*

Projector and screen (or a TV), and a DVD player.

How to link to talk
- The Bible says that we, the church, are the bride of Christ, and Jesus gave his life just to be together with us

BEST MAN FAIL

PREPARATION TIME **5** minutes

Quick summary
This clip shows a wedding that doesn't quite go to plan when the minister and the bride fall in a pool!

Equipment / resources needed
To find the link for this clip, please visit youthalpha.org/lgmedia
You may want to use a projector and a screen in order to show the clip to the whole group

How to link to talk
- The Bible says that we, the church, are the bride of Christ

WEDDING PHOTOS

PREPARATION TIME **10** minutes

Quick summary
If there is a leader from your group who is married, ask if you can show some of their wedding photos to the group.

Equipment / resources needed
Wedding photos.
You may want to use a projector and a screen in order to show the pictures to the whole group.

How to link to talk

- The Bible says that we, the church, are the bride of Christ

ALFREDA

PREPARATION TIME **0** minutes

Quick summary
This true story shows that now that God has cleansed us, we can be the bride of Christ.

Equipment / resources needed
None.

How it works
At the age of twenty-two, Jackie Pullinger travelled out to Hong Kong and began working with drug addicts and prostitutes in the worst part of the city. She tells the story about a seventy-two year-old woman called Alfreda. Alfreda had been a heroin addict and had been involved in prostitution for sixty years. When she was too old to work, she used to sit outside a brothel in a very run down area and poke the sewers with a stick to keep them moving freely. She injected heroin into her back three times a day, because her legs and her arms had been injected too many times. She had no identity card, and as far as the Hong Kong government was concerned, she didn't even exist. A few years, ago she gave her life to Christ and received forgiveness from God. She went to live in one of Jackie's houses and God started to heal her: she began to change. She saw that there were people who were worse off than her, and she tried to help them. Then, Jackie says, Alfreda met a man called Little Wa, he was seventy-five, and they got married! Jackie describes their wedding as 'the wedding of the decade' because this former prostitute and heroin addict walked down the aisle dressed all in white – cleansed, forgiven, and transformed by the love of Jesus Christ.

How to link to talk
- That is a great picture of the Church – before, we were broken sinners but God rescued us, cleansed us, and turned us into his bride. The Bible says that we, the church, are the bride of Christ

---

- Ephesians 5:25 and 32 says: 'Husbands, love your wives, just as Christ loved the church and gave himself up for her to make her holy, cleansing her by the washing with water through the word, and to present her to himself as a radiant church, without stain or wrinkle or any other blemish, but holy and blameless … This is a profound mystery – but I'm talking about Christ and the church'

- The church is the bride of Christ! That's you and me. Jesus gave his life for the bride, for us, so that he can be united with us forever

- Our response should be to love him, to worship him, and to want to live holy lives for him

CONCLUSION

- The church is about people: people in relationship with Jesus, people working together, people looking after one another, people serving and sharing good news with others

- That is why Christians all over the world get together to meet and encourage each other, to pray for each other, and to worship Jesus. We are his people, his family, his body, his temple, and his bride

- Let's pray

QUICK PRAYER TO CLOSE

PREPARATION TIME **0** minutes

Quick summary
Pray to end your session.

Equipment / resources needed
None.

How it works
- I am just going to say a short prayer to close

- Lord, we thank you that we can all be part of the church of Jesus Christ. Thank you so much that you make us part of the people of God, that you accept us as your family: as sons and daughters of God. Thank you that that you allow us to be your body on earth so that people see Jesus through us. Thank you that you make your presence known, and thank you that you love us so much that you call us your bride. Thank you Jesus, Amen

How to link to talk
- Now we're going to have a quick break and then go into our small groups

- Thanks so much for coming to Youth Alpha! It's been great having you as part of this course. We'd love to keep seeing you, so stay in touch

- Do feel free to bring your friends along to our next course, which starts *[insert dates]*

You may want to take a moment to invite the group to a future youth meeting or to a church service with you.

SESSION 10
WHAT ABOUT THE CHURCH?
SMALL GROUP DISCUSSION QUESTIONS

[These can be combined at the end of the talk or interspersed after each teaching point. You can find an additional copy of this sheet online at youthalpha.org/lgmedia]

POINT 1 – THE PEOPLE OF GOD

- How do you feel about being part of the people of God?
- Does this change your view of what church is?

POINT 2 – THE FAMILY OF GOD

- How do you feel about being part of the family of God?
- Does this change your view of what church is?

POINT 3 – THE BODY OF CHRIST

- How do you feel about being part of Jesus' body on earth?
- Does this change your view of what church is?

POINT 4 – A HOLY TEMPLE

- How do you feel about the Bible calling you 'a temple of the Holy Spirit'?
- Does this change your view of what church is?

POINT 5 – THE BRIDE OF CHRIST

- How do you feel about the church being Jesus' bride?
- Does this change your view of what church is?

GENERAL DISCUSSION POINTS

- Can you summarise your experience on Youth Alpha? *[Ask leaders to start by getting one of the most enthusiastic members of the group to answer first]*
- Has your view of the church changed over the last few weeks?
- Do you think you are going to continue your involvement with this group and with the church?
- Would you like to keep meeting up with our group?
- Is there anything that you would like prayer for?

You may like to close by praying together as a group.

SHEET 8
ABSOLUTELY POSITIVELY BINGO WORKSHEET

Get a different person to sign their name in each square of your grid. Choose someone who has the quality described in that square – and tell them that they have it! The first person to fill every square is the winner.

Welcoming person	Natural leader	Amazing footballer	Inspiring person
Kind person	Thoughtful	Good at praying	Great actor
Great singer	Dresses with style	Incredible eyes	Incredible hair
Always encouraging	Amazing dancer	Generous person	Humble person
Very friendly	Great cook	Good at sports	Best smile

SHEET 9
TEAM WORK ACTIVITY

ROLES AND INSTRUCTIONS WORKSHEET

Cut out these roles and ensure that each member of every group is given one before the game starts.

✂ -

   A. You are the speaker. You may talk as much as you like, but you may not move.

✂ -

   B. The only words you may use are, 'Yes', 'No', 'I know' and 'I don't know'. You may not move. The can of fruit is hidden near the window.

✂ -

   C. The only words you may use are, 'Yes', 'No', 'I know' and 'I don't know'. You may not move. The can opener is hidden near the door.

✂ -

   D. The only words you may use are, 'Yes', 'No', 'I know' and 'I don't know'. You may not move. The spoon is hidden near the light switch.

✂ -

   E. The only words you may use are, 'Yes', 'No', 'I know' and 'I don't know'. You may move, but only when you are absolutely sure where the can of fruit, the can opener and the spoon are. You are allowed to touch and carry them, but you must not take them near the leader.

✂ -

   F. The only words you may use are, 'Yes', 'No', 'I know' and 'I don't know'. You may only move if you have the can of fruit in your hand. You are not allowed to touch anything else that contains metal.

✂ -

   G. The only words you may use are, 'Yes', 'No', 'I know' and 'I don't know'. You may only move if you have the can opener in your hand. You are not allowed to touch anything else that contains metal.

✂ -

   H. The only words you may use are, 'Yes', 'No', 'I know' and 'I don't know'. You may only move if you have the spoon in your hand. You are not allowed to touch anything else that contains metal.

SECTION 2

HOW TO RUN A GREAT YOUTH ALPHA COURSE

PLANNING YOUR YOUTH ALPHA COURSE

So you've decided that you'd like to run a Youth Alpha course? That's great! The next thing to do is start figuring out some practical details.

A successful Youth Alpha course will require a fair bit of planning, but don't worry – it's easier than you think. Most of us probably think we can organise a course in less time than it takes in reality, so the sooner you start thinking about it the better.

The more work you do in advance and the better prepared you and your team are, the the more relaxed you'll be on the course itself. This will free you up to spend more time building friendships with people and making them feel valued.

PLANNING – STAGE 1 (3–6 months in advance)

THINGS TO CONSIDER

1. DO I HAVE THE SUPPORT OF MY PASTOR/YOUTH PASTOR/ CHURCH LEADER?

2. WHAT IS THE AIM OF THE COURSE?

3. WHO IS THE COURSE FOR?

4. WHERE WILL THE COURSE TAKE PLACE?

5. WHEN WILL THE COURSE TAKE PLACE?

6. WHO WILL RUN IT?

7. HOW DO WE PAY FOR IT?

8. WHAT ABOUT THE WEEKEND/DAY?

9. SHOULD WE HAVE SUNG WORSHIP?

10. WHO IS MY YOUTH ALPHA ADVISER?

11. HAVE I REGISTERED MY COURSE?

1 DO I HAVE THE SUPPORT OF MY PASTOR/YOUTH PASTOR/ CHURCH LEADER?

We would strongly encourage you to get the support of your church before you set out to run a Youth Alpha course. If you are part of a youth group, this might mean chatting to your youth pastor to get their support. It doesn't necessarily mean you are asking for their help, but you do want their blessing. Ideally, you will need their support in prayer, goodwill and possibly with money.

If you are a youth leader, sit down with your church leader, explain the vision to them and ask for their support.

'How good and pleasant it is when brothers and sisters live together in unity!' (Psalm 133:1).

2 WHAT IS THE AIM OF THE COURSE?

To some, this might seem like a pretty obvious question. Whilst Youth Alpha is an evangelistic course, there are also other ways to use it. Some reasons for running Youth Alpha include using it:

- As a course for those who are outside the church – for evangelism

- As a tool for discipleship

- For renewing and deepening previous faith commitments

- As part of a course to lead up to baptism or confirmation (some denominations) – see page 353

It is important that you decide from the outset what the aim of your course is. Experience shows that if you try to use the course for more than one of these reasons you will probably not be so successful.

3 WHO IS THE COURSE FOR?

Again, this may seem like a pretty obvious question, but it is definitely worth thinking about. Who will you invite on your course?

Possibilities include:

- Your friends

- Those who live in your local community

- Those already involved in your church (if you are using Youth Alpha as a discipleship tool)

- Those who have had some contact with church, but haven't really been involved

- Those in a local club or organisation (eg: YFC centre or youth club)

- Those in a local school (eg: lunchtime or after school club)

4 WHERE WILL THE COURSE TAKE PLACE?

This is an important thing to think about. The venue you choose could be the difference between people feeling comfortable or not, and consequently, people coming or not. We want to remove any potential obstacles that may get in the way of someone coming to Jesus. Here are some ideas and things to think about.

How many people might come? It's worth considering this, as the last thing you want is to have a room big enough for forty people if only five turn up. It is far better to use a small room and squeeze people in. Be realistic about how many people might come along.

Potential venues include:

Churches – for many people running the course, this is the first option that springs to mind. However, just because there is space available at your church, and just because it's probably free, doesn't mean it is the best idea. While it's probably okay if you are running a course for people with a link to the church, for others, going in to a church might be an extra hurdle to overcome.

Community centres – generally these are intended to serve the community and, therefore, are not too expensive to hire.

> '*How good and pleasant it is when brothers and sisters live together in unity!*' (Psalm 133:1)

Sports halls – well worth considering for courses with younger teenagers who will relish the opportunity to play some energetic games. It is also worth considering for courses with guests who are seriously into sport.

Schools – if you are running a lunchtime or after-school course, then asking your school for a classroom to use is probably the best option (for more information on this, please see the article on page 354).

Your/someone's home – if you are aiming to run a small-sized course, then this may well be the best option. Going to either your home, or the home of one of your friends might be more chilled out than an 'official' building.

Fast food restaurants – if the people you want to invite spend lots of time at places like McDonalds, then this is another option. Many restaurants have small side rooms (often used for kids' parties, etc) that they might be willing to let you use/hire (you will probably have to promise to consume a specified quantity of burgers and soft drinks!).

Cafés – similarly, if this sort of dynamic fits your group it may work. We've heard lots of stories about large café chains being willing to let groups hire their cafés after hours if they commit to buying a minimum number of drinks, etc.

Youth clubs etc – if there is a youth club or youth centre in your community you might be able to use this for a minimal fee.

You may well have a much better idea that is different to any of the above – if so, go for it! Don't forget to let us know where you ran a course and how you got on – email youth@alpha.org

5 WHEN WILL THE COURSE TAKE PLACE?

Before settling on a day or a time, you will need to do think about who you are inviting on your course and what their lives are like. For example, you don't want to pick a time and day that clashes with football practice, etc. The first rule of making this kind of decision is to realise that you may never find a time that is perfect for everybody, but try to exclude as few people as possible by considering these questions:

- What time does school finish?

- How easy is it to get to the venue – will guests need a lift or can they get there by themselves?

- What kind of evening/weekend commitments do they already have (clubs, jobs, sports teams, night to go out on the town, homework, family, etc)?

- How do their parents feel about them going out on week nights?

- When are school/college exams?

We would also recommend fitting the course into a school term. Our experience is that if school holidays fall in the middle of the course, it is very difficult to restart and get people back into the course after a few weeks off (if a half-term holiday falls during your course, you may wish to stop for a week if people are going away). It is far better to start at the beginning of term and fit the whole course in to eight or ten weeks. We suggest that you avoid running the course at the same time as major exams.

Ideally, the Youth Alpha Weekend/Day should come after Session 5 and before Session 8 (see course outlines, opposite). Don't forget to schedule the two team training events: Session 1 before the course starts, and Session 2 just before the weekend or day away. For sample timings for your Youth Alpha course, please see Appendix 1 on page 400, or online at youthalpha.org.uk/lgmedia

OPTION 1 – TEN WEEK COURSE (PLUS LAUNCH EVENT)

Team training session 1 – How to lead small groups on Youth Alpha

Introductory session – Christianity: Boring, Untrue, Irrelevant?
Session 1 – Who Is Jesus?
Session 2 – Why Did Jesus Die?
Session 3 – How Can We Have Faith?
Session 4 – Why and How Do I Pray?
Session 5 – Why and How Should I Read the Bible?
Session 6 – How Does God Guide us?

Team training session 2 – How to pray for each other on Youth Alpha

Youth Alpha Weekend/Day

Weekend Session 1 – What about the Holy Spirit?
Weekend Session 2 – How Can I Be Filled with the Holy Spirit?
Weekend Session 3 – How Can I Make the Most of the Rest of My Life?

Session 7 – How Can I Resist Evil?
Session 8 – Why and How Should I Tell Others?
Session 9 – Does God Heal Today?
Session 10 – What about the Church?

OPTION 2 – NINE WEEK COURSE (PLUS LAUNCH EVENT)

Team training session 1 – How to lead small groups on Youth Alpha

Introductory session – Christianity: Boring, Untrue, Irrelevant?
Session 1 – Who Is Jesus?
Session 2 – Why Did Jesus Die?
Session 3 – How Can We Have Faith?
Session 4 – Why and How Do I Pray?
Session 5 – Why and How Should I Read the Bible?
Session 6 – How Does God Guide us?

Team training session 2 – How to pray for each other on Youth Alpha

Youth Alpha Weekend/Day

Weekend Session 1 – What about the Holy Spirit?
Weekend Session 2 – How Can I Be Filled with the Holy Spirit?
Weekend Session 3 – How Can I Make the Most of the Rest of My Life?

Session 7 – How Can I Live Free? *['How Can I Resist Evil?' and
'Does God Heal Today?' combined]*
Session 8 – Why and How Should I Tell Others?
Session 9 – What about the Church?

OPTION 3 – EIGHT WEEK COURSE (PLUS LAUNCH EVENT)

Team training session 1 – How to lead small groups on Youth Alpha

Introductory session – Christianity: Boring, Untrue, Irrelevant?
Session 1 – Who Is Jesus?
Session 2 – Why Did Jesus Die?
Session 3 – How Can We Have Faith?
Session 4 – Why and How Do I Pray?
Session 5 – Why and How Should I Read the Bible?
Session 6 – How Does God Guide us?

Team training session 2 – How to pray for each other on Youth Alpha

Youth Alpha Weekend/Day

Weekend Session 1 – What about the Holy Spirit?
Weekend Session 2 – How Can I Be Filled with the Holy Spirit?
Weekend Session 3 – How Can I Make the Most of the Rest of My Life?

Session 7 – How Can I Live Free? *['How Can I Resist Evil?' and 'Does God Heal Today?' combined]*
Session 8 – What about the Church and Telling Others? *['Why and How Should I Tell Others?' and 'What about the Church?' combined]*

---

6 WHO WILL RUN IT?

So far, there's just you. Who else can help you? What kind of team are you going to need? The more people you can involve in your team, the more people there are praying for the course and inviting people along.

Talks – who will do the talks? Don't just automatically think of asking your youth leaders! We would encourage you to have a go yourself. The sessions in this guide have been written to make it as easy as possible for anyone to give a talk, even if they have never done so before.

Small group leaders – who will be the small group leaders? If you've run the course before, why not ask some of the people who came on the last course as guests to help lead groups?

Food – are you going to need people to help you get or make food?

Set-up/pack-down – what about people to help set-up and pack-down?

It might be the case that there are people in your church who wouldn't see themselves as natural youth leaders, but would still love to support you. They may be willing to help set up, pack down or help you with the provision of food. You could enlist the help of some parents to take turns helping bring food.

Note to youth pastors: we would really encourage you to get as many young people as you can on your team. There is no doubt in our minds that the best people to share their faith with teenagers are teenagers! Traditionally, the church has been slow to learn that, but things seem to be changing. We encourage you to see your role as helping to equip teenagers to reach their friends; Youth Alpha gives you a brilliant opportunity to do that. You may find it is one of the best means of discipleship you've ever found!

7 HOW DO WE PAY FOR IT?

We really believe that running a Youth Alpha course doesn't need to cost the earth. Many of the illustrations require very little in terms of material, though there are some that you will need to buy the odd item for.

One important principle that Alpha has always run on is that the course should be free for guests. We usually suggest that asking people to make a small donation for the food is fine, as is charging for the cost of the Weekend/Day, but ideally, no one should be prevented from attending any part of the course because of money.

It is worth chatting to someone who is good with budgets and making a list of what the course might cost (including the Weekend/Day – venue hire, transport, etc). When you have an idea of the sum of money needed, you could chat to your pastor/church leader or other contacts to see if they can help, or you can do some fundraising yourself. Some churches have a youth or missions' budget that they may be thrilled to use to support what you are doing. You are far more likely to receive some financial support if you explain your needs and apply well in advance.

8 WHAT ABOUT THE WEEKEND/DAY AWAY?

The Youth Alpha Weekend/Day is a key part of the course – there is more information on how to plan it later in this section.

9 SHOULD WE HAVE SUNG WORSHIP?

On an adult Alpha course, worship is considered a viable part of the programme if the course has more than thirty people. We believe that this is the critical mass required for singing songs without embarrassment.

Obviously, the dynamics of a Youth Alpha course are different. Only you will know if worship would be appropriate for your course, and, if it *is* appropriate, what kind of worship would be most natural for your group. It will depend on who is coming on the course, the size of your team, and whether you have a gifted worship leader available to you.

More information on this can be found in 'Worship on Youth Alpha' (see page 351).

10 WHO IS MY YOUTH ALPHA ADVISER?

Thousands of Youth Alpha courses have already taken place across the globe. In many countries there are Youth Alpha Advisers (visit the Alpha website, alphafriends.org to see who is local to you) who can give you invaluable help and advice. As well as giving you advice from their own experience, they may also be able to put you in contact with someone nearby who is already running a successful course, or direct you to a Youth Alpha conference. Chances are that a short chat with an Adviser will save you loads of time and effort in the long run.

11 HAVE I REGISTERED MY COURSE?

We would strongly encourage you to visit youthalpha.org and register your course online. This means that people who are visiting the site looking for a course to join can find you more easily. You'll be the first to hear of new Youth Alpha developments and you'll also get regular updates from the Youth Alpha team.

PLANNING – STAGE 2 (1–2 months in advance)

THINGS TO CONSIDER

1. HOW DO I ADVERTISE MY COURSE?

2. WHAT EQUIPMENT WILL I NEED?

3. WHO IS THE COURSE FOR?

4. WHAT ABOUT A LAUNCH EVENT?

5. HOW DO SMALL GROUPS WORK?

6. WHO SHOULD LEAD THE SMALL GROUPS?

7. DO WE PRAY IN THE SMALL GROUPS?

8. HOW DO I TRAIN MY TEAM?

9. WHAT ABOUT THE PRACTICAL ISSUES?

1 HOW DO I ADVERTISE MY COURSE?

Most, if not all, of the people who attend your course will come because of a personal invitation. While a brochure, poster or invitation on its own is unlikely to bring someone to the course, well-produced advertising can help increase confidence and make it much easier for people to take a risk and invite their friends. In most cases, you and your team will need to invite people personally.

Youth Alpha have produced posters and postcards which can be used to advertise the course. You can get creative and use the internet (sites such as *Facebook* are great) to advertise the course, or you could make a short film advertisement to circulate.

There is a sample information sheet, explaining what the course is about, that can be given to the parents of those you are inviting (see Appendix 2 on page 401. For an amendable version, please visit youthalpha.org/lgmedia).

2 WHAT EQUIPMENT WILL I NEED?

Have a read through the sessions and, based on which illustrational options you choose, figure out what you will need to run the course. For example, you may need a computer, a DVD player, a TV or a projector. Can you borrow any of these items from a church or a friend? Which DVDs will you need over the weeks – can you borrow these from friends? Be organised about planning for this so you don't get caught out at the last minute (see page 349 for more information on how to use multimedia).

3 WHO IS PRAYING FOR THE COURSE?

Is there a group of people you know (perhaps from your church) who might commit to praying for you and your course? Could you ask them?

4 WHAT ABOUT A LAUNCH EVENT?

See page 324 for more information on how to plan and run a Launch Event.

5 HOW DO SMALL GROUPS WORK?

Small groups are a key part of the course. There are two ways to do small groups on Youth Alpha – either in small bursts inbetween the teaching points, or at the end of the talk. The suggested questions at the end of each session are designed to work either way. You will know which option will work best for your group.

Small groups usually have between eight and twelve members, but there should never be more than twelve people in a group. Ideally, each group should have one or two 'leaders' and one or two 'helpers', plus between six and eight 'guests' – people who are there to do the course but aren't on the team.

The leader(s) are there to guide the discussion and host the group. Normally, leaders are Christians who have done the course before. The helpers are there to help host the group and to make guests feel welcome. They may help get drinks and food for people, make introductions and generally be encouraging and helpful, but they shouldn't talk in the discussion.

Allocating people to small groups requires great skill. Depending on the age and maturity of your group, you may wish to form single sex groups, or mix it up (our experience is that younger youth do better in single sex groups and mid/older teenagers do better in mixed groups). We have found that groups work best when teenagers of similar ages are put together. You must also be conscious of the fact that those who have brought friends along may like to be in the same group as their guests. If you know who is coming, it is helpful to allocate people to groups before the course starts, but be prepared to be flexible at the first session.

We would strongly encourage you to do the team training sessions with your team, as the first of these focuses on how small groups work (see Section 4, page 372 for more information).

If you have more than one small group, think about where each group will meet for their discussion time. Wherever they are, everyone in the group must feel comfortable and safe. A useful tip is to ensure that everyone sits on the same level – either on chairs, sofas or the floor, but not a combination of these, as it will make the group dynamic feel odd.

It is vital that all small groups finish on time, if not early. It is better to leave people wanting more than letting them get bored – you can always continue the discussion next time. Be ruthless about sticking to your finish time – even if someone is making the best point ever!

For more information on small groups see 'How to lead a Youth Alpha small group' on page 338.

6 WHO SHOULD LEAD THE SMALL GROUPS?

Having good small group leaders is key to the success of your Youth Alpha course. These are the people who will be hosting the groups and who will have the most contact with the guests who come along.

A good way to decide if someone is right to lead a small group is to ask yourself the question, 'Would I want my best non-Christian friend to be in this person's small group?' If the answer is 'no' then they may not be the best person to have as a small group leader.

Commitment

It is important to make sure that your team are aware of the commitment required to help on Youth Alpha before they agree to take part. Be brave and tell the team up front that they are expected to commit to:

- The launch event
- The whole course (obviously)
- The team training sessions
- The Weekend/Day
- Praying for each member of their group every day

It's a bit like being a part of a sports team or a drama production – if you sign up for it, you need to be able to commit or it won't work. Of course, this only applies to the team, not to the guests.

7 DO WE PRAY IN THE SMALL GROUPS?

One of the goals of the small group is to model praying together, but it is important to remember not to rush into it. There may be people in the group for whom Youth Alpha is their first experience of anything church-related; they may not be comfortable praying with everyone else until later in the course. Go at the pace of the slowest person in your group – if they aren't ready, don't do it.

The earliest we would suggest you try praying together is in Session 4, after the talk 'Why and how do I pray?' If you do decide to have a time of prayer, the leader should test the waters by suggesting that it might be cool if the group prayed together.

Make it clear that no one has to pray aloud, but they're all welcome to. We suggest that the small group leader prays a very short and simple prayer first, something like, 'Thank you, God, for the weather. Amen.' If the leader prays the world's most powerful and beautiful prayer, chances are the group will think, 'Wow, if that's what prayer is, I could never do that.' If we pray a simple prayer, however, the group may think, 'Hey, that was simple. I could do way better than that', and they probably will!

8 HOW DO I TRAIN MY TEAM?

We suggest running two Team Training events – the first, 'How to lead small groups on Youth Alpha' should be held before the course begins, and the second, 'How to pray for each other on Youth Alpha' should be held before the Youth Alpha Weekend or Day.

Training your team is important, even if your group leaders have led small groups before. The training events provide an important opportunity for your team to get together and pray for the course.

Talk outlines for these two training sessions are included in Section 4 of this resource, please see pages 372 and 388 for more information.

9 WHAT ABOUT THE PRACTICAL ISSUES?

At this point, it is worth making a plan detailing how the course will run. This will make things simple rather than stressful! Think about:

- Who will help set up the venue each week?

- Who will sort out DVD clips, online videos/resources and other media? (for more information on this, please see page 349)

- Who will help with food and drinks each week?

- Who will help clear up after each session?

PLANNING YOUR YOUTH ALPHA LAUNCH EVENT

Often, it is a great idea to have some sort of 'launch event' to help advertise your course. The idea behind this is to host a relaxed and fun event to which people can bring their friends – in particular, their friends who aren't already part of the church – so they can hear a bit about Youth Alpha, and hopefully enjoy it enough to join your course.

A launch event can be a good way to give people who may initially be put off by the thought of doing a 'course' a chance to experience Youth Alpha without having to commit. The same applies to those who have never been to a Christian event before.

The general format for a launch event is to focus on the social, fun aspect of Youth Alpha, and, to have a short presentation on the upcoming Youth Alpha course. The presentation should include the testimonies of several people (or just one, if time is tight) and the first talk in the session material entitled, 'Christianity: Boring, Untrue, Irrelevant?'

Obviously, you will want to keep the presentation fairly brief while making it as interesting and thought-provoking as possible. At the end of the presentation or at the end of the event, fliers for, or invitations to the upcoming Youth Alpha course should be handed out, and an opportunity should be given for people to sign up to the course on the spot.

PLANNING – (1–2 months in advance)

THINGS TO CONSIDER

1. WHAT TYPE OF EVENT WILL WE RUN?

2. WHO IS GOING TO HELP US?

3. WHERE WILL WE HOLD OUR LAUNCH EVENT?

4. WHAT SORT OF ENTERTAINMENT DO WE WANT?

5. HOW WILL WE ADVERTISE OUR EVENT?

6. HOW MUCH WILL IT COST?

1 WHAT TYPE OF EVENT WILL WE RUN?

Feel free to create your own type of Launch Event, but to get you started, here are some suggestions. You could organise:

- A performance by a local band, or even a 'battle of the bands' with a number of local youth bands

- A sports competition, eg: five-a-side football, a T20 cricket match, table tennis, basketball, skating … whatever you think would appeal to your group

- A club night with music, videos and drinks (non-alcoholic!)

- A mini-Olympics or an 'it's a knockout competition' with loads of messy games

- A themed banquet

- A '70s or '80s disco

- A film night, with a recent blockbuster projected onto the biggest screen you can muster up (some groups have hired a cinema for this)

Only you know what budget and facilities you have available, and only you know what will appeal to your friends. It is better to do something simple but do it well than to over-reach and find that you don't have the resources to make it work.

2 WHO IS GOING TO HELP US?

You will probably want to ask the team who are helping you to plan your Youth Alpha course to get involved, but feel free to ask if others are willing to help out with this 'one-off' event. Get together early to brainstorm ideas, and make a plan for what you are going to do.

3 WHERE WILL WE HOLD OUR LAUNCH EVENT?

There are two options to consider here. The first option is to use the same venue for the Launch Event as you will use for your course. This will ensure that your guests are familiar with the venue from the start of the course, and it will mean that it is easier for them to find, as they will have been there before.

The other option, however, is to use a venue that you otherwise wouldn't use and to do something bigger and better – giving your event the 'wow' factor (it may also be impractical to have a five-a-side football tournament in your living room).

Either way, don't forget to book the venue early!

4 WHAT SORT OF ENTERTAINMENT DO WE WANT?

Obviously the entertainment you book will depend on the type of event you intend to have. Once this decision has been made, start making arrangements as soon as you can. This may include booking a DJ, band, etc.

5 HOW WILL WE ADVERTISE OUR EVENT?

Be creative with how you advertise your event. There are all the 'old school' ideas such as fliers, posters and invitations, but you should also use media-related methods – create a *Facebook* event, make a video that you can post on *YouTube* or that you can send by text message. Have fun with your advertising! Make as much 'noise' as you can.

6 HOW MUCH WILL IT COST?

Just as you made a budget for your course, so we would advise you to do the same for the Launch Event – start by trying to figure out how much everything will cost. You could ask people for a donation as they arrive, but it is even better if your event can be free. In order to ensure that this is possible, you may want to ask your church for financial help.

PLANNING YOUR YOUTH ALPHA WEEKEND OR DAY

The Youth Alpha Weekend or Day is one of the most important parts of Youth Alpha. Even if you aren't able to run a whole weekend, covering the Holy Spirit material is vital to the success of the course.

If there is one piece of advice that we would give you, it is that you should have a Weekend or Day as part of your course. If this seems daunting, then you can always ask your youth pastor or Youth Alpha Adviser for help in organising it. In some cases, it may be possible for you to join another course's Weekend/Day, providing they are fairly local.

Why is the Weekend/Day so vital? It is the only part of the course that includes teaching on the person and work of the Holy Spirit. It also gives those on the course the chance to be prayed for and filled with the Holy Spirit. Our experience is that the Weekend/Day is the most fun part of the course, and it is also the time when relationships are formed in a much deeper way. We are sure that if you run a weekend you'll never look back!

There are, however, some very good, practical reasons why it may not be possible to run a weekend. These include:

Financial reasons – as we have said earlier, we don't want anyone to be excluded from any part of Youth Alpha because they can't afford it. Therefore, you need to decide in advance whether you have the resources to help those that can't afford to pay the full amount, and if not, it is probably a better idea to go for the cheaper day option, as this will be accessible to everyone.

Practical – if you are running a course on your own without the support of an adult team, you may find there are legal reasons why you can't run a weekend – ie: you don't have any guardians who are over eighteen to supervise the group.

Contextual – if you are running a course in a school it is probably not appropriate to expect the students to go away with you for a weekend. It may be a better idea to incorporate the Holy Spirit material into the weekly sessions.

Relational – if your course will include youth who don't know you well, they (and/or their parents) may be unsure about the idea of going away for a weekend with you. Some will have very genuine concerns that our motives may not be good. Questions like, 'Will my child be brainwashed or inducted into some cult?' might seem slightly funny to us, but could be a real concern for many. Obviously, we should do all we can to dispel such fears by being open in all our planning and communication with parents and guardians, but we might have to accept that a weekend away is simply too big an ask for some.

If you decide that having a weekend away is not the right thing to do, you can still plan a Youth Alpha Day.

PLANNING – STAGE 1 (3–6 months in advance)

THINGS TO CONSIDER

1. WHEN DO WE RUN THE WEEKEND/DAY?

2. WHERE DO WE RUN IT?

3. HOW DO WE AFFORD IT?

4. HOW WILL WE GET THERE?

5. HOW DO WE TRAIN OUR TEAM?

1 WHEN DO WE RUN THE WEEKEND/DAY?

Ideally, the Youth Alpha Weekend or Day should take place some time between week five and week eight of the course. This is roughly at the halfway point. By this time, the guests will have heard about various aspects of the Christian faith, including prayer, the Bible, the cross and so on. Hopefully they will have had some good small group discussions and developed friendships and trust with others in the group.

As you choose the date for your weekend, bear in mind possible clashes: half-term holidays, big school events like fairs or plays, birthday parties and important sporting occasions that you know the group won't want to miss.

2 WHERE DO WE RUN IT?

This is an important decision, and there are resources available to help you find venues that cater for groups of young people. If in doubt, *Google* it!

One key consideration is obviously cost. It is wonderful to go to a purpose-built youth venue with state of the art media and facilities for outdoor activities, but if this is going to make it too expensive for some of your group then it will defeat the object.

A well-planned, well-run weekend with people sleeping on camping mattresses on the floor of a church hall (or similar) can be just as effective, and in some ways, even more memorable. Think about what the needs and desires of your group will be, and try to match that with what they will be able to afford.

You have much greater flexibility if you are planning a day. Although you won't be able to go too far (nor do you need to), it may still be a good idea to get off site and go somewhere new. Think creatively: why not ask a church across town if you can borrow a meeting room? Or ask a member of your church if you can use their home?

3 HOW DO WE AFFORD IT?

As we have said many times, we want the Youth Alpha Weekend/Day to be available to everyone on the course, regardless of how much they can afford. You may choose to set a price for the weekend, but if you have the financial resources (or the offer of subsidy from others), you could make it very cheap, or give people the option to pay only what they can afford. This is left to your discretion. It is our experience that speaking to your church about Youth Alpha's vision is really helpful, as church members may well want to sponsor individuals to go on the weekend.

4 HOW WILL WE GET THERE?

Depending on the size of your course and the desired location of the Weekend or Day, it may be possible to use the cars of adult leaders, if they have them. However, if the group is likely to be large, you will need to hire other transport and this must be booked well in advance. If you want to keep costs down, it might be worth approaching other churches, youth organisations, or a local authority to see if you can find a cheap rental before you go direct to private rental firms or coach companies.

Please note: no financial saving is worth any kind of compromise on safety. You must vet all vehicles, drivers and insurance arrangements carefully before committing to anything.

5 HOW DO WE TRAIN OUR TEAM?

The second Youth Alpha team training session is called 'How to pray for each other on Youth Alpha'. It is essential to do this before the Weekend/Day, as this is the first time that the team will be offering to pray for each member of the group. Training in this is vital, even for those who think they know enough already. The talk outline for this training session can be found on page 388 in Section 4.

PLANNING – STAGE 2 (1–2 months in advance)

THINGS TO CONSIDER

1. WHAT DO WE DO ON THE WEEKEND/DAY?

2. HOW DO WE PROMOTE IT?

3. DO WE NEED PERMISSION?

1 WHAT DO WE DO ON THE WEEKEND/DAY?

The programme for your Weekend/Day should be worked out between one and two months in advance. This will give you plenty of time to put all of your ideas into practice, resulting in an unforgettable weekend for your group! You will find some very basic sample programmes for a Youth Alpha Weekend/Day in Appendix 3 on page 403, or online at youthalpha.org.uk/lgmedia

These are intended to get you thinking about what might work well for your group in the venue you have booked.

Some general points to note

Worship – you may or may not have included worship as part of your course up until now. For some groups, the Youth Alpha Weekend will be the first time that worship is introduced, so it is worth putting a lot of effort into it. Worship is a great corporate activity, and it really helps to bring people into the presence of God.

Afternoon activities – in the afternoon, you may want to give your groups free time, or you may prefer to organise some sports/group games. If you are at a venue that offers instructed activities, this is a great option. If you are running a Youth Alpha Day, a great way to make the afternoon special is to plan a fun group activity that everyone will enjoy.

Evening session – if you are on a weekend away, you can hold the evening session either before or after dinner. In some ways, this is the most important talk of the whole course, so it may be a good thing to do it before dinner when people are more alert. After a meal we can feel lethargic and sleepy, but people's hunger may outweigh that – you should make the call based on your group.

Prayer ministry – it is important to note that on Youth Alpha we never ask people to respond to a 'call' for prayer by raising their hand, or coming forward – we simply offer to pray for everyone. It is a good idea to have group leaders sitting with their groups so they can easily offer prayer to each person. There should be no pressure on anyone to be prayed for. If you are running

a weekend, we suggest having another time of ministry on Sunday after the talk.

Talks – there are three talks included for use on the weekend. The third talk, 'How Can I Make the Most of the Rest of My Life?' will probably not fit into a single day programme, so could be done either at the next Youth Alpha session, or at the end of the course.

2 HOW DO WE PROMOTE IT?

We recommend that you start talking about the Weekend/Day on the second session of the course. The Weekend/Day will be an exciting time, but some people may feel intimidated by the idea of it on the first week. You should aim to have a flier, booking form and parents' information sheet available for your guests by week two or three of the course. We would suggest mentioning the Weekend/Day at every session, and during the two sessions before your Weekend/Day, ask your small group leaders to encourage their groups to come.

As with the course invitation and Launch Event, you could use media such as videos and social networking sites to create a 'buzz' about the Youth Alpha Weekend or Day.

3 DO WE NEED PERMISSION?

With teenagers under eighteen it is vital to get permission from their parents/guardians before you can take them anywhere. In Appendix 4 (page 405) of this *Leaders' Guide* you will find a sample parents' information sheet/booking form. An amendable copy of this form can be found at youthalpha.org/lgmedia, which you can adapt and use to ensure that all parents/guardians are aware of your arrangements. Anyone who does not have permission from a parent/guardian cannot attend the Youth Alpha Weekend/Day. In the UK, all of your adult helpers will need a Criminal Records Bureau (CRB) check. For more information on these checks, please see the article, 'Staying safe on Youth Alpha' on page 360. You should also ensure that at least one of your leaders/team is a qualified first aider.

For your Youth Alpha Weekend/Day, we recommend a minimum of one adult for every six under eighteen year olds.

PLANNING – STAGE 3 (2–4 months in advance)

1. WHAT DO WE NEED TO TAKE ON OUR WEEKEND/DAY?

2. WHAT INFORMATION SHOULD WE GIVE OUT?

3. WHO IS DOING WHAT?

1 WHAT DO WE NEED TO TAKE ON OUR WEEKEND/DAY?

You should liaise with the venue to figure out what you need to bring. Ask things like:

- Is any bedding provided? What about towels?

- Do you have a DVD player/computer/TV/ projector we can use?

- What sports facilities are there?

- What cleaning duties do we need to do?

- Who cooks/what cooking facilities are there?

It's also a good idea to take a stack of Bibles with you.

2 WHAT INFORMATION SHOULD WE GIVE OUT?

It is useful to put together a pack for everyone who is coming on the Youth Alpha Weekend or Day. It should include all of the information they will need, such as a list of what they should bring, exact details of where and when everyone is meeting, how they will travel, and exactly when and where they will be dropped off when the weekend or day is over.

You'll also want to make sure that the parents of your group are really well informed about the Youth Alpha Weekend/Day. We suggest you put together a pack for parents, including the venue details and contact numbers (both for the venue and your group leaders), a timetable, and the parents' information sheet/ booking form – see Appendix 4 on page 405 for samples of these. Amendable versions of these sheets and forms can be found online at youthlapha.org.uk/lgmedia

3 WHO IS DOING WHAT?

Make sure that your team are clear about who is doing what on the weekend/day. Well in advance, you should decide who is speaking, and, if you plan on having worship you should decide who will lead it.

In some cases, you may feel like you need some extra support and expertise on your Youth Alpha Weekend or Day. You might like to invite a guest speaker, a guest worship leader or another type of specialist to help with a particular part of the weekend/day. A local Youth Alpha Adviser might be able to help with some recommendations if you don't already have the contacts. Such people tend to be busy, though, and you will need to book them well in advance. The only thing to be mindful of is that it usually takes time for young people to develop trust – before you invite a guest, ensure you are confident that the group will not feel threatened by having someone new come into their midst.

We suggest giving one person the responsibility of hosting the sessions and making announcements, etc, for the whole weekend/day, so it is clear to everyone that someone is in charge.

You can also assign responsibilities to others on your team for:

- Catering (if not taken care of by the venue)

- Entertainment (organising a talent show or similar?)

- Games and ice breakers

- Sports and activities

PLANNING – STAGE 4 (1 week in advance)

1. WHERE WILL PEOPLE SLEEP?

2. DO THE VENUE HAVE ALL THE INFORMATION THEY NEED?

3. HAVE I GOT EVERYTHING PLANNED AND WRITTEN DOWN?

1 WHERE WILL PEOPLE SLEEP?

It is much better to draw up a bedroom plan for the weekend before you leave rather than trying to do it upon arrival. This can be a work of art in itself – but just remember that you can't please everybody all of the time.

A few hints

- Try to keep small groups together as much as you can

- It might be helpful to put girls and guys in separate areas of the venue, eg on different floors if appropriate

- Try to spread leaders and other trusted individuals around the venue evenly to keep things calm. Note that leaders and teenagers should not share rooms

2 DO THE VENUE HAVE ALL THE INFORMATION THEY NEED?

Make a call to the venue to give them final numbers for rooms/catering (if appropriate) and let them know what time you will arrive, etc.

3 HAVE I GOT EVERYTHING PLANNED AND WRITTEN DOWN?

Making sure you have everything written down is really important, especially if you are going off site. We would suggest you draw up a master list that includes:

- The name of each person who is coming

- Any allergies, medical or dietary requirements

- Parents'/guardians' names and contact details

- Contact details for each person's doctor, as well as contact details for a local doctor

- How each person is travelling to and from the venue (which car, train, bus, etc)

- Whether they have paid and what they owe

- Which room they will sleep in

- Which small group they are in

- Any duties they are assigned to (for leaders/helpers only)

- A separate list of what equipment you need to bring (including the required equipment for talk illustrations)

Finally, after all of your planning and preparation, don't forget to pray. Enjoy your Youth Alpha Weekend or Day and watch God move!

PLANNING YOUR FOLLOW-UP

Before you begin running a Youth Alpha course, it is worth giving some thought to what will happen at the end of your course.

Jesus' commission to us is to 'make disciples', not just converts. Follow-up after a Youth Alpha course is vital, and we need to be willing to commit to that before starting a course.

There are, of course, many different ways to follow-up from Youth Alpha. If you are part of a local church and/or youth group then it may be that your Youth Alpha group can easily join up with one or both of these. Certain denominations will have programmes that help new Christians join their particular church.

> 'Therefore go and make disciples of all nations, baptising them in the name of the Father and of the Son and of the Holy Spirit, and teaching them to obey everything I have commanded you. And surely I am with you always, to the very end of the age' (Matthew 28: 19–20)

It is important that you continue to be a part of everyone's journey, not just those in the group who have made a commitment to Jesus. It has been said many times that faith is a journey, and this journey doesn't start or end on Youth Alpha. If we suddenly stop talking to someone because they didn't make a decision for Jesus on our course, then that doesn't speak a great deal about our love for them.

Keep praying for your group and make arrangements to get together fairly regularly. Involve them in your church and invite them to your youth group. Your church or youth group may need to adapt slightly in order to make services/meetings more accessible to young people who are new to the Christian faith – this is not always easy to address, but these conversations are always very healthy.

Keep your eyes open for any practical needs that your friends may have in order to continue their journey. For example, do they have a Bible that they can read? Is there an appropriate Bible reading guide you can get them? Can you start a follow-up or discipleship group so that you can all continue meeting together in a similar context?

There are many Christian organisations that have produced great youth resources which could be used as follow-up programmes to Youth Alpha. Visit youthalpha.org and look under the 'friends' section for links and information.

One great way of engaging people in the journey of faith is to invite some of those who did the last Youth Alpha course to come and help you run the next one. Why not ask them to be involved as small group leaders, speakers, or behind-the-scenes helpers? We've seen many cases where returning to help on a course has sparked someone's faith more than when they attended the course as a guest.

EXPERT ADVICE ON RUNNING YOUTH ALPHA

HOW TO LEAD A YOUTH ALPHA SMALL GROUP

By Matt Costley

The British band Coldplay wrote a song called 'Square One'. It goes like this: 'From the top of the first page/To the end of the last day/From the start in your own way/You just want somebody listening to what you say/It doesn't matter who you are.'

I think these words pretty much sum up the way a lot of our generation feel about life. We just want to know that someone cares about what we have to say.

Over recent years, we've seen a massive rise in the use of social networking and media-sharing websites such as *Facebook*, *Twitter*, *MySpace* and *YouTube* (to name a few). One of the reasons that so many of us are using them is that they affirm the idea that 'my life matters' and that 'the rest of the world needs to hear what I am doing and thinking'.

On Youth Alpha, we want to make time to hear what everyone on the course thinks and feels. We believe that their life and their opinion do matter, even if we don't agree with them. We want to use the course to get to know each other and to build relationships. That's why, in many ways, small groups on Youth Alpha are the most important part of the whole course.

AIMS OF SMALL GROUPS

There are two main aims of small groups – to discuss, and to build relationships.

1 TO DISCUSS
On the first week of one of the courses I was involved in, a thirteen-year-old guy in my small group came out with a well-presented, three-point argument for why there was no God. I was impressed – he sounded like he knew

what he was talking about. Someone asked him how he had come to those conclusions, and he froze. He repeated the same argument. Again, someone asked why he believed this, but he couldn't explain it. It turned out that he had learnt the three points from a teacher at school, but he didn't really understand what they meant.

> We have one golden rule in small groups: no question is too simple or too hostile

In many ways, this is what the church has done to young people for years – we have given the 'answers' without helping people to figure out *why* they are the answers.

It's important on your Youth Alpha course that you don't just feed people information, but that you give them time to find the answers for themselves. If we allow this to happen, then the fruit will be long-lasting and life-changing, rather than short-term and shallow.

John 16:13 says, 'But when he, the Spirit of truth, comes, he will guide you into all truth.' Discussion helps truth to rise to the surface, making it easier for everyone to discover for themselves. Talking together in a small group allows everyone to express their opinions. We don't need to be afraid of questions – actually, we embrace them. As that verse says, the Spirit will lead us into truth, and if something is true, it will stand up to any amount of questioning. We have one golden rule in small groups: no question is too simple or too hostile. In fact, the first time you get together in your group, it can be a good thing to identify in your head who the most hostile person might be and invite them to speak first – this will give permission to others to be honest too.

2 TO BUILD RELATIONSHIPS
When I first moved to London I didn't know a single person. Soon after I arrived, I did

an Alpha Course at my church and, during that time, became good friends with the people in my group. Eleven years later, those guys are still my best friends and we are doing life together.

Someone once said that people go to church for many reasons, but only come back for one – if they make friends. Hopefully the people in your small group will really enjoy hanging out and getting to know each other better. This aspect of the Youth Alpha course is so important; it's essential to spend time getting to know each other and letting friendships form.

FIVE TOP TIPS FOR SUCCESSFUL SMALL GROUPS

1 LEADERS ARE THERE TO FACILITATE DISCUSSION

Remember that the role of the small group leader is not so much to try to answer people's questions as it is to facilitate discussion. The best thing a leader can do is ask questions. A great one is, 'So what do the rest of you think?' When someone offers a thought, it's not the leader's job to jump in with their own views or an answer, but instead to throw it open to the rest of the group.

The small group is for the guests on the course to have their say, not the leaders

The small group leaders on Youth Alpha are more like group facilitators than instructional gurus. A facilitator is simply another member of the group who is helping to keep the discussion going. Our views are no more important than anyone else's, and we are not looking to judge people or their opinions. It is our aim to guide and steer the group, so ask lots of questions!

2 THEY'VE ALREADY HEARD A TALK

This is a key point to grasp. Remember that by the time we get to the small group time, everyone has already heard a talk – they don't want to hear another one. So any kind of preaching is banned! This can be really hard, especially if you are listening to people ask questions that you think are really easy to answer. You might be in a group where it seems that they have just managed to disprove all of Christianity – even so, don't try and defend it. The small group is for the guests on the course to have their say, not the leaders.

3 LOOK FOR OPINIONS NOT ANSWERS

Try to avoid asking closed questions – questions that have either 'yes' or 'no' as an answer. Instead, ask open-ended questions that require an opinion for an answer. Not only will this help to keep the discussion flowing, but it also means that there can be no right or wrong answer. A good thing to ask is, 'What do you think/how do you feel about that?' as this makes it a more personal question.

There are lots of suggested questions listed at the end of the course sessions – feel free to use these if they are helpful for getting discussion going.

4 VALUE EVERY OPINION

Don't take sides in your group's discussion, but value every opinion that is shared. Even if someone says something that seems crazy or ridiculous, we want them to know that what they think matters to the group. You could say something like, 'That's interesting. What does everybody else think?' This allows you to affirm them without having to agree, and it gives others in the group a chance to respond for themselves.

5 DON'T BE AFRAID TO LOSE THE ARGUMENT

This is one of the hardest things to do and it may go against every fibre of your being, but it is really important. We won't and don't have to 'win' every discussion, sometimes it is better to lose! I have seen groups tear apart everything that was said in a talk, but still return week after week to hear the next topic. Many of the people in these groups came to faith because they had been given space to discuss things. We need to trust that if truth is truth, it will always come out.

DOS AND DON'TS

DON'T

- Ask a question and then answer it yourself. This devalues the question you have just asked

- Put somebody else's answer into your own words: it invalidates their explanation

- Be afraid to gently challenge or tease out a response, eg: 'Can you explain what you mean by that?' or 'Can you give an example?'

- Be afraid of silence. Allow time for the group to think about questions/issues raised. Allowing silence shows that you value thoughtful and considered responses. Someone will talk eventually!

DO

- Think about your group as you prepare your questions. Make the questions as relevant to them as possible

- Affirm responses neutrally, if possible, eg: 'Yes' or 'Thank you'. This shows that you welcome further responses from others

- Answer questions with questions

GROUND RULES FOR YOUR SMALL GROUP

The last thing anyone wants is for their small group to feel like school, but it can be helpful to set some group ground rules on the first week to make sure everyone has a good time. Here are four that might help you:

1 NO PUT-DOWNS
We want everyone to respect each other. It's okay for the group to attack ideas, but not each other.

2 THERE'S NO SUCH THING AS A STUPID QUESTION
We want everyone to know it's okay to ask *any* question without being laughed at.

3 NO ONE HAS TO TALK, BUT ONLY ONE PERSON TALKS AT A TIME
We won't force anyone to speak, but we do want to respect each other and that means listening to what others have to say without talking over them.

4 WHAT IS SAID IN THE GROUP STAYS IN THE GROUP
If someone shares something personal in the group, there needs to be an understanding that it is not going to be passed on to others at school or anywhere else.

Lastly, don't forget to have fun in your groups, and always make sure that you finish on time or early – it's better to leave people wanting more than not wanting to come back because they got bored. If someone doesn't come back, don't worry – it's unlikely to be your fault. Keep praying for them anyway.

> *We need to trust that if truth is truth, it will always come out*

My experience is that being part of a Youth Alpha small group is by far the best element of the course – the friendships formed in those groups can last a lifetime.

Matt Costley is the Youth Pastor at HTB in London, and is the former Head of Youth Alpha.

htb.org.uk

HOW TO GIVE A GREAT YOUTH ALPHA TALK

By Gavin Calver

Leonard Sweet, an American writer and theologian, suggests that communicating to today's teenagers requires us to be **EPIC**:

Experiential – let them experience God.
Participatory – let them participate in the talk.
Image-driven – our talks should be image-heavy: whether in the form of movies, *YouTube* clips, pictures or images described using words (stories), teenagers respond to images.
Connected – we must be community-centred (small groups).

[Adapted from Leonard Sweet, *Postmodern Pilgrims* (Broadman & Holman Publishers, 2000).]

The thing I love about Youth Alpha is that it lends itself to being EPIC. The opportunity to communicate the gospel in a way that our friends will understand is very exciting, but also challenging. On Youth Alpha, all the talks are given live – there is no fallback DVD option! Your aim is to bring out the session's subject with the help of video clips, icebreakers and other creative aids.

> *On Youth Alpha, all the talks are given live – there is no fallback DVD option!*

Preparing and presenting a live talk every week can initially seem daunting, but it's actually one of the real strengths of Youth Alpha. Live talks help you to gauge exactly where your group are at week by week, helping you tailor the way you present the material to them. My aim here is to share some practical advice that may be helpful to consider before you start your Youth Alpha course. The real key is to prepare properly and to pray.

> *The better prepared you are, the shorter your talk will be*

MAKE IT SHORT

Whatever else you do, always know exactly how you will start and finish your talk. It can be helpful to try to remember the first and last few sentences of your talk so that you can start and end confidently. Be incredibly disciplined about keeping to your allotted time, no matter how tempting it may be to run over.

The typical Youth Alpha guest doesn't have a huge attention span. Think of it a bit like a TV programme – TV producers know we concentrate better in small bursts, so they use commercial breaks to split programmes into more manageable chunks. Likewise, try to make your points quickly, using an illustration to break up the presentation and keep the group's attention. Use plenty of the suggested illustrations and do all you can to keep your young people engaged.

If you have had experience of speaking at an adult Alpha course, you now have to think shorter, shorter and even shorter. This can be hard; it seems easier to explain 'Why Did Jesus Die?' in forty-five minutes, than to explain it in fifteen or twenty minutes. However, twenty minutes is actually quite a long time, and this should be seen as the absolute maximum talk length on Youth Alpha.

The better prepared you are, the shorter your talk will be – the less prepared you are, the more you will waffle! Why not ask a friend to listen to your talk beforehand and get them to offer suggestions?

MAKE IT MEMORABLE

Make use of illustrations, media clips and examples. The ones listed in this resource are great, but do not feel constrained by them. If you have other ideas that are suitable, use them instead (and share them online so other leaders can use them too).

Make use of simple words and expressions that your group will understand. Don't use 'Christian-speak' that those in the church may be used to. If you have to use 'Christian' words like 'redemption', 'grace', 'sin', 'blood' and 'repentance', explain them so that everyone understands their meaning.

Be yourself. Don't try to be something you're not. Your group will see straight through it. Be true to your personality: don't try and be funny if it doesn't come naturally to you. People respect authenticity, so be genuine without being too heavy or intense. Remember, it's not about being cool – it's about loving people and drawing them closer to the kingdom of God.

Make use of the Bible, but don't expect the group to know anything about it. Assume that even the most common Bible stories are unknown to them. This can actually be a help, as hearing the stories for the first time often has a powerful impact on people.

MAKE IT PERSONAL

Make use of your own experiences in your talk. Personal stories are often the ones that young people remember afterwards, so these are an important part of the talk. You could also involve other leaders in sharing stories from their lives if they are relevant to the talk (make sure you check them beforehand). Don't underestimate the power of personal testimony. If we are vulnerable in our story telling then this can have a profound effect on a Youth Alpha group.

Don't forget that, whatever your age, you are a great example. The group may have forgotten what you said by next week, but they *will* remember what kind of person you are and how you live your life.

Sometimes you might not get much of a response from the group. That doesn't mean that you have given a bad talk (but do ask for feedback from your friends). My experience is that a lot can be happening in a person, even if they don't immediately respond to your words. The Holy Spirit works in people's hearts even if we can't see it. If we do our best, then God does the rest.

Gavin Calver is the National Director of British Youth for Christ.

yfc.co.uk

HOW TO PRAY FOR EACH OTHER ON YOUTH ALPHA

By Mike Pilavachi

When I first became a Christian I learnt that Jesus didn't just *say* wonderful things, he also *demonstrated* wonderful things: he *taught* the good news and he *lived* the good news. I learnt that part of what he did was to set people free by praying for them in various ways. Jesus' ministry of healing people and setting them free didn't end when he died and rose from the dead: he gave that ministry to his church, to his people.

For a while, the only group prayer I had ever seen modelled involved queuing up in front of a few super-spiritual Christians on a stage and waiting to receive prayer. I thought that if these people (they usually wore white suits and spoke in American accents) prayed for me I'd be blessed, but if a neighbour or someone sitting next to me at church prayed for me, well, that just wasn't the same.

A few years ago, I turned up at a church just outside London and I discovered that prayer isn't meant to be like that. At the time, I was really broken: a lot of things had gone wrong in my life. At the end of the service, the vicar (it was an Anglican church) said, 'If anyone would like prayer for anything then come forward and the ministry team will come and pray for you.' I was curious, as I'd never seen anything like this before.

People went forward, and the ministry team prayed for them in a really relaxed way. It looked so calm! Lots of different things seemed to happen – some were really obvious and some were less so. Some people started to cry, and at first I thought, 'Oh no, they're upset, why isn't anyone comforting them?' Others started to laugh and I *really* didn't get that. Some people started to shake a little bit, and some people even seemed to fall down, which scared me the first few times. The next week, there were testimonies from some of the people I had seen receiving prayer, and they would talk about the amazing things that God had done to them on the inside while they were being prayed for.

I realised that until that moment, I had only looked at what was happening on the outside, when all the while God had been working on the inside. My immediate thought was, 'Wow, this ministry team are so holy and spiritual, I could never be like that.'

I was desperate to meet with God, so regardless of what they asked people to go forward for, I'd go anyway! If the vicar asked if people wanted to respond to a call to be an evangelist, or a pastor, or to go to outer Mongolia as a missionary, I'd go forward to get prayed for. The amazing thing was, perhaps because I was desperate, God would meet with me, often in very real ways.

> *I thought, 'Oh no! I can't pray on my own, I'm not spiritual, I'm not holy, nothing will happen'*

I still stood in awe of the ministry team – I thought they were so spiritual and amazing. Then one Sunday night, the vicar said to me, 'Mike, I'd like you to join the ministry team.' I thought, 'The man's an idiot! He doesn't know what I'm really like; he doesn't realise that I'm not spiritual', so I said okay before he found out and changed his mind.

I started out by praying in a 'tag team' with a more experienced man from church (probably to prevent me killing anyone by mistake). We prayed for people, but I really believed it was the other guy's prayers that counted, not mine.

One Sunday, there were loads of people wanting prayer. The person leading the ministry said, 'Mike, we don't have enough people to pray, you're going to have to pray on your own tonight.' I thought, 'Oh no! I can't pray on my own, I'm not spiritual, I'm not holy, nothing will happen.' I just panicked and hoped that the person I was going to pray for would only have something small, like a headache. The guy I went up to asked me to pray for two things: a bad back and really bad depression. I said, 'Okay, let's pray for the depression first' (I chose this because I thought it would be harder to tell whether or not he was healed. That way he wouldn't notice that my prayers didn't work). I put my hand on his shoulder, and said some words. Inside I was thinking, 'Oh go on Lord, please. Just this once. I'll do anything, even be nice to my sister', but outside I was trying to look very spiritual. I thought I'd pray for a short time and then explain why sometimes people don't get healed.

> *Praying for others is something we can all do*

Suddenly, the guy opened his eyes and said, 'That's amazing – my depression's lifted, I feel like I can laugh for the first time in ages!' I tried to look very confident, as if I'd expected that and I said, 'Shall we go for the double and pray for your back too?' I put my hand on his back and prayed inside my head, 'Go on, go on Lord, do another one.' After a while, he opened his eyes and said, 'Thank you for praying for me.' I thought, 'That means his back's not healed.' Still, I was pretty pleased, because one out of two ain't bad!

Later, I was talking to someone else when the same guy ran up and said, 'Look, I've just realised I can do this', and he started doing all sorts of things with his body – his back was healed. I left that night walking on air. I suddenly realised a great truth: 'I'm spiritual, I'm holy, I heal people', and I couldn't wait for next Sunday. The next week, I prayed for someone with great faith – I rebuked the disease, I blessed the person, I prayed quietly in a whisper and then I rose to a crescendo. When he opened his eyes, I said, 'Well?' He replied, 'Nothing's happened, except

my legs hurt because I've been standing here for so long', and he left.

I was really confused. I thought, 'God, last week when I didn't have much faith, you healed someone, but this week nothing! Why?' At that moment a verse of scripture came into my mind (it's in Proverbs, James, and 1 Peter): 'God opposes the proud but gives grace to the humble.' At that point I knew exactly what it was all about.

Praying for others is something we can all do. It's not about people who think they are spiritual and holy or those who stand on platforms. This is a ministry for the whole body of Christ, for the whole church – for everybody. The people God loves to use the most seem to be the people that know that they can't do it on their own. They know that if God doesn't show up, they're in trouble.

One of the things I love about Youth Alpha is that it gives people on the course the chance to be prayed for. This first happens on the Youth Alpha Weekend or Day, and later in the course, during the session on healing. In our groups, we want to model how to pray for each other in a simple way that is easily replicable. This will show people that they, too, can begin to pray for others. While there may be 300 different ways to pray for someone, I want to give you a really simple model that all of us can use, regardless of experience.

FOUR VALUES OF PRAYER MINISTRY

I want to suggest four values we should hold on to as we pray for people:

1 WE VALUE THE CROSS OF JESUS CHRIST

The death of Jesus Christ on the cross is central to everything. Everything we receive is because of the cross, not because of us. At the foot of the cross, we are all the same size; we're all the same. This helps us realise that it's not about you or me, and it's not about an 'anointed' person who comes to town – it's about the anointed person who is Jesus.

It's his anointing, his gifts, his power; it all comes from him and it's all because of the cross. If we value the cross of Jesus Christ, we realise that the ultimate and best healing is forgiveness – coming into relationship with him: that's the root of everything else. When we value the cross of Jesus we don't pray prayers like this, 'Lord, bless and heal Jane because she is such a good person and she really deserves it.' Instead we will pray, 'Lord, bless and heal Jane because you are such a wonderful God, because you've already done it and you've already earned it.' We value the cross of Christ and that puts everything else in its place.

2 WE VALUE THE BIBLE AS THE WORD OF GOD

The Bible is our final authority on all matters of faith and conduct. That doesn't mean that there aren't other authorities, but these all fall under the final authority, which is God's word. That means the way we pray needs to come under the scrutiny of scripture and conform to what the Bible says.

We sometimes hear bizarre stories about what God is doing. If we value the Bible as God's word, we take those stories we hear, and we check them with the book. There's certainly enough bizarre stuff *in* the Bible to keep us going for ages before we need to start looking for bizarre stuff *outside* it! Like Jesus spitting on mud and rubbing the paste in a man's eyes to heal him – what's that about?

Yet Jesus Christ is our model for ministry as revealed in the Bible, so we've got to be people of the book; people who read and study the Bible.

3 WE VALUE THE PERSON AND WORK OF THE HOLY SPIRIT

What does that mean? That means it is *his* work and not ours. Actually, that is amazing news – we are released from the burden of feeling like *we* have to do something. It's God that does it, not us. When we're praying for people, we need to look at ourselves like waiters and waitresses in a restaurant. The customer comes in, and we go up to them and say, 'What is your order, Sir/Madam?' They may say, 'A bad left knee, healed please.' We write down, 'Bad left knee healed', and we take the order to the chef. Only the chef can make up the order, and in the same way, only God does the healing.

We get to be involved, we get to be waiters and waitresses, but Jesus does the healing – he does it with us. That's great news: if it's God's work and not ours, we don't need to stress, just keep it simple.

4 WE VALUE THE DIGNITY OF THE INDIVIDUAL

It's really important that we treat people with respect and dignity, just as we would like to be treated. If we are praying for someone, the worst thing we can do is get distracted and stop concentrating, that is not affirming and valuing an individual.

> *When we're praying for people, we need to look at ourselves like waiters and waitresses in a restaurant*

The ultimate goal is that the people we pray for meet with Jesus. Sometimes when we pray, it will all seem very gentle. At other times, it might be less gentle – people may laugh or cry, shake or fall over. All of this is okay, we respect their dignity.

PRACTICAL TIPS

We always encourage guys to pray with guys and girls to pray with girls. This just makes it easier for people to be honest with each other. We all know there will be some things guys wouldn't want to talk about in front of girls and vice versa.

First of all, **invite** the Holy Spirit to come. The Holy Spirit has been there the whole time, but now we're asking him to bring his presence to the person we're praying for. We can pray three words: 'Come Holy Spirit.'

The trick then is to **wait**. The temptation is to cover the silence with words – sometimes we find silence embarrassing – but actually, we just need to wait for the Lord.

Then we **watch**. We can keep our eyes open: in Biblical times they prayed with their eyes open. Jesus told the disciples to 'watch and pray' (Matthew 26:41). Jesus said, 'I only do what I see my Father doing, I only speak the words my Father gives me to speak.' This means, 'I want to follow him, I want to see what he is doing and I want to join in with that.' I wasted many years of my Christian life saying to God, 'Lord, this is what I want to do, would you bless that?' It's actually much more fun to find out what God's already doing and just joining in with that – it takes the stress away.

Sometimes the first thing that the person receiving prayer feels is a sense of peace. Then, really calmly, you may want to pray. If, for example, it's a bad left shoulder you are praying

for, just put your hand gently on the shoulder and ask for healing in Jesus' name: 'Lord would you bring healing here.' You don't need to do anything weird, just keep watching and waiting. Often, you don't see anything happening, and yet the person gets healed.

I want to remind you to only lay your hands on appropriate parts of the body (I won't go into details about this!). The only way to get better at praying for people in these ways is by doing it, so try!

When you have finished praying, you can ask what happened. If they say, 'Actually, I don't think anything happened', do not respond by saying, 'Nothing?! That's odd. You're the tenth person I've prayed for tonight and all the others were miraculously healed and set free. What's wrong with you?' If we treat people like that, they will leave discouraged. We should simply encourage people that God's Spirit always comes when we ask him, but we don't always sense what he is doing.

Praying for each other on Youth Alpha is an opportunity to cooperate with God and bless others with *his* blessing. It's not something reserved for only a few people – it's for all of us.

> *The ultimate goal is that the people we pray for meet with Jesus*

Mike Pilavachi is the Founder and Director of Soul Survivor.

soulsurvivor.com

PRAYING FOR YOUR YOUTH ALPHA COURSE

By Pete Greig

Well, it's been a long, slow process, but recently I got converted. Evangelists have been telling me for ages how much better my life will be if I see things the way they do. They've explained that I won't fully understand until I take the leap of faith, and they've testified to their own personal experiences. In the end I'm not sure if I was won over, or merely ground down. Anyway, I finally did it: I upgraded my battered old mobile for a sleek black iPhone.

To be honest, my old phone really wasn't that bad. If you want to see a bad mobile, you should check out the one my mum uses on the Isle of Wight. It's the size of a brick, and at times, she has to stand on one leg on the front doorstep, with the phone about twelve inches from her ear just to make the wretched thing work. Compared to hers, my old mobile was fine, so I guess I was a reluctant convert.

Despite the fact there have been no blinding lights and no angelic choirs, now I've made the switch I must admit that my iPhone really is better. I'm even telling my friends about it, and I actually caught myself advertising an Apple course at the church of All Things Apple.

My old phone was functional, but my iPhone is fun too. What's more (bear with me here), it's actually taught me things about communicating with God. My prayer life can easily become merely formal and functional, when it's meant to be fascinating, enjoyable, intuitive and expansive.

What I'm realising more and more is that prayer isn't just a way of getting things done and making things happen (a healing here, a heavenly memo there and a parking space at the supermarket on a Saturday afternoon). Prayer is the life-giving heartbeat of a dynamic,

Prayer isn't just a way of getting things done and making things happen

colourful, intuitive, intelligent, fun interaction with Jesus Christ.

When he was very little, my son Danny came into my study one day and started playing with my hole-punch. He was very taken with it, very impressed, and he spent a long time driving it around the floor like a car and snapping it like a crocodile. It was a long time before he turned to me and said, 'Daddy, what is this for?'

We can often treat our faith like that – enjoying it, admiring it, using it for all sorts of things but never really stopping to wonder, 'Father, what is it for? Why have I been saved? What is the point? Now that I am Spirit-filled, baptised, and helping on a Youth Alpha course – what now?'

I sometimes wonder what Adam and Eve talked about with God every evening in the Garden of Eden before the Fall. After all, there was no sin to fight, no sickness to heal, no gospel to preach, no transformation of society required. They didn't pray to make stuff happen, they prayed because they enjoyed sharing their lives with God – it was the most natural thing in the world. It was what they were made to do.

We are not Christians because of some cosmic strategy, and we do not pray merely to get things done while functionally serving the Lord. My wife Sammy and I did not have children as a 'child-raising strategy', but as an expression of our intimacy: we desired to lovingly raise children to maturity. We pray because we're wired for delightful intimacy with God.

I'm so excited that you're setting out on this journey of running a Youth Alpha course. I would encourage you to simply find a friend or two and get together to pray for your course. It's a good thing to pray for the course in the months and weeks leading up to it, as well as throughout the course itself. Ask others to pray for you and your course, too. If you ask God to do specific things, you'll be amazed at the miracles you'll see!

There are no secrets to this stuff, but I would encourage you to try to make it fun as well as functional. Why not include worship, or write down, draw or paint your prayers, or maybe use some visual aids such as photos as you pray for people. Try sticking your small group list on the bathroom mirror, or setting your phone alarm to remind you to pray a one-liner for them at a certain time each day? You can

> *We pray because we're wired for delightful intimacy with God*

also visit www.24-7prayer.com for more ideas and encouraging stories, or get hold of my book *Red Moon Rising* which will really help you get excited about the power of prayer.

Let's upgrade our prayer lives by daring to ask big things of God, and making prayer as creative and enjoyable as possible – the word 'functional' only makes sense with those first three letters (fun!) at the start.

I hope that as you run Youth Alpha for your friends you also celebrate and grow in your relationship with God, by making time to walk and talk with him each day. That is something my iPhone will never really help me with, but that's what I'm here for and that's all that really matters.

Pete Greig is one of the leaders of the 24-7 Prayer movement and is also Director of Prayer for HTB and Alpha International in London.

24-7prayer.com

USING MULTIMEDIA ON YOUTH ALPHA

By Phil Knox

There is a fascinating moment in the book of Acts when Paul is preaching the gospel in Athens. He notices an altar 'to an unknown God' and basically says, 'I know this God, he has a name, and his name is Jesus.' Paul uses the things that are around him to communicate the good news in a way that people will understand.

Today we live in a multimedia-filled society. Technology is everywhere, and if Paul was communicating the gospel in the 21st century I am sure he would still be using things around him to help. So how do we make the most of this massive area of technology?

FILM CLIPS

Every Youth Alpha session contains a selection of film clips to choose from that will help you illustrate the message. They can be powerful, memorable, entertaining and they can enhance your talk. Unfortunately, due to copyright restrictions, Youth Alpha cannot provide these film clips for you, so the first step is to decide which films you want to use, followed by borrowing or renting them.

> *For more ideas (including films released since this resource was written), visit youthalpha.org*

Top tips

- Source and check video clips well in advance. Make sure they are appropriate. For more ideas (including films released since this resource was written), visit youthalpha.org

- Make sure the clip is cued, the sound level is right and the lighting is adequate. Check the timecodes – we have done this for you in this resource, but in some DVD regions this may be out by several seconds

- Think carefully about how you will introduce and talk about the clip. Make sure you fill in the necessary background for those who have never seen the film but don't give away what happens altogether

- Don't feel you need to use a popular, recent film – sometimes a film the group haven't seen before can be more powerful in making the point

- Check that you have the right licence to show film clips – in the UK, most churches and schools will have a licence already. See www.ccli.co.uk for information

INTERNET VIDEO CLIPS

Internet videos, along with wireless internet, have exploded in the last few years, meaning that the use of online videos has become a possibility in Youth Alpha sessions. To this end, we have included some links to relevant clips on our website (youthalpha.org), but do search for new clips yourself.

Top tips

- There are several programmes on the internet that can help you download a *YouTube* video rather than streaming it – this can be useful, especially if there is no internet access in your venue

- Make your own videos. This creates a great sense of ownership and community. *YouTube* is all about participating and contributing, even though the quality is not always that great. Get some of your team to film vox pops on the week's subject, or film a five minute mock documentary

- If you do make videos or find any good clips to use, share them online at youthalpha.org so others can access them

- It is worth noting that the terms and conditions of *YouTube* say that clips are licensed for private and personal use only. If you wish to show these clips to your youth group you should always seek permission to do so from the copyright holder

POWERPOINT

Powerpoint can be a great way of keeping attention and building momentum through a session. It helps people keep track of what they are learning, and can be especially useful as each Youth Alpha session has a number of clear points to communicate.

Top tips

- Make sure the text is big enough to read

- Use powerful images from the internet.
  We live in an image-rich culture and our generation will engage better and remember more if there is a memorable image with each point. There are many websites offering free images such as www.freefoto.com

- Go through the presentation beforehand so you know it works and matches your talk

- Print off the order of your slides so you know what is coming next

MUSIC

Music can also be a great way of connecting with teenagers, and there may be some great tracks that really communicate a key point of a session.

Top tips

- Be aware that music, almost more than anything else, divides as well as unites. Be careful not to alienate half your group with choice of a particular style

- If you use some contemporary Christian music, try to look at it through the eyes of a teenager who has no experience of Christian worship – is it relevant?

- Playing a whole four minute track may be too long to engage a group in just listening. Consider playing just part of a track, or using a visually rich Powerpoint presentation to accompany the music

PRACTICAL ADVICE

Make sure that your media will work when you want it to. The biggest piece of advice we can give you as a leader is to get someone else to help. There are loads of people who love technology, and this can be a great way of getting them involved in serving. Make sure you prepare adequately and fully brief the person you ask – it is well worth having a practice run through so they know when to play each clip.

> *Make your own videos. This creates a great sense of ownership and community*

Top tips

- If you are using a laptop to play a DVD, you can bookmark the scene you want – this means that it will remember where to start from even if you play another DVD first

- Factor in the amount of time it will take to change and cue the next DVD (if you're using more than one)

- Try not to cue up a DVD scene on screen while the speaker is talking – it will be distracting. If you can use another monitor, that is better

We are really passionate about exploring the meaning of life and communicating the good news in a relevant and accessible way. Technology is a great way of doing this. Have fun with using multimedia in your sessions; we hope they communicate the life-changing message of Jesus in a relevant way.

Phil Knox is the Evangelism Resources Senior Manager at British Youth for Christ.

yfc.co.uk

WORSHIP ON YOUTH ALPHA

By Al Gordon

Worship is key to what Alpha is all about – giving people the chance to meet Jesus. When I was eighteen, a friend gave me a tape of worship music that had been recorded at a gathering of about 10,000 young people. I remember putting the tape into my walkman (retro, I know), and being blown away by the presence of God that seemed to fill my bedroom. That was the first time I experienced the Holy Spirit, and I remain convinced of the importance of worship.

Surprisingly, perhaps, worship plays a central role in an Alpha Course. The key question is, how on earth can you ask a bunch of people who don't believe that God exists to worship?

THE FATHER SEEKS WORSHIPPERS

Evangelism is about restoring correct worship. Worship is one of those things that everyone does instinctively: it's a first order human activity, like breathing, eating and sleeping. Jesus came to restore right worship so that everyone can find purpose and meaning in a loving relationship with their heavenly Father.

The Westminster Catechism says, 'The chief end of man is to glorify God and enjoy him forever.' At what point do we let people know this? When they've been hanging around church for a while? If our main purpose is to be worshippers, then worship must be at the heart of our gospel message: worship and evangelism go hand in hand.

WORSHIP DRAWS PEOPLE TO GOD

There's a brilliant story in Acts 16:25, where Paul and Silas have been thrown in jail for telling people about Jesus. They start worshipping, God intervenes supernaturally, the doors of the jail are blown off and half of the prison is converted. Worship can have a powerful impact on people who don't know God, because he is present.

WORSHIP IS WHAT WE DO

We're the church. We worship. It's a fact. It's been this way from the start of our story. People know this about us and there's no point in pretending we don't worship. We do. Because we're the church.

When people come and hang out with us, wanting to find out a bit more about what we believe, we shouldn't start pretending that the things we really value aren't important to us. That would be lacking in authenticity.

> *Worship and evangelism go hand in hand*

We want our evangelism to give people a taster of what church is like, and 'what-you-see-is-what-you-get' is a really important principle. We don't need to try and pretend we don't love to worship. We do, however, need to think about how we introduce people to worshipping Jesus, given that the whole worship-earthquake-chains-coming-off thing is quite rare.

YOUTH ALPHA

We suggest you introduce some sort of worship on week one of Youth Alpha. We tried having no form of worship. That's hard, because by the end of a ten week course, people have pretty much formed their understanding of what Christians do. They rock up to church after Alpha, you're all singing, and it becomes weird.

We tried introducing worship on the Weekend Away, and it was weird then too; people already had enough going on, being away with a bunch of strange Christians and all.

So, we recommend starting worship on the first night, because at least then everything is weird. You could start with a couple of songs led by someone on a guitar or by a band, or you could just listen to a worship song on CD.

When I lead worship for the first time on Youth Alpha, I normally say, 'Hi, my name is Al, I am your worst nightmare, a Christian with a guitar.' And they laugh, because it's true. Then I say, 'Would you like to stand, we're going to sing together.' I sing two songs and say, 'Would you like to sit down?' That's it. I don't pray, start explaining stuff ('I wrote this song the day my dog died') or 'coach' people in worship. John Wimber used to say, 'Worship is better caught than taught' and there's a lot of truth in that. People will figure it out, and the teaching material of the course covers worship, so there's no need to add anything extra. Let them be. They probably won't sing for weeks.

WHO SHOULD LEAD WORSHIP?

On Youth Alpha, the ideal person to lead is someone of a similar age to those doing the course. They don't have to be as good as Tim Hughes, the most important thing is that they have a heart for God and can carry a tune.

WHICH SONGS SHOULD WE SING?

If you look at the fifty top songs your church sings, they will fall into two loose categories: objective songs (he is good) and subjective songs (I love you, Lord). For the first few weeks

I would recommend you use objective songs. On the weekend, I would recommend that you begin to introduce some of the more subjective songs, as people are beginning to have an understanding of what a personal relationship with God looks like.

ALTERNATIVE IDEAS

People often ask us what they should do with a small Youth Alpha course, if, for example, there are only ten people having a course in someone's living room? There does come a point when it is just not practical to do sung worship, but if you can do something to reflect the values I've been talking about here, it will really help ground people in worship. Perhaps play a worship DVD or song, or have worship music playing in the background, just to introduce people to the concept of worship. See youthalpha.org for more ideas.

Don't worry if it feels really awkward: it feels just as awkward with hundreds of people, the only difference is that there are more people feeling awkward

Finally, don't worry if it feels really awkward: it feels just as awkward with hundreds of people, the only difference is that there are more people feeling awkward. We've got to take the long view. This is a ten week course that may be the start of a life-long journey for those who come to faith. Worship on Youth Alpha may not seem (superficially) the most inspiring, but in many ways it is the most significant worship for our church's life. Behind the scenes, even if people look like they're having a horrible time, the Spirit of God is at work, breaking captive hearts out of jail. Bring it on!

Al Gordon is Associate Director of Worship Central and Director of Sunday Services at HTB in London.

worshipcentral.org

USING YOUTH ALPHA FOR CONFIRMATION

By Louisa Jacob

Youth Alpha can work very well as a pre-confirmation course, encouraging teenagers to ask questions and discover what they really think about their faith.

We have seen Youth Alpha successfully incorporated in the run up to confirmation across different denominations, with the specifics of confirmation being taught additionally at the end of the course.

Youth Alpha can also work well as a post-confirmation course, encouraging those who may be wondering 'what next?' to continue exploring the questions they may have.

If you are a teenager who has been through confirmation, then you may want to run Youth Alpha for others who are either thinking of being confirmed, or who are already confirmation candidates.

> *As the emphasis in Youth Alpha is on small group discussion, we have found that, after confirmation, the group will often want to carry on meeting*

As the emphasis in Youth Alpha is on small group discussion, we have found that, after confirmation, the group will often want to carry on meeting. Whether this is in a church or school context, it is a great opportunity to keep exploring these important issues together. Youth Alpha should always be run with a view to having a follow-up plan.

Louisa Jacob is the former head of Youth Alpha and Student Alpha at HTB in London.

htb.org.uk

USING YOUTH ALPHA IN SCHOOLS

By Helen Lawson

Many teenagers today lead incredibly busy lives. They are involved in so many clubs, sports and activities that finding time to go along to another evening event may prove difficult. Running Youth Alpha in a school provides students with an opportunity to come along in a lunch break, or for a short period of time after school, to ask questions and explore Christianity.

If you are a student in a school, then you are probably the best person to run a course for your friends! It is fantastic that you want to share what you believe with others. I'd encourage you to run a course with another friend or two, and make sure you have support from parents, your youth pastor, or a supportive teacher.

GET PERMISSION

If you're a student, you will probably need permission to run a course. This might be from the head teacher, from the chaplain (if there is one) or from another senior teacher. Most schools allow different forms of student-led lunchtime clubs, and Youth Alpha is simply another of those. Hopefully your school will be thrilled that you want to contribute to school life in this way.

If you are a youth worker, it might be a good idea to see if there are Christian contacts already involved in the school (ie: chaplain, Christian Union or Christian teachers) and work with them. The most effective way to work in a school is by partnering with those who are already there, and building positive relationships with them. They will be your best support network for Youth Alpha.

If there are no Christian contacts in the school, check out what other groups run at lunchtime and after school. It is important not to run Youth Alpha in competition with things that are already in place.

If you are approaching a head teacher, have a clear picture of what you want to do, and be honest. Make it clear that you are coming to bless the school and to serve them as a community, not to demand entry. Also, ensure that you dress and act appropriately in accordance with teachers from the school. You need to make sure that you are aware of the school's child protection policy. Check with the leadership at the school and at your church to make sure you are covered for every eventuality.

TIME AND SPACE

So where do you start? Think about where you are going to run your group and at what time – lunchtime or after school? Ensure that you have all of the resources and materials that you need. For example, are you using multimedia that will require a DVD player/computer? Make sure you have everything on hand so that each session can run smoothly.

> *You are probably the best person to run a course for your friends!*

Think about the timing of your session. The students who come along at lunchtime or after school will, no doubt, be tired from lessons. You want to make the sessions fun and interactive so you can keep their attention.

Different schools will have different length breaks. It is possible to fit Youth Alpha into a thirty minute time slot – it could look something like this:

0–5 minutes: time to build relationships, eat together, relax and chat

5–15 minutes: give your talk

15–25 minutes: small group discussion time

25–30 minutes: end with some social time and invite guests back next week

Make sure that you have some social time at the beginning so students are not coming from one class to another 'class'. Try to make it engaging, but also try to create a relaxed space where the young people can feel comfortable and at ease.

You also need to think about the length of your course. Running the standard ten week course may not be possible within the school term. We would recommend that you don't cut out any of the topics though, it is better to merge some together. Please remember that Youth Alpha is very flexible and can be run in eight, nine or ten weeks.

Think about who will give the talks. If you are a student, I would encourage you and your friends to do some of them. You might want to ask others from your church (if the school are happy for this to happen) or ex-pupils to come and be 'guest speakers' at some sessions.

PUBLICITY

Publicising your course is vital so that every pupil in the school knows it is happening and knows that they are invited to come along. The best way to advertise is to be creative! You could promote the course with posters – make sure they look professional and fun; try to change their locations often so that they don't get stale.

You could try advertising each session individually rather than advertising the whole course at once, eg: 'At 1 pm today, Fred Smith with be speaking on "Does God Heal Today?" followed by discussion and debate.'

You might like to have some sort of 'Launch Event' to start your course. Many schools will allow students or schools workers to speak in assembly. Maybe you could have a local Christian 'celebrity' (ie, a footballer or actor) come in and and introduce Youth Alpha. Or, if assembly or celebrities are not an option, you could just have a special lunch – perhaps order a takeaway pizza and then do the introductory session.

YOUTH ALPHA WEEKEND/DAY AWAY

In this area in particular, every school is different. You may feel confident and able to take your group away for the weekend in order to cover the teaching material on the Holy Spirit. If you can, and the school and parents are happy, then that is great.

For those who are unable to take the group away, don't worry! There are other options. One option would be to join with another local school /church running Youth Alpha and go somewhere for a day or afternoon (see page 326 for more ideas). If you can't get away outside of school hours, try to make these talks special in some other way. You could change your meeting from lunchtime to after school and extend it slightly, for example. Again, providing food is a good way to make it fun. One group I know ran their course each week in the school's Physics Department, but for their Holy Spirit session, they simply merged the talks together and held a special lunch in the Art Department! They didn't go far, but it made those sessions significant and different from the others.

The main thing about running Youth Alpha in a school is to have fun together. Make it engaging, build relationships, be flexible and enjoy!

> *Make the sessions fun and interactive so you keep their attention*

Helen Lawson is the former Director of Youth Alpha and Student Alpha in Scotland.

uk.alpha.org

AM I TOO YOUNG TO RUN A YOUTH ALPHA COURSE?

By Brad Hawkes

These days, the word 'temple' doesn't really pop up that often, and when it does, we probably think of ancient places of worship in the Far East, or a tourist attraction we've seen on the Travel Channel. But the Bible speaks about temples over and over again. Back in the day, the temple was 'the place where God lived', where people could come to get hold of him. The temple was a big, visible reminder that God wanted to make himself available to his people and to make sure everyone knew where to find him.

In modern terms, you could liken the temple to a mall, a supermarket or a fast-food joint; each of them visible with their neon signs and billboards, all claiming to have what you need to make you happy. Whether it be the golden arches with their promise of a quick burger or a Happy Meal, a Nike ad subtly suggesting that their latest high-tops are all you need to make that dunk, or another smooth iPod commercial wooing you into the world of digital downloads. All of them with something on offer. All of them visible. All of them available.

Ask any young European today if they know where they can get a fast-food fix, find a packet of cigarettes or buy a new pair of Chuck Taylors, and they'll point you in the right direction. But try getting them to give you directions to the nearest church, or asking if they know where to find Jesus and the percentages drop. Thanks to media and technology we have pretty much everything at our fingertips, yet God appears to be less and less visible. Less and less prominent. Less and less available.

Recent surveys say that over eighty per cent of European teenagers are interested in topics regarding religion and faith. Read that again – over eighty per cent! That means young people are out looking for something, and there's more on the market to choose from than ever before. In the meantime, we Christians seem to be suffering from acute invisibility!

1 Corinthians 6:19 tells us that we are temples of the Holy Spirit. That means we are mobile, modern-day venues where God can dwell. We are living neon signs displaying God's name; walking, talking billboards making God available to our generation in our schools, universities and workplaces. Every young person standing up for Jesus is like a 21st century temple, a point-of-contact between heaven and earth. When Sam and his Christian Union in Derby put up that poster of themselves with the words 'We're all Christians, ask us why!' in their college, they turned themselves into a contact-point. When Lina from London stood up at assembly and announced that she was a Christian, or when those girls from Nottingham put up hearts with Christian messages written on them on Valentine's Day, God didn't just see a poster, a trembling girl, and red pieces of cardboard ... God saw temples!

> *We are living neon signs displaying God's name; walking, talking billboards*

So, my answer is *no,* you're not too young to run a course for your friends. By deciding to be visible in your school, college or community, you can join together with thousands of other young people across the UK, Europe, and the world, who are helping Jesus to reach a generation that he's longing to touch. You can be the point-of-contact in your world, and show your friends where to find God. You can help make God visible again in your generation.

Brad Hawkes is the International Leader for the New Generation International team.

newgenerationuk.com

RAISING UP YOUNG LEADERS

By Pete Wynter

Developing young leaders is an essential part of any thriving youth ministry, and Youth Alpha provides the perfect opportunity for young people to step up and lead among their peers. Although the Bible is clear that leadership is a gift, it's important to realise that we are all called to lead. If someone becomes a true follower of Jesus, it won't be long before they find themselves leading. That may mean leading an individual to know Jesus too, or influencing the communities or culture around them. Some will lead a few and others will lead many, but all leaders will be resourced and discipled well if we release them into roles of responsibility and purpose.

Youth initiatives that release young people into positions of leadership have experienced an increased ownership and commitment. As young people have been encouraged to put faith into action, use their gifts and influence others, they have grown as effective missionaries and disciples far more so than when they were spoon-fed from the front of an exciting programme of performance-driven dazzling lights and loud music. It doesn't take long to see that youth who are given opportunities to lead and take responsibility mature at a 'greenhouse' pace compared to those who dutifully sit through week after week of activities designed to equip them for some future that they really should be living now.

The way we release young people into leadership must, therefore, be carefully considered. It's not always good to throw them in at the deep end, sending them out along the tight rope of leading their peers, without safety nets to catch them if it goes wrong due to failure or missed opportunity. Equally, it isn't good to put so many 'safety nets' in place that your youth are forced to wonder if they will ever

> *Youth who are given opportunities to lead and take responsibility mature at a 'greenhouse' pace*

get to actually walk down the tight rope at all (this tends to be the greater problem in most youth ministries).

There are three safety nets: mentoring and accountability, training and a culture of encouragement. There are also three tight ropes: real contexts, vision that releases vision and external engagements.

Before we briefly explore each point, it's important to understand that if you are the leader of a group, then you are at the centre of what is released. God breathes through you, and will use your particular gifts and character to inspire those around you. For that reason, you must always be seeking to live the kind of life that you expect the young leaders around you to live out. When considering each of the following tight ropes and their safety nets, you should first ask yourself if they are all in place in your own life before seeking to establish them in the lives of those around you. In the past, youth leaders have spoken to me asking for the five keys to effective youth ministry, or for the latest top ten tools to ensure they're doing their job properly; really, all they need to do is get their own life in order and not rely on the latest gimmick or wise words. Always remember that you are at the centre of all that you seek to inspire in others, and if Christ is at the centre of you then you are off to a flying start!

SAFETY NETS

1 MENTORING AND ACCOUNTABILITY

This is where it all starts. The book of James speaks about confessing our sins to God, and to one another, in order to see healing. Intentional mentoring (group or individual) is the best context to be real, deal with character and relational issues and to build a trusted and teachable relationship with young leaders. If you begin to mentor those you seek to release, you will develop an accountable and valued relationship that will enable young leaders to know you are committed to them and are happy for them to be real about how they are and how their faith is growing. Too many leaders go through life without really walking closely with anyone. They become increasingly isolated in their role and then struggle even more with issues that have never been brought into the open. Then, when they fall from the tight rope, we all feel let down and wonder how on earth they ever managed to be there in the first place.

2 TRAINING

If we want to grow, we need to keep learning. Any leader who stops learning will stagnate and live on yesterday's experiences. Too often, when we see a gift for leadership in a young person, we want to get them going immediately. It is essential that you build some kind of training into a young leader's regular experience so that they are consistently reflecting and adding skill to the passion that we see in them. Hosting monthly 'leadership schools' or connecting to leadership training organisations will fuel what you are doing locally, and ensure that young people continue to take their responsibility seriously.

3 CULTURE OF ENCOURAGEMENT

People 'fly' when they know they are valued. If a young leader feels nervous that people will laugh at their risk, they will inevitably shy away from it and be disillusioned with the consequence of their leadership not being what they hoped it would be. If a culture of encouragement is built, then people step up even more, knowing that even if they fail, they will be brushed down and encouraged to try again. Do whatever it takes to build encouragement – write notes, give feedback, value effort, play icebreakers that inspire the best in people.

TIGHT ROPES

1 REAL CONTEXTS

Beware of calling 'token' readings at the front of church or serving in the back room leadership. These things may well be part of a leadership role, but most young people will eventually walk away if that's all their 'leadership' consists of. Leadership is about team building, inspiring vision, problem solving, developing creativity and strategy and inspiring hearts and minds. If we can release these kinds of contexts and give real responsibility to young people then they will grow fast. Youth Alpha courses provide an ideal context to involve young leaders in planning, strategising and team building, both through small group leadership, speaking, setting up and hosting an inviting venue.

> *Leadership is about team building, inspiring vision, problem solving, developing creativity and strategy and inspiring hearts and minds*

2 VISION THAT RELEASES VISION

Are you clear about where you are going? If you aren't, then you can't expect those who lead alongside you to get inspired and step up. If you have a clear vision or mission statement then people around you will 'get it' and run hard with it. They will understand the dreams that need to be fulfilled and the sacrifices that need to be made, and they will likely do all they can to be a part of making something inspiring happen. Work at communicating the vision you have, so that young leaders can capture it, and maybe even come up with their own vision within that context. For example, you may have a vision to host an incredible Youth Alpha course, they may catch that and fulfil their own vision to bring as many friends from the local college or school as possible.

3 EXTERNAL ENGAGEMENTS

If you want young leaders to develop, you need to take them out of their comfort zones and away from their 'normal' environments from time to time. The world is bigger than our local context, and when we see that, we begin to see a bigger need for our leadership. Uncomfortable platforms validate true gifting. If a young person feels that their leadership is valued by people they don't know in a place that is unfamiliar, it's amazing to watch the increase in confidence, expectancy and desire to grow. When a young leader has some experience under their belt, make arrangements to take them with you to an event where they can play a part in leading, be it a school, youth service or conference.

Establishing each of these six points will ensure that you have a context where young leaders can really lead, but, when they wobble and fall from time to time (as most of us do), they will be caught by the safety nets and made ready for their next attempt in the adventure of the tight ropes. Watching young leaders grow is one of the most rewarding experiences as a youth worker. Knowing that you are passing on experience and skill in a way that you wished had been done for you at that age, means that the next generation of leaders will totally surpass our own. And that's exactly what we want, isn't it?

Pete Wynter is the Director of Onelife.

onelifeonline.org.uk

STAYING SAFE ON YOUTH ALPHA

By Rachael Heffer and Simeon Whiting

Working with young people may well be one of the most exciting and challenging things anyone can do. Not only is it both fun and hard work at times, but it also carries a significant level of responsibility. A youth leader may, at any one time, need not only to be conscious of the programme, timing and activities taking place in the venue, but also of the potential risks or hazards that there may be around them. Leaders must know how to deal with any accident or incident that may occur.

Therefore, spotting anything that could put the health and safety of a young person or a member of the team at risk is vital. For this reason, there are guidelines – and in some cases, legal requirements – which we must adhere to. For instance, if you are working with young people in England, there are policies in place (such as the *Health and Safety Act* and the *Child Protection Act*) that must be followed in all youth work settings. These policies help to safeguard both the young people and the youth leaders present. Wherever a youth activity is taking place,

> *The guidelines are largely a simple matter of common sense*

whether it's a regular event or a one-off, whether it's in a church, school, park or other venue, Youth Alpha group leaders will need to adhere to the policies that deal with concerns such as health and safety and child protection. Take some time to familiarise yourself with these policies, and to think about what you must do to make sure your youth work operates within them.

Having said that, please do not be daunted by this responsibility, and do not become convinced that something is bound to go wrong! Accidents and incidents are actually very rare, so there is no need to be paranoid. All we must do is make sure that every possible precaution has been taken in order for our young people to have fun and learn in a safe environment. The guidelines that are in place to help us do this are largely a simple matter of common sense.

To help you, outlined below are nine areas that you should bear in mind as you plan your Youth Alpha course. Obviously, not all of them will apply to your situation, so just be mindful of the ones that are relevant to you.

1 RISK ASSESSMENT
It is essential to assess the risk factor of any venue you may wish to use for a youth activity, meeting or event – regardless of where it is. Ensure you have thoroughly checked out any potential hazards and assess how problematic any highlighted areas could be. Where possible, Risk Assessment forms should be used and completed fully for your back-up and records.

Consider the likelihood of anything going wrong and ask yourself what the consequences would be should any concern turn out to be a real issue? Once these areas have been highlighted, find ways to minimise or remove the risks. If you have any doubts, make sure you seek extra advice before proceeding with your activity.

2 FIRST AID
As far as it is possible, you should have a qualified first aider on your team (make sure everyone knows who this person is), and a first aid box that is easily accessible and stocked with all the basic equipment. Keep a check that all content – creams, etc – are in date.

Ensure that you have an easily accessible 'Accident and Incident Book' where all accidents and incidents are recorded. Everything, from a cut finger to an emergency requiring a 999 call, needs to be logged, written down (details included) and kept on file. This is not only to safeguard the young people, but also yourselves as youth leaders in case any complaint or query from parents (or others) is raised after an incident. Ensure that your whole team is aware of this book and that they use it adequately – filling it in as soon as possible following any incident or accident.

3 FOOD HYGIENE
If you are going to be providing food on your course, think through the basics of food hygiene – talk to an expert about the essential basics you will need to take into consideration.

Some of the vital issues include how to keep the kitchen and equipment clean and safe, how to prepare food using the right knives and chopping boards, how to store food safely and serve it at the correct temperature and making sure hot drinks are carried properly. Whilst this may not seem like a top priority when running a Youth Alpha course, it is a key part of ensuring that your young people are kept safe and well in their environment.

4 FIRE PROCEDURES
Wherever your course takes place, the whole team should know what to do if there is a fire. This includes knowing where the fire exits are and where the assembly point is once you've left the building. Always follow fire procedures if a fire alarm goes off, even if you know it is a false alarm. If you need to leave a venue, quickly count your group to ensure that everyone is with you. Keep fire exits clear and unlocked, and keep extinguishers in their right place. Know how to use the fire alarms, how to turn them off and how to reset them. Seek advice on this ahead of your course starting if this is unknown or unclear.

5 PARENTAL CONSENT
It is essential to obtain written permission from parents or carers before taking young people anywhere other than your usual venue.

Details of where you are going, timings for your departure and return, what you'll be doing, etc, are all essential to include in your letter to parents. These details could be put in a letter with a tear-off slip for the parent to sign and give back to you. Do not take young people out without this permission (see Appendix 4, page 405 for a sample form, or visit youthalpha.org.uk/lgmedia for an amendable version). You may also wish to ask parents' consent for you to make very basic decisions on behalf of their child in an emergency medical situation. Ask parents to include their mobile contact numbers in their consent forms.

> *Find ways to minimise or remove the risks*

6 RELEVANT INFORMATION
When you work with young people, it is useful to have facts about each person on file so that you can easily access key information about them. Try to include information such as: full name, address, phone number, date of birth, name of parent or carer, contact details for parent/carer, emergency contact number, email address, any medical needs, allergies, or dietary requirements.

Keep this information secure and confidential, and do not share it with other agencies without the permission of the young person's parent or carer. (To do so would be to contravene data protection guidelines.)

7 TRANSPORT
When travelling in a car or minibus, everyone must have a seat and seat belts must be worn – this is a legal requirement. Try and make sure an adult travels in the back of the minibus with the young people. Make sure your vehicle is working properly and that it is fully covered by insurance.

To adhere to *Child Protection Guidelines*, if you are travelling in a car with only one young person, ensure they sit in a rear seat (the only exception to this is if you are driving a two-door car, in which case the young person should sit in the front passenger seat).

8 CHILD PROTECTION

Anyone who is running a Youth Alpha course should be fully trained in the basics of the *Child Protection Guidelines*. Stories of child abuse and neglect seem all too common, and sadly, the church is often seen as part of the problem, not part of the solution. This means it is essential that we act responsibly. The church, school or other venue in which you meet should have basic *Child Protection Guidelines* which your team must follow. In the UK, any person working with young people or children must undergo an Enhanced Disclosure in your group's name, through the Criminal Records Bureau. (This sounds intimidating, but is actually very straightforward.) If you need any help with this, your denominational head office, your diocese or the Churches' Child Protection Advisory Service (www.ccpas.co.uk) should be able to help you. Even if you know every person involved in your course really well, it is essential that everyone undergoes this procedure.

Make sure the team is clear about how to express any concerns they may have about the possible neglect or abuse of a child, and who they should talk to. As much as possible, make sure the team know who is with who and what they are doing at all times – be accountable to each other. Try not to work on your own with young people but always as part of a team (even if it is with only one other leader). Never take young people out or away with fewer than two of you. If you do have to work with a young person on your own for any reason, do it in public view, making sure there are other people around, keeping the door open. Basically, be aware of how your actions look to others.

> *Don't get paranoid, but do be careful*

If a disclosure of some kind is made by a young person to a member of the team, ensure that the team member writes down the full details of what was shared by the young person as soon as possible after the event. You will need to have some forms accessible to you for the logging of such conversations. Encourage your team only to speak to the overall course leader about what was shared, not with other team members if there is no need. If, at any point, follow-up is required with Social Services or the police etc, written records are valuable forms of evidence.

Don't get paranoid, but do be careful, for your own protection as well as for that of the young people you work with. These simple steps can help protect you, your young people and your team.

9 CONFIDENTIALITY

DO promise your youth a safe place to talk, and guarantee to them that you will not gossip about what you are told, but NEVER promise complete secrecy. There may be things you need to pass on if a child's safety is at risk. If ever you feel out of your depth in talking to a young person, never be afraid to ask a fellow team member to assist you and join the conversation.

Hopefully the issues noted in this article will provide some basic guidelines for you to think about when you are planning your Youth Alpha course. In all things, remember that while it brings great responsibility, it is also a privilege to work with young people and to see God so at work in their lives.

Simeon Whiting and Rachael Heffer work for British Youth for Christ.

yfc.co.uk

YOUTH MINISTRY 3.0 – A MANIFESTO OF CHANGE

By Mark Oestreicher

There's a series of commercials on American TV for a hamburger chain. The commercials show ordinary people – often guys – wearing the long red braids of the chain's logo character, and having countercultural epiphanies about burgers and other fast-food realities. My favourite of these commercials opens with an aerial shot of a massive hole in the ground, and hundreds of people are running toward it from all sides. When they get to the hole, they all jump in.

Then the shot changes to catch the face of one guy (wearing the red wig) who's running amid the crowd. As he's running, we can hear his thoughts as he realises that something isn't right. He then starts to speak as it dawns on him that he doesn't have to have his burgers cooked ahead of time and kept warm under a heat lamp. He slows to a stop, and a few others also stop to listen – but most of the crowd continue to run into the hole. The few who stop with him all decide that they want their burgers to sizzle! They cheer and start running back – against the flow of the crowd.

It's a funny commercial. But I have to admit that every time I see it, it reminds me of the church. We have all this momentum. We perceive things are going well. Our megachurches are more mega than ever. Our youth ministries are better funded than ever. Youth ministry is receiving more respect than ever. We have better resources and training events and celebrities and credibility than we've ever had.

So why does it seem like we're racing into a hole?

I want to be part of that countercultural band of youth workers who stop. I want to be part of that 'wait a second' group who doesn't just accept the way things are. I want to join with others who notice that we're heading down a path toward obsolescence and complete ineffectiveness, and turn around to ask, 'What should we change?'

I believe we're at a crossroad in youth work. In order to be effective – in order to be true to our calling – we need to change. We need to turn at this crossroad, but I'm afraid we're passing right through it, assuming that the way we've always done things will continue to work.

The problem is this: the way we're doing things is already not working. We're failing at our calling, and deep down, most of us know it. This is why we need an epochal shift in our assumptions, approaches, models, and methods.

It's time for Youth Ministry 3.0.

AN EXTREMELY SHORT HISTORY

Adolescence is a cultural phenomenon, and it's fairly recent. It's only in the last 100 years or so that our Western cultures have acknowledged a period of time between childhood and adulthood. And youth culture itself is even more recent – it's really only about sixty years old.

Sure, this is a generalisation, but it's not unfair to break modern youth culture into three epochs. We could say that the first epoch was post World War Two until about 1970 (I've started calling this 'Youth Culture 1.0'). The second epoch was roughly between 1970 and the turn of the millennium ('Youth Culture 2.0'). And we're living in the third epoch now ('Youth Culture 3.0').

> *I believe we're at a crossroad in youth work*

THE THREE TASKS OF ADOLESCENCE

All teenagers, at least those who live in a culture that acknowledges adolescence, wrestle with three 'tasks': identity, autonomy and affinity. I refer to them as tasks, though they're wrestled with almost completely semiconsciously. The older a teenager gets, the more self-aware they become of this wrestling, of these tasks (and certainly more so these days since adolescence now stretches into the twenties). But the tasks present themselves at the onset of adolescence.

Identity is the, 'Who am I?' question. Simply put: one's identity is the sum of one's self-perceptions. This includes self-perceptions about character, values, purpose, and potential in life; caste; emotional makeup; appearance and body type; intellectual, spiritual, and emotional strength or weakness; relationship to family, friends and culture at large as well as many other factors.

Children and pre-teens aren't intellectually capable of this kind of third-person thought. A nine-year-old cannot stand apart from herself and perceive herself – she cannot form opinions of herself based on self-perception. She can form opinions about herself based only on what she likes or doesn't like, and what others have said about her.

This is why identity is such a major task in adolescence. The reality is that by the time an adolescent reaches her mid-twenties, her identity will be mostly formed. (And, remember, this is the whole point of culture giving teenagers a respite between childhood and adulthood.) Sure, we continue to shape and refine our identities throughout adulthood, but the core formation work is done. The course is mostly set.

Autonomy simply refers to something's separateness – its independence. In adolescent-development terms, autonomy is wrestling with the questions, 'How am I unique and different?' and, 'What's my unique contribution?'

In psychological terms, this is often referred to as *individuation*. The process of individuation is becoming oneself: unique, and separate. This process is primarily (though not exclusively) the issue of separating from one's family.

Mixed into this progression is the ancillary question, 'What's my unique contribution?' The 'contribution' in that question plays out in a variety of arenas: family, friends, and other relationships; school; youth group; community and the world. As a teenager begins to see her uniqueness, she's better equipped to understand her role and influence in relationships and the world around her. As she begins to see how that influence plays out, she's better equipped to grasp her uniqueness.

Affinity, as a word, simply means likeness or attraction. We use it in a developmental sense to refer to people's connection to others who are like them in some way. This 'likeness' may be external – a teenage boy may find affinity with guys who are into skateboarding or science, or a teenage girl may find affinity with a group of kids who like a certain style of music. But the likeness can also be more internal. A teenager can find affinity with others who share the same values or the same outlook on life, or he can find affinity with his family based on shared experiences and stories.

This final task of adolescence almost seems in opposition to the task of autonomy. But, in reality, they go hand in hand – two apparent opposites in a dependent dance, with identity looking on. Autonomy and affinity are the yin and yang of identity formation, really, informing and framing that first task.

It's easy to see this quest for affinity in teenagers. They desperately desire to be included, to be part of a social network, to feel as though they belong somewhere. Young and middle teens, especially, commonly have multiple affinity groups to which they belong (or aspire to belong). This is all a normal (sometimes healthy, sometimes not) part of the process of figuring out who they are.

SHIFTING PRIORITIES

I believe (and I'm finding good support for this idea from those more academic than me!) that these three adolescent tasks have remained constant, but their prioritisation has shifted over the three epochs of youth culture. In Youth Culture 1.0, 'the long leg of the three-legged stool' (as I've started to call it) was identity. Youth culture was new, and was trying to figure out who it was. It was still very much a sub-culture of culture at large, and not dramatically influential to the world of adults.

Ever since caring adults started trying to connect with teenagers, youth work, has been cross-cultural, missional work. In many ways, the earliest modern youth workers (during those post World War Two days, when Youth Culture 1.0 was just getting some traction) were motivated almost purely by missionary zeal. They wanted to bring the love of Christ to a different cultural grouping of people, and thought long and hard about how to embody the gospel in ways that were culturally appropriate. We could say that Youth Ministry 1.0 was proclamation-driven, and had key values of *evangelism* and *correction*.

But in the late 1960s, as youth culture came into its own, and was clearly no longer a passing cultural fad, the priorities of the three adolescent tasks went through a shift. Youth Culture 1.0 was already 'other' and 'different', which gave it a natural sense of autonomy. But as youth culture became more accepted and normative, the adolescent need for autonomy exerted itself and became the leading task. Identity and affinity started to be worked out *in the context* of autonomy.

Youth work also went through a dramatic shift as youth workers, trying to be true to their calling, shifted their assumptions, approaches and methods to reach teenagers. Youth workers responded (appropriately, it's important to remember) with new tools to build

autonomous youth groups. Youth Ministry 2.0 became *programme*-driven, with key values of *discipleship* and *building a positive peer group*.

But a third shift in youth culture has taken place. We might say that Youth Culture 2.0 was so successful in its quest for autonomy that it left a 'belonging vacuum'. As youth culture became the dominant culture in our society (with adult culture now looking to youth for cues in almost every arena), youth culture responded by splintering. We now find ourselves in a time when there is no longer one monolithic youth culture. There are now multiple youth cultures, each with its own values, behaviours, attitudes, styles, music, language, and relational norms.

> *Youth Ministry 1.0 was* proclamation-*driven, and had key values of* evangelism *and* correction

Youth Culture 3.0 is defined by a priority of affinity, the need to belong. For today's teenagers, identity and autonomy are worked out *in the context* of the quest for affinity.

AND HERE'S THE RUB

Many of us have sensed that something is wrong with how we're doing youth work. We've been like those people in the commercial, running towards the big whole in the ground, utilising our finely tuned programs in an attempt to reach teenagers who just don't give a rip about our games, entertainment and well-crafted youth sermons, but thinking there must be a different way of living out our calling.

We see the current dropout rates of teenagers after youth ministry, and we think (with our Youth Ministry 2.0 mindsets): 'We need to add cooler programmes! We need a big youth centre – on the other side of the parking lot from the church! We need better games! We need a state-of-the-art sound system!'

We see kids in our ministries with shallow, unarticulated faith, and we think, 'We need a better curriculum! We need more mission trips to shock them! We need a small groups programme – let's see how HTB or Soul Survivor does it! We need to increase the youth budget so we can do better stuff!'

Alas, our thinking is stuck in – let's face it – the previous millennium. We *cannot* build a great youth ministry to reach Youth Culture 3.0 teenagers with Youth Ministry 2.0 methods or thinking.

YOUTH MINISTRY 3.0

Instead of the evangelism and correction themes of Youth Ministry 1.0 or the discipleship and create-a-positive-peer-group themes of Youth Ministry 2.0, we need to embrace the key themes of *communion* and *mission*.

COMMUNION

For teenagers desperate to define their identities through affinity, we need to help them experience true community. True community doesn't mean once-a-week, highly programmed youth group meetings. True community *might* take place in the context of a small group – but the practice and programming of small groups does not ensure true community. True community is life-on-life, whole life, eating together, sharing journeys, working through difficulties, wrestling with praxis (theology in practice), accountability, safety, openness, serving side-by-side, cultivating shared passion and holy discontent, mutuality, and a host of other variables. True community *is not* a programme. It's not something people sign up for. It's not something we force.

But 'community' doesn't seem to completely capture Youth Ministry 3.0 thematically. Instead, let's make the subtle but significant shift to the value of *communion*. Communion is true community with Christ in the mix. Communion is both the *essence* and the *action* of a Christ community.

MISSION

'Mission' and 'missional' have become buzzwords over the past few years. I'm concerned they're becoming faddish, which would be a great loss as they're so massively pregnant with truth, value, and scriptural integrity. For our purposes here, let's describe 'missional' as 'joining up with the mission of God in the world'.

Mission, in this context, is *not* about having a purpose or mission statement. It's not about being purposeful (although that's not a bad thing) or purpose-driven. And I'm *definitely* not using the word 'mission' to describe starting a programme of missions. Mission, in this context, starts with the assumption that God is already actively working on earth, bringing redemption, restoration, and the transformation of all creation. Therefore, a missional ministry seeks to discern, observe, and identify what's close to the heart of God and where God is already at work – and then *joins up* with the work of God already in progress.

> *Youth Ministry 2.0 became* programme-*driven, with key values of* discipleship *and* building a positive peer group

Combine these two themes – communion and mission – and you have a youth ministry that could be described as communion on a mission: a Christ-infused, true community seeking to engage the world in God's redemptive work-in-progress. Can you see how this provides meaning and direction to all three adolescent tasks?

'My identity is a follower of Jesus Christ, framed in real community with others who have a synergistic, shared passion for the work of God in the world.'

'My uniqueness (autonomy) is found both in the individuality of my own story, as well as in the unique ways in which my contextualised community seeks to live out faith in Christ, together and for others.'

'My affinity is with these people, for these people, with Christ, and for the active work of God in the world.'

Whereas Youth Ministry 1.0 was proclamation-driven and Youth Ministry 2.0 was programme-driven, Youth Ministry 3.0 needs to be … not-driven. It's time to do away with being driven or driving. That metaphoric language might work for herds of cattle, but it doesn't work for a fluid, missional community.

> *Youth Ministry 3.0 needs to be … not-driven. It's time to do away with being driven or driving*

Instead, let's say *present*. Present to the work of God in our lives and in the world. Present to the moment, not just living for a day when we leave a horrible world. Present to one another – to those experiencing communion with us, to those who aren't (yet), and even to those who never will be in our community. Present to life in the way of Jesus.

Figuring out what all of this looks like in real youth work is going to take lots of experimentation and failure. We'll need to be passionate about contextualisation and not just copy each other. Let's remember these fantastic words that Jesus said as he was sending out the disciples: 'Don't think you have to put on a fundraising campaign before you start. You don't need a lot of equipment. *You are the equipment*, and all you need to keep that going is three meals a day. Travel light' Matthew 10:9–10 (*The Message*, emphasis mine).

Mark Oestreicher is the former president of Youth Specialties. This article is based on Marko's book, *Youth Ministry 3.0* (Zondervan/Youth Specialties, 2009).

SECTION 4

YOUTH ALPHA TEAM TRAINING

TEAM TRAINING SESSION 1

HOW TO LEAD SMALL GROUPS ON YOUTH ALPHA

TEAM TRAINING SESSION 1
HOW TO LEAD SMALL GROUPS ON YOUTH ALPHA

SUMMARY

AIMS OF THIS SESSION

- To equip team members to run a fantastic Youth Alpha course

- To explain how small groups work

- To empower team members to lead small groups confidently

NOTES

- We strongly recommend that every Youth Alpha course includes the following team training session. Why not get together one evening, have a meal, work through this training material and pray for your course together?

- This session should be held before the course begins

SESSION OVERVIEW

- Food
- Welcome
- Worship
- Talk
  - Introduction
  - Point 1 – Youth Alpha course overview
  - Point 2 – Aims of the small group
  - Point 3 – Practicalities of small groups
  - Point 4 – Tips for leaders
  - Point 5 – Ground rules for your small group
  - Point 6 – Praying in your small group
  - Conclusion
- Group activity – Small group role-play

INTRODUCTION

- Welcome to the Youth Alpha course team training! It's great to have you as part of our team!

- The aim of this session is to give you an idea of what will happen on the course and to equip you to be able to lead a Youth Alpha small group

If your team don't know each other very well, you may wish to start with an ice breaker game to help them start to learn some names.

POINT 1 – YOUTH ALPHA COURSE OVERVIEW

1. WHY ARE WE RUNNING THIS COURSE?

- Some of you may have lots of experience with Youth Alpha, others will have done a course, and some won't know anything

- So let me quickly tell you why we're running the course

- The aim is to give our friends a chance to hear more about what we, as Christians, believe, and to give them a chance to experience what being a part of a Christian community is like. Our hope is that as they hear about Jesus and discuss what they think, they will find that it is true and they may want to set off on a journey of faith with God

- Here's what this course is not:

    - a place where we only want certain opinions voiced

    - a chance to 'Bible-bash' our friends

    - a place to pressure people into making a decision for Jesus

    - a guaranteed way to 'convert' people

- Youth Alpha is a tool we can use to offer our friends a chance to explore the Christian faith and learn about the person of Jesus Christ

2. HOW DOES THE COURSE WORK?

- The course runs over eight/nine/ten sessions/weeks *[delete as appropriate]*

- Each session will have the following elements:

Food

- We'll start each session by eating together. *[Explain the context of this – whether it will be a meal, snacks, or another option you have chosen]*

- We believe that there is something spiritual about eating together – Jesus did a lot of his ministry around meals. It's a great way to build community, too

Fun

- The aim is for every session to be fun. This course is not meant to be heavy or intense. If you have any ideas on how we can make it more fun, please share them

- We might play a game or show a funny video to start the session. We believe that you can learn about Jesus and have fun at the same time!

Talk

- Each session, one of us will give a talk

- That's our chance, as a team, to say what we want to about Christianity – and it's our *only* chance. If it isn't said in the talk, it doesn't need to be said at all

- Each talk will be on one of the suggested Youth Alpha topics

- The idea is that the talks should be appealing and relevant to the group. We will use illustrations and different media to make it interesting

Small groups

- Every Youth Alpha session has small group discussion time. This is the most important part of the whole course, and it's vital that we get this right

- That's really why we're doing this training session – so we are all equipped and ready to host and lead the small groups

- So those are the four components of the course

- There's also a Youth Alpha Weekend/Day in the middle of the course which you should already have in your diary. We'll talk more about that in a few weeks at our next training session

- For the rest of this session, we're going to look at how Youth Alpha small groups work and how we can lead them well

POINT 2 – AIMS OF THE SMALL GROUP

- Let's start by having a look at how a small group might work

AUSTIN POWERS　　　　　PREPARATION TIME　**5**
　　　　　　　　　　　　　　　　　　　　　　　　　　minutes
Quick summary
In this clip we see a number of people having group therapy. This is an example of how a small group shouldn't work!

Equipment/resources needed
A copy of the film Austin Powers: International Man of Mystery, *New Line Cinema, 1997. Certificate 15.*

▷ *Chapter 8: 0:51:18*　　　☐ *Chapter 8: 0:54:37*

Projector and screen (or a TV), and a DVD player.

How to link to talk

- That's an example of how your small group shouldn't work! A Youth Alpha small group has quite a different feel – it is not like a self-help group. No matter how annoying the people in your group may be, it's a good thing to *not* want to kill them!

- So why do we have small groups?

- Jesus had small groups! He had a group of twelve guys that he hung out with, and they certainly asked lots of questions (in a way, you could say the disciples were the first Youth Alpha small group!)

- There are two main aims of small groups – to discuss, and to build relationships

1. TO DISCUSS

- The British band Coldplay wrote a song called 'Square One' which goes like this:

  'You're in control, is there anywhere you wanna go?
  You're in control, is there anything you wanna know?
  The future's for discovering
  The space in which we're travelling
  From the top of the first page
  To the end of the last day
  From the start in your own way
  You just want somebody listening to what you say
  It doesn't matter who you are.'

- This pretty much sums up the way a lot of people think these days. On one hand, we are in control of our own lives, but on the other hand, we really just want someone to listen to our thoughts

- Youth Alpha gives people the chance to express their views on life and faith. The best way to do this is through discussion

- This is very important – we want people to be able to say what they really think

- Youth Alpha is about helping people to make the right decisions, rather than just telling them the right answers. We don't just want them to know the facts, we want them to be able to figure stuff out and find the answers for themselves

- If we allow this to happen, then the fruit will be long-lasting, rather than short-term

- Discussion helps truth to rise to the surface, making it easier for people to discover it for themselves

- In John 16:13, it says, 'But when he, the Spirit of truth, comes, he will guide you into

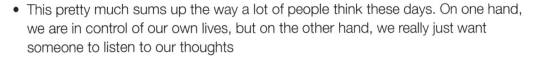

all truth. He will not speak on his own; he will speak only what he hears, and he will tell you what is yet to come'

- We don't need to be afraid of people's questions. As that verse says, the Spirit will lead us into truth – and if something is true, it will stand up against any amount of questioning

- We have one golden rule in small groups – **no question is too simple or too hostile**

- We need to make it easy for people to discuss whatever they like, including questions about faith and Christianity, or issues that the course material might have raised for them

2. TO BUILD RELATIONSHIPS

- Someone once said that people go to church for many reasons, but only come back for one – if they make friends

- Hopefully the people in your small group will really enjoy hanging out and getting to know each other better

- This aspect of the Youth Alpha course is so important; it's essential to spend time getting to know each other and letting friendships form

POINT 3 – PRACTICALITIES OF SMALL GROUPS

1. WHEN ARE THE SMALL GROUPS?

If you are aiming to have small groups after the talk:

- After the talk, we will split into our groups and go to different parts of the venue for our discussion time. *[It might be good to have more drinks and biscuits available for this]*

- Wherever you are situated, you must make sure that everyone in the group feels comfortable and safe. We need to ensure that everyone sits on the same level – either on chairs, sofas or the floor, but not a combination of these, as it will make the group dynamic feel odd

- It is vital that all small groups finish on time, if not early. It is better to leave people wanting more than letting them get bored – you can always continue the discussion next time. Be ruthless about sticking to your finish time – even if someone is making the best point ever!

- Finishing on time offers people security, especially if they're feeling unsure about being on the course in the first place. There's nothing worse than people not coming back because the group went on so late the first week

- Do use the suggested questions in the *Leaders' Guide* as a starter for your small group discussion, but feel free to talk about whatever you'd like

If you are planning to have small groups within the talk, after each teaching point:

- The person giving the talk will tell you how long you have for each block of discussion – probably no more than five or ten minutes. Small groups will stay in the main room for discussion, otherwise too much time will be spent going to and from groups

- Do use the suggested questions in the *Leaders' Guide* as a starter for your small group discussion, but feel free to talk about whatever you'd like

2. WHO IS IN THE GROUP?

- Small groups usually have between eight and twelve members, but there should never be more than twelve people in a group

- Ideally, each group should have one or two 'leaders' and one or two 'helpers'

- The leaders are there to guide the discussion and host the group. Normally, leaders are Christians who have done the course before

- The helpers are there to help host the group and to make guests feel welcome. They may help get drinks and food for people, make introductions and generally be encouraging and helpful

- There should be between six and eight guests per group – people who are there to do the course but aren't on the team

- If you are a helper, there is one really important thing to remember: **you should not talk** in the group discussion unless the leader specifically asks you to. You're there as a silent support to the leader – it may well be that some of the guests don't even realise until halfway through the course that you are on the team, which is fine!

3. HOW DO WE START THE GROUP ON THE FIRST NIGHT?

- On the first night when you get into your small group for the first time, I'd suggest you start with some sort of group ice breaker game. This may seem really cringey but it is worth doing

- The important thing is to learn each person's name in a way that helps everyone else remember it

- Suggestions include *[please feel free to suggest your own]*:

  1. **The name game:** starting with the group leader, each person must say their first name preceded by a word that starts with the same letter. The word must describe their personality, for example: Macho Matt, Super Sarah, Phunny Phil, etc. The next person must start by saying the name(s) of those before them, and then say their own, so that the last person has lots of names to remember!

  2. **Favourites:** each person must say their name, and then tell the group what their favourite film/book/TV programme/song is

  3. **The lift game:** each person must say their name, followed the name of the

person they'd most like to be stuck in a lift with (this person could be famous, dead, alive ... there are no restrictions)

4. **The desert island game:** each person must say their name, and then tell the group what one luxury item they'd take with them if they were stranded on a desert island

- It can also be a good to ask why each person has come to Youth Alpha. If you know anything about your group beforehand (maybe through chatting while you eat) then start by asking someone whom you know will give a negative response

- This will allow everyone else to be as honest as they like. If the first person says, 'I just want to know Jesus better', chances are that everyone else will feel too embarrassed to say what they really think. What you want is someone who can say, 'I'm only here because my friend dragged me along. I would rather be anywhere else in the world than here. I'm an atheist and this is all a load of rubbish.' That would be perfect!

POINT 4 – TIPS FOR LEADERS

1. WE'RE THERE TO FACILITATE DISCUSSION

- Remember that the role of the small group is not so much to answer people's questions as it is to facilitate discussion

- The best phrase you can use is, 'What do the rest of you think ...?'

- So when someone offers a thought, it's not your job to jump in with your views or an answer, but to throw it open to the rest of the group. Let me demonstrate what I mean

BALL SKETCH

PREPARATION TIME **0** minutes

Quick summary
In this illustration, you (and six or seven volunteers) will demonstrate the 'perfect' Alpha small group discussion time.

Equipment / resources needed
Enough chairs for six or seven people.
A ball.

How it works
Ask for six or seven volunteers (this could be all of your team, which would be great).
Get them to sit in a semi-circle facing the rest of the group (you can either ask them to bring a chair, or have some already set up). Get hold of a ball. Then explain:

- These six/seven people represent a Youth Alpha small group, and we are going to demonstrate how an ideal discussion should work. I am the small group leader

- Normally a group would sit in a circle – just so you know

- We're going to demonstrate visually how a discussion works, so let's pretend that whoever has the ball is the person who is speaking

- There are three ways a small group *could* work:

MODEL 1 – WRONG

- So I have the ball, and I would start off by saying something like, 'What did everyone think of the talk tonight?' Someone would hopefully answer that *[throw someone the ball – they don't actually have to answer. Ask that person to throw it back to you – then throw it to them, and ask them to throw it back to you – keep doing this]*

- Now you can see that if the small group works like this, then there are two of us having a great discussion – but the rest of the group are bored

- This is how NOT to do your small group on Youth Alpha!

MODEL 2 – WRONG

- Another way of running your small group is like this *[quietly tell your group to always throw the ball back to you]*:

- I can start off the conversation by asking *[insert name]* a question. S/he passes it back to me, so I pass it on to *[insert name of someone else]*. S/he passes it back to me *[keep this going]*

- Although the whole group is involved in the conversation, it's still all about me, the leader. This is also NOT how the ideal small group works

MODEL 3 – RIGHT

- Here's how the ideal small group goes *[quietly tell your group to pass the ball amongst themselves, occasionally returning to you]*:

- Again, I start off the discussion, but this time the group chats amongst themselves

- Occasionally it may return to me, but I simply ask another question or say, 'What do others think?' to keep the conversation focussed on the group.

- This is the perfect small group discussion! The conversation is flowing and everyone is contributing by saying what they really think

How to link to talk
Ask for a round of applause for your volunteers, thank them, and ask them to return to their seats.

- So, a small group leader is more of a facilitator than an instructional guru. A facilitator is simply another member of the group who is helping to keep the discussion going. Our views are no more important than anyone else's, and we are not looking to judge people or their opinions. It is our aim to guide and steer the group, so ask lots of questions!

- Remember the key question for leaders: 'And what do the rest of you think?'

2. THEY'VE ALREADY HAD THE TALK

- This is a key point to grasp. Remember that by the time we're ready for our small group discussion, everyone has already heard a talk; they certainly don't want to hear another one. Preaching of any kind is banned in the group

- This can be hard, especially if people are asking questions that you consider easy to answer – but don't do it

- You might be leading a group who seem to have disproved every aspect of Christianity. Even so, don't try and defend it

- You might get asked lots of questions and want to answer them – don't! Far better to say something like, 'That's a great question – what do the rest of you think?'

- By session six (or so) of the course, your group may want to know what you think about certain subjects, and only then might it be appropriate to share. We need to earn our right to talk by listening for the first half of the course

3. LOOK FOR OPINIONS NOT ANSWERS

- Avoid asking closed questions – questions that have either 'yes' or 'no' as an answer. Instead, ask open-ended questions that require an opinion

- This helps to keep the discussion flowing, but it also means that there can be no right or wrong answer; you are asking for an opinion and because we respect each person, no one can be incorrect

- I'd suggest you ask what people *think* or *feel* in order to keep things open

4. VALUE EVERY OPINION

- Don't take sides in the discussion, but value every opinion that is shared

- Even if someone says something that seems crazy or ridiculous – we want them to know that what they think matters to the group

- You could say something like, 'That's interesting. What does everybody else think?' This allows you to affirm them without having to agree, and it gives others in the group a chance to respond for themselves

5. DON'T BE AFRAID TO LOSE THE ARGUMENT!

- This is also really important. If you get to the end of the night and your small group have, say, disproved the resurrection, don't worry! Actually – this is great! You may be discouraged, but the chances are that your group will come back next week in order to disprove the next topic. Just remember – if truth is truth, it will always come out

- This is a really hard thing to do, and takes discipline on your part as leader

You may wish to include the following optional extra, but it is not essential

OPTIONAL EXTRA – GOING DEEPER

'FEELING DISCOURAGED' TESTIMONY

If you have a story about a time when you were feeling discouraged by a small group discussion, regardless of whether everything worked out or whether you felt that you failed, then share it now. It will encourage those who are nervous about getting it wrong.

POINT 5 – GROUND RULES FOR YOUR SMALL GROUP

- Youth Alpha is not supposed to be like school (at all!) but it might be helpful to set some ground rules, as a group, on the first week. These could include things like:

1. NO PUT-DOWNS

- We want everyone to respect each other. It's okay for the group to attack ideas, but not each other

2. THERE'S NO SUCH THING AS A STUPID QUESTION

- We want everyone to know it's okay to ask *any* question without being laughed at

3. NO ONE HAS TO TALK BUT ONLY ONE PERSON TALKS AT A TIME

- We won't make anyone speak
- We want to respect each other, and that means listening to what others have to say and not talking over them

4. WHAT IS SAID IN THE GROUP STAYS IN THE GROUP

- If someone shares something personal in the group, there needs to be an understanding that it will not be passed on to others at school or anywhere else

POINT 6 – PRAYING IN YOUR SMALL GROUP

- One of the goals of the small group is to model praying together

- It is always good to remember not to rush into prayer, though. Go at the pace of the slowest person in your group – if they are not ready, don't do it

- There's nothing worse than trying to have a time of prayer that goes a bit like this:

MEET THE PARENTS   PREPARATION TIME   **5**
                                                                                         minutes
Quick summary
This clip shows Greg saying grace before a family dinner. This is an example of an unsuccessful prayer.

Equipment/resources needed
A copy of the film Meet the Parents, *Universal Studios, 2000. Certificate 12.*

▶ *Chapter 5: 0:23:27*   ☐ *Chapter 5: 0:25:11*

Projector and screen (or a TV), and a DVD player.

How to link to talk
- You see, when we put people on the spot it can be embarrassing for them – we don't want that!

- There may be people in the group for whom Youth Alpha is their first experience of anything church-related; they may not be comfortable praying with everyone else until later in the course

- The earliest we would suggest you try praying together is after the talk 'Why and how do I pray?' – Session 4

- If you do decide to have a time of prayer, the leader should test the waters by suggesting that it might be cool if the group prayed together

- Make it clear that no one has to pray aloud, but they're all welcome to. We suggest that the small group leader prays a very short and simple prayer first, something like, 'Thank you, God, for the weather. Amen'

- If you are in your small group and you feel a long and eloquent prayer coming on, do pray it, but not until you get home!

- If the leader prays the world's most powerful and beautiful prayer, chances are the group will think, 'Wow, if that's what prayer is, I could never do that.' If we pray a simple prayer, however, the group may think, 'Hey, that was simple. I could do way better than that', and they probably will!

CONCLUSION

- To conclude, small groups are an absolutely key part of the course

- If we get them right, they will be the most enjoyable part too, and our groups will love being together

- Remember:

  - it's a discussion, not a question and answer session

  - no preaching

  - value all people and their opinions

  - finish on time, no matter what

- In a minute we're going to have a go at practising being part of a small group

- Before we do that, let's look at one final video – about how *not to* lead an Alpha small group

HOW NOT TO RUN A SMALL GROUP

PREPARATION TIME 5 minutes

Quick summary
This clip shows a 'computer simulation' of how to run a small group – or not. (This film stars Jamie Haith, head of Student Alpha, who does all the voices, too.)

Equipment/resources needed
To find the link for this clip, please visit youthalpha.org/lgmedia
You may want to use a projector and a screen in order to show the clip to the whole group.

How to link to talk
- So that's how not to do it!

GROUP ACTIVITY

SMALL GROUP ROLE-PLAY

PREPARATION TIME 15 minutes

Quick summary
A small group role-play demonstrating how, and how not, to lead a group.

Equipment/resources needed
One envelope per group.
Eight cue cards to go inside each envelope. You can find the cue cards on Sheet 10 at the end of this session, or online at youthalpha.org/lgmedia

How it works

Get people into groups of eight (there are eight cue cards in each envelope).

Each person must take a cue card at random from the envelope – this will tell them which 'character' they are to be.

Tell the groups:

- In each group there is one helper and one leader – please identify yourself if this is you

- No one else should identify themselves – it's more fun that way

- 'Guests', I want you to pretend that it is the first week of Youth Alpha, and that you have just listened to the talk 'Who Is Jesus?'

- 'Leaders', the first thing you need to do is introduce everyone, and play some sort of ice breaker game (maybe the 'name game'?)

- Leaders, you should ask each of your group why they have come – and the rest of you must make up a reason that fits your character

- Then, start to discuss the talk, and you *must* stick to the role you have been given

- We will give you thirty minutes *[or set another time limit]* to do both the welcome game and the discussion – then we'll hear some feedback about how you got on

CLOSE OF SESSION

Once everyone is finished, get feedback from groups (maybe ask one or two people from each group to speak for their 'team')

- How did you get on?

- What was difficult about that?

- What was easy about that?

- Which character was the hardest to handle?

- In what way is leading a Youth Alpha group different from leading other types of group *[if relevant]*?

You might like to close in prayer, praying for the team and the course.

This training session is based on the article 'How to lead a Youth Alpha small group' by Matt Costley. To read the article in full please see page 338.

SHEET 10
CUE CARDS –
SMALL GROUP ROLE-PLAY

Print as many copies of this sheet as you think you will need, depending on the number of groups. Insert one copy of each character into each group's envelope, ensuring there are only eight roles in total.

THE LEADER
You are the leader of this group. Your role is to facilitate the discussion, and make sure that everyone has an opportunity to speak. Don't let anyone dominate the discussion, and remember to follow the guidelines you were given earlier.

THE HELPER
You are the helper. You may not speak unless the leader asks you to.

THE ATHEIST
You don't believe in God, or in any 'higher power'. You think anyone who believes in such things must be crazy and illogical. Argue this point in a non-hostile way.

THE THINKER
Your big question (which you should come back to often) is, 'If there is a God, why is there so much suffering in the world?'

THE OVERLY-SINCERE CHRISTIAN
You are a super-keen Christian and cannot believe that anyone could doubt there is a God. You know your Bible backwards and you should quote Bible verses to the group as often as you can get away with.

THE TALKER
You are going to be loud and slightly obnoxious – you don't think you believe in God, but aren't really sure. However, you love to hear the sound of your own voice and should try to speak as often as you can, over the top of others if need be.

THE QUIET ONE
You are quiet and you don't like to say *anything*, even if asked. You should refuse to answer questions – just sit there and look awkward.

THE SEEKER
You are genuinely interested in discussing this theme, and want to know what others think. You will support the leader if any disputes arise, and you just want to be able to have a good, interesting discussion.

TEAM TRAINING

SESSION 2

HOW TO PRAY FOR EACH OTHER ON YOUTH ALPHA

TEAM TRAINING SESSION 2
HOW TO PRAY FOR EACH OTHER ON YOUTH ALPHA

SUMMARY

AIMS OF THIS SESSION

- To equip team members to run a fantastic Youth Alpha Weekend/Day

- To explain how the weekend/day prayer ministry time works

- To empower team members to pray for each other and their groups

NOTES

- We strongly recommend that every Youth Alpha course includes the following team training session. Why not get together one evening, have a meal, work through this training material and pray for your course together?

- This session should be held a week or two before the Youth Alpha Weekend/Day

SESSION OVERVIEW

- Food
- Welcome
- Worship
- Talk
    - Introduction
    - Point 1 – Youth Alpha Weekend/Day overview
    - Point 2 – What is prayer ministry?
    - Point 3 – Four values of prayer ministry
    - Point 4 – Practical tips
    - Conclusion
- Group activity – Prayer ministry time

INTRODUCTION

- Welcome to the second Youth Alpha team training session!

- The aim of this session is to give you an idea of what will happen on the Youth Alpha Weekend/Day and to equip you to be able to pray for the people in your Youth Alpha small group

If your team don't know each other very well, you may wish to start with an ice breaker game to help them start to learn some names.

POINT 1 – YOUTH ALPHA WEEKEND/DAY OVERVIEW

1. WHY DO WE HAVE A WEEKEND/DAY?

- The weekend is the only part of the course that includes teaching on the person and work of the Holy Spirit

- It also gives us the chance to pray for our groups to be filled with the Holy Spirit. It's a chance for them to experience the love of God

- It is often the most fun bit and I think you'll find that the relationships in your group become much stronger as a result of the Weekend/Day *[delete as applicable]*

2. HOW DOES THE WEEKEND/DAY WORK?

- We're going to be holding the Weekend/Day at *[venue]* from *[date/time]* to *[date/time]*

- We're getting there by *[insert mode of transport]*

- And here's how the programme will work:

[Describe the programme for the your weekend/day – see the sample programmes in Appendix 3 (page 403 or visit youthalpha.org/lgmedia*) for example timetables that will help you plan.]*

- At the end of the talk, 'How Can I Be Filled with the Holy Spirit?' we will have a chance to pray for our groups

- This session is to help train and equip us so we know how to pray for each other

POINT 2 – WHAT IS PRAYER MINISTRY?

- Prayer ministry is where we pray for each other by the laying on of hands

- Jesus prayed for people by placing his hands on them (Luke 4:40)

- The early church prayed for people by placing their hands on them (Acts 8:18)

- Paul tells us to do the same (2 Timothy 1:6)

- People can sometimes be scared about prayer ministry, because they have a false view of who the Holy Spirit is

THE SIMPSONS

PREPARATION TIME **5** minutes

Quick summary
In this Simpson's clip, we see the faith healer come to town. He is showy and does a rap, while Bart 'heals' Homer of having a bucket on his head! This is an example of how the Holy Spirit can be incorrectly portrayed.

Equipment/resources needed
A copy of The Simpsons: *'Faith Off' (season 11, episode 11), Twentieth Century Fox Film Corporation, 2000. Certificate PG.*

▷ *Chapter 4: 0:08:48*   ☐ *Chapter 4: 0:09:34*

Projector and screen (or a TV), and a DVD player.

How to link to talk
- People can have a false view of the Holy Spirit and prayer ministry because of how it is sometimes portrayed

- We don't need to be worried though, our model of ministry is designed to make it as simple and clear as possible, with no hype

---

- Prayer ministry is about cooperating with God in what he is doing

- I'm always encouraged by the story of Moses parting the dead sea (Exodus 14)

- When we look at the story, we read that all Moses had to do was stretch out his staff

- It was God who parted the sea! God does the hard bit – we have the easy part

POINT 3 – FOUR VALUES OF PRAYER MINISTRY

1. WE VALUE THE CROSS OF CHRIST

- We want to value the death of Jesus Christ on the cross, because that is central to everything

- Everything we receive is because of the cross, not because of us

- At the foot of the cross we are all the same size

WE'RE ALL THE SAME

Quick summary
Use this analogy to demonstrate to your team that we are all the same at the foot of the cross.

Equipment / resources needed
None

How it works

- If I compare myself with someone like *[insert the name of one of your friends]* I may think, 'Hey, I'm not doing too badly! Compared to him/her, I am a pretty good person.' Compared to *[insert name]* I can feel pretty good about myself

- But, if *[insert name]* and I are both at the foot of the cross looking up, we're exactly the same

How to link to talk

- That helps us realise that it's not about you or me, and it's not about some 'anointed' person who comes to town – it's about *the* anointed person: Jesus

---

- It's his anointing, his gifts, his power; it all comes from him and it's all because of the cross

- If we value the cross of Jesus Christ, we realise that the ultimate and best healing is forgiveness – coming into relationship with him: that's the root of everything else

- When we value the cross of Jesus we don't pray prayers like this, 'Lord, bless and heal Jane because she is such a good person and she really deserves it.' Instead we will pray, 'Lord, bless and heal Jane because you are such a wonderful God, because you've already done it and you've already earned it'

- We value the cross of Christ and that puts everything else in its place

2. WE VALUE THE BIBLE AS THE WORD OF GOD

- The Bible is our final authority in all matters of faith and conduct

- That doesn't mean that there aren't other authorities, but these all fall under the final authority, which is God's word

- That means the way we pray needs to come under the scrutiny of scripture and must conform to what the Bible says

- We sometimes hear bizarre stories about what God is doing. If we value the Bible as God's word, we take those stories we hear, and we check them with the Bible

- There's certainly enough bizarre stuff *in* the Bible to keep us going for ages before we need to start looking for bizarre stuff *outside* it! Like Jesus spitting on mud and rubbing the paste in a man's eyes to heal him – what's that about?

SMITH WIGGLESWORTH

PREPARATION TIME 0 minutes

Quick summary

This true story shows how God used Smith Wigglesworth to perform incredible miracles, but that we look to Jesus, not other people, as our model.

Equipment / resources needed

None

How it works

There was a guy called Smith Wigglesworth, he was born in 1859 and he was a plumber from Bradford, England. He couldn't read or write, but when he became a Christian, his wife taught him how to read as they studied the Bible. He had a simple but profound faith, and he took God at his word. Let me tell you two short stories about what he did.

He once got called to pray for someone, but they died before he got to them. Smith decided that he wasn't going to let death stop him. He went to the morgue, picked up the corpse, held it against the wall and said, 'In Jesus' name, I speak life to you and I rebuke death.' Then he let go, and the corpse fell to the ground. Now, if that had been me, I'd have looked at the corpse and said, 'Well, I had a go, it didn't work – never mind, let's move on.' But not our friend Smith. He picked up the corpse, put it against the wall and prayed again, 'I speak life to you in Jesus' name.' He let go again, and once more, the corpse fell down. He did this a third time, and on the third attempt, the corpse started walking around! Amazing!

On another occasion, Smith Wigglesworth met someone with stomach cancer. As he prayed for them, he punched them really hard in the stomach, and the cancer was healed! (I bet there are some people you'd like to pray for using that method!)

How to link to talk

- Now, we could think 'that's a good model for ministry'. God used Smith Wigglesworth in some remarkable ways, but Smith is not our model for ministry

- Jesus Christ, as revealed in the Bible, is our model for ministry, so we've got to be people of the book; people who read and study the Bible

3. WE VALUE THE PERSON AND WORK OF THE HOLY SPIRIT

- What does that mean?

- It means it is his work and not ours

- Actually, that is amazing news – we are released from the burden of feeling we have to do something. It is God that does it, not us

WAITERS IN A RESTAURANT

PREPARATION TIME 0 minutes

Quick summary

This analogy which likens us to waiters/waitresses and God to a chef, shows how he is responsible for all the actual work, but how we can help.

Equipment / resources needed
None

How it works

- When we're praying for people we need to look at ourselves like waiters and waitresses in a restaurant

- The customer comes in and we ask them, 'What is your order?' and they may say, 'A bad left knee, healed please.' We write down, 'Bad left knee healed' and then we take the order to the chef

How to link to talk

- Only the chef can create the order

- In the same way, only God does the healing and the ministry

- The great thing is that we get to pray – we get to be waiters and waitresses!

JESUS RAISES LAZARUS

PREPARATION TIME 0 minutes

Quick summary

This story shows how prayer is a team effort – we pray, God heals!

Equipment / resources needed
None

How it works

- I love the story in the Bible when Jesus raises Lazarus from the dead (John 11:38–44)

- It was a 'team effort' – Jesus and the disciples worked together! In fact, the disciples did two thirds of the work and Jesus only did a third

- Who rolled the stone away? The disciples

- Who took the grave clothes off? The disciples

- The only bit that Jesus did was say, 'Lazarus come forth!'

How to link to talk

- We get to be involved – we get to pray – but Jesus does the healing!

- That is great news – it takes away all the burden and stress

- If it's God's work and not ours, we don't need to worry – he will take care of everything. Just keep it simple

4. WE VALUE THE DIGNITY OF THE INDIVIDUAL

- This is really important. We must treat people with respect and dignity, just as we would like to be treated

- If we are praying for someone, the worst thing we can do is get distracted and stop concentrating, that is not affirming and valuing an individual

- The ultimate goal is that the people we pray for meet with Jesus. Sometimes when we pray, it will all seem very gentle. At other times, it might be less gentle – people may laugh or cry, shake or fall over. All of this is okay, we respect their dignity. We don't need to draw attention to it or make it into a spectacle

- When you have finished praying, you can ask them what happened

- If they say, 'Actually, I don't think anything happened', don't be negative. We should simply encourage people that God's Spirit always comes when we ask him, but we don't always sense what he is doing

- We always say that guys pray with guys and girls pray with girls. This is about respecting people's dignity and making it easier for them to be honest. We all know there will be some things guys won't want to talk about in front of girls and vice versa

POINT 4 – PRACTICAL TIPS

- So, on the weekend, when the speaker ends their talk and invites us to pray to be filled with the Spirit, we will wait on him for a bit

- The speaker/leader will tell you when to start praying

- No one will be asked to respond, so it's up to you, as leaders and helpers, to offer to pray for each person in your group. It helps if you are already sitting with your group during that session

- You can pray on your own for someone, or in pairs, but no more than two of you should pray for one person at a time, or it can seem a bit intense

- Remember, guys pray with guys, girls pray with girls

- Ask the person if you can pray for them – if they say no, then that's cool, just move on

SAVED   PREPARATION TIME **5** minutes

Quick summary
This clip shows people being bundled into a van and being forced to receive prayer – this is not how we want to pray for people!

Equipment / resources needed
A copy of the film Saved, United Artists, 2004. Certificate 12A.

▷ *Chapter 14: 0:38:14*   ☐ *Chapter 14: 0:39:39*

Projector and screen (or a TV), and a DVD player.

How to link to talk
- This is how not to pray, obviously! We never pressure anyone into receiving prayer

The best way to pray for someone who wants it is to:

- Place your hand on an appropriate part of their body – their shoulder is probably fine

- **Invite** the Holy Spirit to come. Pray simply, 'Come Holy Spirit'

- Then **wait.** This is actually harder than you might think

- Resist the temptation to cover up silence with words. We just need to wait for God to do it

- Then we **watch**. I want to encourage you to pray with your eyes open. This can seem unnatural, but Jesus told the disciples to 'watch and pray' (Matthew 26:41). Jesus said, 'I only do what I see my Father doing, I only speak the words my Father gives me to speak'

- Keep your eyes open and watch for what God might be doing

LADY WITH WIG

PREPARATION TIME **0** minutes

Quick summary
This story demonstrates why it's important to pray with your eyes open!

Equipment / resources needed
None.

How it works
This is a story that Mike Pilavachi tells, which may or may not be true – I really hope it is true!
A lady came up for prayer at a church meeting and a guy started praying for her (remember, *we* would always encourage guys to pray with guys and girls with girls).
He held her head in his hands, closed his eyes and started praying. After a while, he thought she seemed a lot lighter, so he opened his eyes. To his horror, she'd fallen down under the power of the Holy Spirit and he was left holding her wig in his hands while she was lying bald on the floor!
In his panic, he quickly stuffed the wig back on her head before she opened her eyes. When she did open her eyes she started screaming because she thought she'd gone blind – in his haste, he had put the wig on the wrong way round!

How to link to talk
- So we want to pray with our eyes open and watch what God is doing!

- As you pray, if you sense that God is saying something to that person, and it is strengthening, encouraging and comforting (1 Corinthians 14:3), you can share that

- When you sense they have finished, or that God has done what he wanted to do for now, you can ask them what they sensed/felt

- Then go and pray for someone else!

CONCLUSION

- In a minute we're going to practice praying for each other so that we are all equipped when the weekend comes around

- To summarise, prayer ministry is about cooperating with God

- We need to remember that we value the cross of Christ – so we are ministering to someone on our own level, not someone lesser or better than ourselves

- We need to value the Bible as God's word

- We need to value the work of the Holy Spirit – it is the Spirit who does the work, not us

- We must value the dignity of each person – we want to bless them and build them up in Christ

- So shall we have a go?

You may close this part in prayer and ask God to minister to you all by his Spirit.

GROUP ACTIVITY

PRAYER MINISTRY TIME

Ask people of the same sex to get into groups of three (you can do pairs if you prefer). Tell the group that they should each take turns praying for each other – one person 'receives' while the other two pray and wait, and then they should swap.

As the leader, you should coach them – while they pray for someone, remind them to:

- Place a hand on the person's shoulder

- Ask God's Spirit to come and meet with that person

- Keep your eyes open (you may need to move around to check this – it is usually the most common mistake to make, we naturally close our eyes)

- Remember to wait on God, don't worry about silence

- Watch what God is doing and be open to him

- When you think you've finished, ask the person what they sensed/felt

- Now swap over

Bring all the groups back together, and ask for some feedback. Ask them:

- How did you get on?

- What was difficult about that?

- What was easy about that?

- Do you feel you could do that with your group on the Youth Alpha Weekend/Day?

Ask anyone who has any questions or concerns to meet you at the end.

CLOSE OF SESSION

You might like to close in prayer, praying for the team and the Weekend/Day.

This training session is based on the article 'How to pray for each other on Youth Alpha' by Mike Pilavachi. To read the article in full please see page 343.

APPENDICES

APPENDIX 1

SAMPLE YOUTH ALPHA COURSE TIMINGS

The following timings are samples to show you how your course could run in either ninety minutes, two hours, or in a thirty minute school lunch break.

A typical afternoon session could look like this:

3.45 pm	Team arrive, set up venue and pray
4.30 pm	People arrive, food/drinks/snacks served, time to chat
4.55 pm	Introduction to session from leader
5.00 pm	Ice breaker game
5.10 pm	Talk/teaching material presentation
5.30 pm	Small group discussion time
6.00 pm	Session ends

A typical evening session could look like this:

6.30 pm	Team arrive, set up venue and pray
7 pm	People arrive, food/drinks/snacks served, time to chat
7.30 pm	Introduction to session from leader
7.40pm	Ice breaker game
7.50 pm	Talk/teaching material presentation
8.10 pm	Small group discussion time
8.45 pm	Chill-out time
9.00 pm	Session ends

A typical school lunchtime session could look like this:

12.30 pm	People arrive, eat together, relax and chat
12.35 pm	Talk/teaching material presentation
12.45 pm	Small group discussion time
12.55 pm	Chill-out time
1.00 pm	Session ends

APPENDIX 2

YOUTH ALPHA COURSE – SAMPLE PARENT INFORMATION SHEET

This is a sample hand out only. You can find an amendable template online at youthalpha.org/lgmedia which can be adapted to fit the context of your course.

[INSERT NAME OF CHURCH, EG: ST STEPHEN'S CHURCH] YOUTH ALPHA COURSE – PARENT INFORMATION SHEET

WHAT IS YOUTH ALPHA?

Youth Alpha is a fun, informative and relaxed course that offers teenagers the chance to explore some of the bigger questions of life, while teaching the basics of the Christian faith.

Youth Alpha is based on the Alpha Course, which is now running in over 160 countries worldwide. Over 18 million people have attended a course, and it is running in every major Christian denomination around the world.

For more information please visit alpha.org

WHAT HAPPENS AT YOUTH ALPHA?

Each session of Youth Alpha has four main elements – food, fun, a short presentation, and discussion in small groups.

At each session, one of the team will give a short presentation on a different aspect of the Christian faith (covering topics such as 'Who Is Jesus?', 'Why and How Do I Pray?', and 'What about the Church?' among others).

Following the presentation, there will be discussion time in small groups. Here, the groups are encouraged to be completely honest, say exactly how they feel about what has been said and debate the topics together. All opinions are considered valid, and there is no pressure to think or act in a particular way.

It is worth mentioning that no session is compulsory, and guests are welcome to leave the course at any point. The course provides an opportunity for anyone, regardless of background, to make an informed choice for themselves.

WHO IS RUNNING IT?

This Youth Alpha course is being run by [insert name(s)] and a team from [insert church or youth centre name (if applicable)].

WHAT ARE THE PRACTICAL DETAILS?

Youth Alpha will run weekly on [insert day and time of day, eg: Wednesday evenings] from [insert start time, eg: 7 pm] to [insert end time, eg: 9 pm] at [insert venue details].

There is an optional weekend/day [delete as appropriate] in the middle of the course which we would love your teenager to come to. We are currently finalising arrangements for this, and more information will be provided near the start of the course.

DOES IT COST MONEY?

The course itself is totally free – food will be provided for an optional donation of [insert suggested donation, eg: £2]. There will also be a suggested cost for the weekend/day [delete as appropriate] which we will confirm soon, but we would hate anyone to miss out due to financial reasons so please speak to us if this may be a problem.

WHO CAN I CONTACT FOR MORE INFORMATION?

Please contact [insert name] on [insert phone number] or by email on [insert email address].

If you are interested in the topics covered on Youth Alpha and would like to find out more about attending an Alpha Course yourself, please just ask one of the team or visit **alpha.org** to find a local course.

We hope this answers your questions. If not, please feel free to contact us; we would love to speak to you.

APPENDIX 3

SAMPLE YOUTH ALPHA WEEKEND PROGRAMME

FRIDAY

7 pm onwards	Arrive
8 pm	Evening meal
9 pm	Short introductory session*, including:
	• Ice breaker games
	• Short time of worship
	• Brief overview of weekend, prayer
Late activity	Bonfire, late night hike, big-screen movie, etc

SATURDAY

9 am	Breakfast
10 am	Weekend Session 1, including:
	• Ice breaker games
	• Worship
	• Talk – 'What about the Holy Spirit?'
11.30 am	Break
12 pm	Small groups
1 pm	Lunch
2 pm	Afternoon activities, sports, or visit to an attraction
4.15 pm	Afternoon tea (for those who are starving)
5 pm	Weekend Session 2, including:
	• Ice breaker games
	• Worship
	• Talk – 'How Can I Be Filled with the Holy Spirit?'
	• Prayer ministry
7 pm	Evening meal
8 pm	Entertainment: movie, talent show, etc

*The suggested weekend introductory session is entirely optional, and no teaching material has been produced for this. We would suggest you simply welcome people to the weekend, run through the programme for the weekend, and introduce the theme of the person and work of the Holy Spirit. It should not be a full talk – just opening remarks.

APPENDIX 3 (continued)

SUNDAY

9 am	Breakfast
10 am	Small groups
11 am	Weekend Session 3, including:

- Ice breaker games
- Worship
- Talk – 'How Can I Make the Most of the Rest of My Life?'
- Prayer ministry

1 pm	Lunch
2 pm	Travel home

SAMPLE YOUTH ALPHA DAY PROGRAMME

9.30 am	Arrival and breakfast
10 am	Weekend Session 1, including:

- Ice breaker games
- Worship
- Talk – 'What about the Holy Spirit?'

11.30 am	Break
11.45 am	Small groups
12.30 pm	Lunch
1.30 pm	Afternoon activities, sports, or visit to an attraction
3.30 pm	Weekend Session 2, including:

- Ice breaker games
- Worship
- Talk – 'How Can I Be Filled with the Holy Spirit?'
- Prayer ministry

5 pm	Drinks and snacks
5.30 pm	End of day

APPENDIX 4

YOUTH ALPHA WEEKEND/DAY – SAMPLE PARENT INFORMATION SHEET/BOOKING FORM

This is a sample hand out only. You can find an amendable template online at youthalpha.org/lgmedia which can be adapted to fit the context of your course.

[INSERT NAME OF CHURCH, EG: ST STEPHEN'S CHURCH] YOUTH ALPHA WEEKEND/DAY [DELETE AS APPLICABLE] – PARENT INFORMATION SHEET

WHAT HAPPENS AT THE YOUTH ALPHA WEEKEND/DAY? [DELETE AS APPLICABLE]

The Youth Alpha Weekend/Day [delete as applicable] offers teenagers a chance to continue their Youth Alpha journey with a bit more time to hang out together. The Weekend/Day [delete as applicable] will be packed full of fun activities, as well the usual Youth Alpha sessions, including more presentations and small group discussions.

The Weekend/Day [delete as applicable] will focus on the work of the Holy Spirit in the lives of Christians. There will also be an opportunity for the group to pray together. As always, we can assure you that there will be no pressure on anyone to pray, sing or participate in anything that they do not wish to. The weekend is entirely voluntary, and it is up to you whether your teenager comes.

Activities such as [insert activities you intend to do here] will form a major part of the Weekend/Day [delete as applicable] and all meals will be provided from [Friday dinner] through to [Sunday lunch].

WHO IS RUNNING IT?

This Youth Alpha course is being run by [insert name(s)] and a team from [insert church or youth centre name (if applicable)].

All adult helpers have had a Criminal Records Bureau (CRB) check [UK only] and we will have a qualified first aider with us.

DOES IT COST MONEY?

Obviously, it does cost money for us to run the Weekend/Day [delete as applicable]. We are suggesting that people pay a fee of £__ [insert decided fee] to attend (includes all meals, accommodation and activities), but bursaries are available for anyone who cannot pay the full amount. Please speak to one of the team for information regarding bursaries [if applicable to your course]. The fee is payable in [insert methods of payment accepted, eg: cash, cheque (remember to include details on who to make the cheque payable to), etc].

WHAT ARE THE PRACTICAL DETAILS?

We will be holding the Weekend/Day [delete as applicable] at [venue name and address details]. We will be travelling there by [insert mode of transport] together. We will meet on [insert date, eg: Friday 24 September] at [insert time, eg: 6 pm] to leave at [insert time, eg: 6.15 pm] and plan to return to the same point at [insert time, eg: 9 pm] on [insert date, eg: Sunday 26 September].

WHO CAN I CONTACT FOR MORE INFORMATION?

Please contact [insert name] on [insert phone number] or by email on [insert email address].

The emergency contact for the venue is [insert number].

HOW CAN WE BOOK?

Each person attending needs to fill in a booking form which must be signed by a parent or guardian. Relevant medical and dietary information must be included. Please return the form and payment to one of the Youth Alpha team as soon as possible in order to guarantee a place.

We hope this answers your questions. If not, please feel free to contact us; we would love to speak to you.

[INSERT NAME OF CHURCH, EG: ST STEPHEN'S CHURCH] YOUTH ALPHA WEEKEND/DAY [DELETE AS APPLICABLE] – BOOKING FORM

GUESTS' PART

Name:
Address:
Postcode:
Email:
Mobile number:
Date of birth:

I would love to come to the Youth Alpha Weekend/Day [delete as applicable] at [insert name of venue]. I agree to abide by all the rules of the Weekend/Day under the leadership of the Youth Alpha team.

Signed: _____   Date: _____

PARENTS' PART

Parent/guardian name(s):
Address (if different from above):
Postcode:
Email(s):
Home telephone number(s):
Mobile number(s):
Other emergency contact (24 hrs):
Medical requirements:
Dietary needs:
Allergies:
Doctor's name:
Doctor's phone number:

☐ I agree to _____ attending the Youth Alpha Weekend at [insert name of venue] from [insert start date, eg: 24 September] – [insert end date, eg: 26 September] [insert year, eg: 2010] and entrust them to the leaders' responsible care while they are participating in the Youth Alpha Weekend/Day [delete as applicable] Away programme. I understand that they will be travelling by [insert mode of transport].

☐ I give my permission for the leaders or venue staff to treat my child for minor medical needs, including administration of pain medication (such as Paracetamol and Ibuprofen) as needed.

☐ I enclose cash/a cheque for the sum of [£ insert decided fee] (payable to '[insert name to whom the cheque is payable]').

☐ I have described any relevant medical, dietary and allergy details above. In case of an emergency, I can be contacted at the number(s) above.

Signed: _____ (parent/guardian)   Date: _____

PLEASE RETURN THIS SLIP TO [INSERT LEADERS' NAME] **WITH THE CORRECT PAYMENT AS SOON AS POSSIBLE TO ENSURE A PLACE.**

Lightning Source UK Ltd.
Milton Keynes UK
UKOW06f0618110215

246082UK00006B/25/P